4TH OF JULY,
ASBURY PARK

4TH OF JULY,
ASBURY PARK

A HISTORY OF THE
PROMISED LAND

DANIEL WOLFF

BLOOMSBURY

Published by Bloomsbury Publishing, New York and London
Distributed to the trade by Holtzbrinck Publishers

All papers used by Bloomsbury Publishing are natural, recyclable
products made from wood grown in well-managed forests.
The manufacturing processes conform to the environmental
regulations of the country of origin.

Library of Congress Cataloging-in-Publication Data

Wolff, Daniel J.
4th of July, Asbury Park : a history of the promised land /
Daniel Wolff.—1st U.S. ed.
p. cm.
ISBN 1-58234-509-0 (hardcover)
ISBN-13 978-1-58234-509-3
1. Arts—New Jersey—Asbury Park—History. 2. Rock music—New Jersey—
Asbury Park—History. 3. Rock groups—New Jersey—Asbury Park—History.
4. Asbury Park (N.J.)—History. 5. Asbury Park (N.J.)—Intellectual life.
6. Asbury Park (N.J.)—Social conditions. I. Title: Fourth of July, Asbury
Park. II. Title.

F144.A6W65 2005
974.9′46—dc22
2004026965

First U.S. Edition 2005

1 3 5 7 9 10 8 6 4 2

Typeset by Hewer Text Ltd, Edinburgh
Printed in the United States of America
by Quebecor World Fairfield

For the ones who have a notion

Fellow Citizens: Pardon me, and allow me to ask, why am I called to speak here today? . . . This Fourth of July is yours, not mine.

—Frederick Douglass
Rochester, New York
July 4, 1852

INTRODUCTION

THIS IS THE history of a place that never existed.

This is a history of the promised land.

There *is* a city called Asbury Park, a place on the Jersey shore occupied by real people, where actual buildings stand in various stages of decrepitude and renewal, where the Atlantic Ocean breaks on the sand. And this book tells what happened there over the past 130 years.

But the purpose of this book is to tell the history of what Asbury Park promised.

These days, most of us know that promise through the music of Bruce Springsteen. If we've heard about the city at all, it's as the beat-up shore town where Springsteen came of age. From his first album (which he called *Greetings from Asbury Park, N.J.*) to his breakthrough record, *Born to Run*, Springsteen's jangly, almost ragtime rock & roll kept evoking the vision of a collapsing seaside amusement park. Lovers threw each other in the sand; calliopes wheezed in the background. And as his sound evolved, he also refined the way he used Asbury Park. It became a "town full of losers," the ultimate backwater, the exhausted remains of the American dream. Against that romantic landscape, Springsteen cast himself as the young rock & roller "pulling out of here to win."

The music made Springsteen famous—and Asbury Park famous, again. Soon millions of fans here and abroad could sing along with every word. When Mary's dress waved on "Thunder Road," when her front door slammed, audiences cheered the dream of breaking free. Somewhere out on the highway, Springsteen promised, there was the chance to see if love was real. And though he made it clear that chance involved *leaving* the dusty beach town, Asbury Park was where it all started: the beginning of the run toward freedom.

Farm kids who had never seen the ocean, kids from nice suburban homes who were born to stay put, took Asbury as their own. We recognized the fortune-teller, Madam Marie, and could find our way along the dinging boardwalk. When Springsteen sang about driving the circuit—down Kingsley Avenue and back up Ocean—we were with him, steering with one hand, nonchalant. We knew the backstreets, the darkness at the edge of town.

And that's because Asbury Park never existed.

At the peak of its popularity, in the early twentieth century, it wasn't really a city at all but an amusement. The economy was driven by spectacle: one hundred thousand people showing up to watch the annual Baby Parade, where hundreds of toddlers dressed up as adults and competed in a kind of miniature Miss America.

Before that, the great American writer Stephen Crane saw his hometown of Asbury Park as a symbol of the young nation's hopes and its hypocrisy, late-nineteenth-century America summed up in the smiling, sunburned tourists paying to ride wooden horses in circles.

And even before that, at its founding, Asbury Park was as much vision as reality. The contradictions were built right into its name.

It was Asbury to honor Bishop Francis Asbury, the pioneer of American Methodism. The town rose on the Jersey dunes as a model religious community: a sort of mirage shimmering above earthly temptations. At the same time, the city's founder, James Bradley, saw it as a park. Not a community for its residents as much as an attraction that aimed to draw, entertain, and milk distant urban populations. For years, Asbury Park condemned "fun" as just another drug to corrupt the masses, meanwhile pushing that drug with every Ferris wheel and band concert.

So when Springsteen arrived, a hundred years after the founding, he moved into a city that was already a symbol. It had been put up not just as a place to live but to *mean* something. Generations of musicians had already used that symbol to make popular music. From turn-of-the-century oompah bands through the early days of jazz to the beginnings of rock & roll, Asbury Park had been part of a shore sound—beach music—that was all about the sometimes contradictory ideas of freedom and fun and democracy.

If anything had changed by Springsteen's time, it was the understanding of what those promises meant—and how they'd been broken. Even as his E Street Band was forming, Asbury's ghetto erupted into flames. Visitors tanned on the beach while the inner city burned, and the *New York Times* editorialized that this racial violence had a "particular irony." But that was only true for those who had refused to see behind the grinning mask of amusement. For the people who lit the fires, Asbury's runaway American dream was as old as its history.

While this book traces that history in some detail, the narrative skips from decade to decade. That's because it's following the idea of the place: the changes in meaning. How the Methodist dream became a stronghold of the Ku Klux Klan. How the principles of capitalism were rooted in the Mob. The different signals that Asbury is giving, today, when it promises a "shorefront revival."

The specifics are the story, and Asbury Park is a unique place. But this isn't just a local history. The brand of Northern racism that characterizes Asbury Park is only exceptional to the degree that it was publicly debated and held up as a national example. Other characteristics that seemed to set the nineteenth-century resort town apart became, in the twentieth century, commonplace. Asbury pursued the trickle-down theory of economics before the name had been invented. It ran a service economy while much of the United States still saw its future in manufacturing and agriculture. It helped create the model for Las Vegas, Disney World, the mall.

Is Asbury Park, then, a typical American city? At first glance, no. Although, like communities across the country, it was shaped by the major issues of the day—from Prohibition to the Great Depression to the invention of the teenager. Maybe Asbury isn't as special as it's always claimed? Maybe every city, from Dubuque to Paris, is a kind of promise?

Easier to answer is the question of whether Asbury Park's history can stand in for the nation's history—the way Springsteen used it. The answer is yes, of course. That's what the place was built to do.

Finally, this book is, in a couple of senses, rock & roll history. For one thing, Asbury's music has always been key to what's going on, and the story of the city inevitably traces the origins of the rock & roll sound and attitude. But also, the history of Asbury Park has the shape and feel of rock & roll. It keeps jumping to what moves us, hurrying to the next climax, deliberately repeating itself as it tries to get and keep our attention.

So, this is the history of a particular city on the Jersey shore. Which is a history of the promised land. Which is a place that never existed—and has proved almost impossible to leave.

FOURTH OF JULY, 1870

A BURNT-OUT, middle-aged businessman is walking down Broadway. Day in, day out, for more than a decade, he's run a brush factory: hairbrushes, horse brushes, paintbrushes, scrub brushes. The business, which he started from scratch, has made him rich—and has taken its toll both physically and spiritually. He's just turned forty, is married but childless. Self-made, he wonders why he worked so hard and sacrificed so much. Even his deep Methodist faith doesn't seem able to sustain him.

Coming up Broadway, he notices a fellow Methodist, and the two men stop to chat. The friend is the treasurer of a brand-new real estate venture on the Jersey shore. The businessman asks how it's going, and his friend is all optimism. Well, very well; in fact, if he puts his name down now, early, he can have his choice of building lots at a special price.

The last thing the brush manufacturer wants is more responsibility. But for a while now, his doctor, his wife, and his friends have been advising him that he needs a break. They all seem to agree that sea air and a trip out of New York City would make all the difference. In fact, he'd been planning a trip to Europe.

"Well," he answers, without giving it much thought, "put me down for two."

A few days later, he and some of his friends decide they'll go look at the development and pick out his new lots. Taking a ferry across New York harbor to Port Monmouth, he rides from there to Eatontown, New Jersey, by train, has dinner in a country inn, and then travels on what he calls "one of the worst roads that could well be imagined." It's a turnpike, a new one, but in May of 1870 even a new road is a backbreaking mixture of sand, mud, plank supports, and potholes. And the most common means of transportation, something known as a Jersey wagon, is a square, straight-sided contraption with hard flat seats and unforgiving wooden springs. "As free from graceful lines as those of a ready-made coffin," one contemporary described it, and it helped make the trip down the shore "a weariness to the flesh and spirit." At the end of the long ride, "the more robust were generally able to climb out but the feebler ones . . . had to be lifted." Given the businessman's health, he may have needed assistance.

He's set down in a stretch of empty sand and scrub oak. Construction on the new town hasn't begun, and between the green flies buzzing around his head and the dunes stretching on like a desert without shade or structure, the businessman might well have turned right around, gone back to the city, found his so-called friend, and asked for his money back. Instead, he is, in his words, "completely taken" and decides to return as soon as possible and set up camp.

The very emptiness calls him. It appeals to his sense of adventure, his nose for business, and his religious beliefs: the qualities that have carried James A. Bradley this far in life. Born on Valentine's Day, 1830, at the Old Blazing Star Inn, in Rossville on Staten Island, Bradley was the son of an Irish farmer with a drinking problem and an English mother. He was baptized a Catholic. When he was five, his father died, probably from drink. Two years later, his mother married Charles Smith, and they followed the stream of people moving into Manhattan. In those years before the Civil War, the city's population was exploding, from 130,000 people to more than a million.

The Smiths moved to Cherry Street on the Bowery, once a fairly exclusive neighborhood catering to "Gentry and Seafaring men alike." But in 1837, the year they moved, a general economic panic had embraced the city. That April alone, 128 firms went under. Railroads fell, banks collapsed, and building construction stopped. The city's working class crowded into tiny, miserable tenement apartments. The poor sewer system and primitive health services led to massive outbreaks of typhus and cholera. Bradley's stepfather set up a notions store to sell a little bit of everything: groceries, meat, clothing, shoes. He and his seven-year-old son (now known as Jim Smith) had a peddler's wagon. Their favorite spot was down on Catherine Street outside the new specialty store, Lord & Taylor.

The panic of 1837 fed a growing evangelical movement. Preachers predicted doomsday and railed against the evils of drink. They also attacked the immigrant religion, Catholicism. New York City's Catholic community was still small—accounting for only eight of the city's 150 churches—but it was easy to blame the "papist" minority not only for corrupting morals but for taking jobs. At grade school, Jim Smith would have studied textbooks full of anti-Catholic prejudice. Did people know he was Catholic? Sometime in those early years, he began insisting that people call him Bradley, but it isn't clear whether he let on about his religion.

As a teenager, Bradley hung with a rowdy, immigrant crowd. He was a Bowery Boy (which designated both the geographical area and one of the gangs that ran the Lower East Side) and soon developed what he called "a fondness for wine." That was only one of Cherry Street's temptations. By the early 1840s, the Bowery had become a working-class pleasure zone. Cockfights were staged next to billiard halls. Hookers waited outside former mansions. And the small hotels offered free "vaudevilles" to attract customers. These included a little bit of everything, from ventriloquism to dancing, circus acts to comics.

The young Bradley loved the shows, often going to three a week. As a thirteen-year-old, he was in the right place to have witnessed the development of one of the most popular styles of the day: the minstrel show. In a Bowery theater in February 1843, a quartet of white performers put on blackface and, using a heavy "nigger" accent, helped start what would become a national fad. The Virginia Minstrels played reels and jigs, told down-home planta-tion jokes, and loped across the stage in what they called the Virginia Jungle Dance. Negroes were barred from Bowery theaters, but minstrel shows became the rage.

Soon, Bradley's mother, Hannah, decided that her teenage son was learning too much too fast and needed a change of scene. She shipped him out to Bloomfield, New Jersey, across the river and north of Newark, where a friend from her childhood owned a farm. Jim spent a year in Jersey milking cows and feeding chickens. He hated it. Twice he ran away and was caught trying to catch a ferry back into the city. Finally, at the age of sixteen, he returned to the Lower East Side. Apparently, he'd been straightened out. He got a job, anyway, as an apprentice to a local brush manu-facturer and began his career.

It was hard, hot work in a cramped space that stunk of hog bristle and glue. The animal hair had to be washed by hand, dried in a hot room, bleached, sorted for length, shaped, tied, glued, and inserted into a handle. Depending on the type of brush, a man might make six to eight dozen a day. The hours were long, and when work was over, Bradley returned to a crowded, narrow tenement life amongst thousands of others fighting to survive.

His transformation from worker to successful businessman began when he was eighteen. That year, his older sister died. At the funeral service—held at a Methodist camp meeting outside Brooklyn—Bradley saw the light. His mother was Methodist, and now he converted to what was, in that era, a "distinctively middle-class creed." Leaving behind his immigrant religion was a move up and out—a chance to reinvent himself—and Bradley went at it with a fervor. He became a model employee. By the time he'd turned twenty-one, he was foreman at the brush factory. He married Helen Packard, an educated Rutgers student: timid, gentle, and devout. The two of them resolved to start their own business and, through extraordinary self-discipline, managed to save one thousand dollars. That, a visitor would recall, was an enormous sum, especially from "one of a class which save so little."

The Bradleys were determined to leave that class behind. In 1857, they completed payment on a lot uptown. Then, borrowing the capital, the twenty-seven-year-old Bradley launched his own brush company. He couldn't have picked a worse time. Stock market speculation, enormous monopolies in railroads and other industries, the surge of new immigrants—all combined to produce a nationwide panic. Unemployment skyrocketed; financial institutions closed. In New York City, the only currency anyone would accept consisted of bank bills depreciating at five to twenty-five percent a day. By December of 1857, the city had lost an estimated $120 million, and nearly a thousand businesses had gone under. The panic led to the Third Great Awakening (also known as the Businessmen's Revival), where thousands gathered for prayer meetings and denounced the addiction to moneymaking. Backlash against immigrants revived, too, with editorials to "shoot down any quantity of Irish or German." Meanwhile, the tenements exploded, as starving workers lashed out at the system. Unemployed workers occupied City Hall, and the government eventually had to call in the marines to restore order.

The only thing that kept the Bradleys' business afloat was their bankers' decision not to call in the loans, and that may have been based on the couple's single-minded perseverance. Bradley, a visitor recalled, was "a vigorous and large built man, rather rough in his appearance but full of energy." While his wife kept shop, he was upstairs cutting, shaping, and gluing brushes. Later in life, he'd reminisce how lunch in those days was often a slice of bread coated with molasses. By the end of his second year in business, Bradley had cleared his losses, and soon, he "added considerably to his capital." The main reason was war. When the South seceded from the union, the North passed tariffs to protect its manufacturers. New York's economy took off, creating an enormous demand for, among other things, brushes: to clean cannons, curry horses, groom officers' uniforms. New York City was home to a few dozen millionaires in 1860; by 1864 there were several hundred. When the Civil War ended, Bradley's firm had sales of $400,000 a year.

The war put the Bradleys into a new class of American capitalists—not as incredibly wealthy as John D. Rockefeller or Diamond Jim Brady, but full-fledged participants in what would come to be known as the Gilded Age. The Bradleys moved the factory to larger quarters on Pearl Street in Manhattan and bought a "fine house" on Brooklyn's Bedford Avenue. If James Bradley had taken his Methodism seriously before, he now became a major donor and the superintendent of the new Central Methodist Church in Williamsburg. At that time, the most popular religious figure of his day, the abolitionist Reverend Henry Ward Beecher, was attracting huge "privileged audiences" to his Brooklyn church.

While Beecher often called for social reforms, his sermons also amounted to "reassurances," as one historian puts it, ". . . that social inequalities generated by the free market system were divinely sanctioned and morally justifiable." At the same time, the born-again evangelist Reverend Dwight L. Moody was conducting his own mammoth revivals, arguing that the suffering of the city's tenement dwellers was a direct result of their having "drifted away from God."

So, at age forty, Bradley has the comfort both of his success and his religion. Still, he finds himself deeply and strangely exhausted. He buys the building lots on the Jersey shore and resolves, that summer of 1870, to leave the city to become, in his words, "an inhabitant of the wild woods." That empty stretch of undeveloped beach, he decides, is "where my wearied body and brain might rest, lulled to sleep by the murmuring sea at night, and awaked in the morning by the songs of birds in the pine trees surrounding my couch." It's a vision far from his tenement past, from the sorting of hog bristle, from his fine house in Brooklyn. Early on the morning of June 9, he sets off with a pair of horses, a carriage, a tent, and John Baker, whom he describes as "my colored man."

Aboard the steamer *Red Bird*, Bradley crosses New York harbor, cuts inside Sandy Hook, and steams up the Navesink River to the town of Red Bank. Along the way, he falls into conversation with a man named Shaw. Only later does he discover that it's Henry Ward Shaw, best-selling author (under the pen name Josh Billings) of the *Farmer's Almanac*. Billing's way with an aphorism has made him even more successful than his contemporary Mark Twain. "What the moral army needs just now," Billings wrote, "is more rank and file and fewer brigadier generals." Maybe even more apropos to the exhausted brush manufacturer in search of a dream: "Building air castles is a harmless business as long as you don't attempt to live in them."

Bradley disembarked in Red Bank, leaving Baker to take care of the horses, and walked over to the Globe Hotel for a meal. It's there that his revelation began. He no sooner sat down at the table than "a feeling of freedom and satisfaction swept over him." As the feeling grew, he recognized it as an awakening, a heaven-sent miracle. Speaking of himself in the third person, he would tell his biographers, "tears rolled unrestrainedly down his face."

The epiphany, if startling, wasn't totally unexpected. This kind of moment had, after all, launched the religion Bradley believed in, Methodism. A hundred and thirty years earlier, in London, John Wesley had felt his heart "strangely warmed," and rediscovering the Christ that had been hidden to him by the rituals and conventions of the Church of England, he'd cried out—much as James Bradley would cry out upon reaching *his* promised land— "I believe!"

This born-again moment was at the core of the young Methodist Church. Shucking questions of doctrine like baptism and confession, John Wesley had seen his mission as "carrying religion and morality to the submerged classes." He advocated open-air preaching, going directly to the new working class of the industrial revolution, and leaving the details of how they wanted to practice their faith up to them. "One condition, and one only, is required," Wesley wrote: "a real desire to save the soul."

Not surprisingly, a religion that rebelled at the Church of England and championed a fresh, democratic approach had immense and widespread appeal in the American colonies. In the years before the Revolutionary War, the 250 original subscribers to New York City's first Methodist congregation ran the gamut from "Negro servants to the Livingstons, Delanceys, and Stuyvesants." During those years, American Methodism was a passionate, evangelical sect driven by a band of circuit-riding preachers. The colonies' best-known and most successful, Francis

Asbury, left England for Philadelphia in the fall of 1771. As a young man of twenty-six, he asked himself some of the same questions that Bradley must have during his much shorter crossing on the *Red Bird*—and ended with a similar determination. Aboard ship, Asbury wrote in his journal: "Whither am I going? To the New World. What to do? To gain honor? No, if I know my own heart. To get money? No. I am going to live with God and to bring others to do so."

Asbury went on to organize the first American Methodist Conference. He spoke not only in churches but in pioneer cabins, in prisons, town halls, and anywhere else people would listen. It worked. There were less than five thousand Methodists in the colonies at the time of the Revolutionary War. By 1790, the new nation had more than forty-five thousand white members and nearly twelve thousand "colored." While New York City was a British stronghold, mostly Church of England, New Jersey was far more open to the new sect and its emotional revivals. Asbury, ordained a bishop by John Wesley, presided over what were called Love Feasts. One report, from around 1776, described the whole congregation as being "bathed in tears," with the cries so loud you couldn't hear the preacher. "Some would be seized with trembling, and in a few moments drop on the floor as if they were dead; while others were embracing each other with streaming eyes, and all were lost in wonder, love, and praise."

Bradley's moment of revelation was part of his religious tradition. And, as he began his long, bumpy ride down the Jersey shore, the ex-Catholic envisioned himself as carrying that revelation with him: a kind of modern pilgrim on a quest into "the wild woods."

Except the shore, even then, wasn't exactly wilderness. From Red Bank to Long Branch, Bradley rode a train line that had been established six years earlier. Granted, the railroad ran so close to the beach that, as one observer noted, "the surf blends with the rattle of the cars and the shriek of the locomotive whistle; and at times in high tide, the waves have washed over the tracks." Still, the train link had already created a real estate boom and promised a much greater one. The population of the New Jersey shore, some fifty-six thousand in 1850, doubled over the next thirty-five years.

And according to a *New York Times* correspondent, Long Branch in 1870 was "the favorite watering place of the United States," always presenting "a gay and animated spectacle." The robber barons of the day—Diamond Jim Fisk and Jay Gould—were staying there that summer. The West End Hotel boasted six hundred rooms, and there were vast summer "cottages" on two-hundred-acre plots. "The Branch" was where Josh Billings was headed and where President Grant would vacation later in the summer.

Bradley's wild woods were eight miles south of Long Branch. In between was a barren stretch of seafront where only one family managed to eke out a living. So although he was only a long carriage ride away from a thriving resort town, it felt awfully remote. When he and Baker arrived at dusk, it was too dark to cut tent poles. They threw a piece of canvas over the beams of one of the first buildings going up, made their "couch" of horse blankets and carriage cushions, and after a supper of dry crackers, fell asleep in the construction site. The next morning, they woke and looked out over nothing but sand and sea. "Mr. B," sighed the unhappy Baker, "this is a wilderness place."

Bradley, on the other hand, was energized by the sight. After breakfast, they rode down to look over his new property, which sat at the edge of a small natural lake. The land, according to one historian, was "a wild, wave-lashed solitude of sand, overgrown with pines and oaks and cedars." There, they pitched their tent and, in Bradley's words, "began our Crusoe life."

The worn-out brush manufacturer so loved that image that he

later named an uninhabited bit of land on nearby Sunset Lake "Robinson Crusoe Island." Daniel Defoe had described his 1719 novel as a story of the "religious application of events . . . to justify and honor the wisdom of Providence." Bradley saw himself on a similar mission. He was a noble pilgrim (deliberately) shipwrecked on the New Jersey shore, creating out of wilderness a brand-new life based on born-again Christian principles. Which left Baker, his "faithful old colored servant," in the role of Friday.

There's no record of how Friday felt about this job description. John Baker had been a slave in Virginia at the start of the Civil War. When federal troops launched an attack near his owner's plantation, he managed to escape to Washington and, from there, made his way north to New York. Among the city's thousands of escaped slaves, he'd somehow "drifted into the employ" of the Bradleys. The devout couple had taken on Baker as a special project. Mrs. Bradley set about teaching him how to read and, placing a Bible in his hands, began the work of conversion. It's not clear whether the colored man, then in his mid-forties, was a Baptist or a nonbeliever, but the proselytizing made him uneasy.

"You are trying to do right," James Bradley would exhort him. "You want God to be your friend and to live to be good and do good."

"Ah yes," Baker would answer and, then, touching his heart, add, "but I don't feel right just here."

This fit perfectly with Bradley's seashore adventure. Not only would he start a new life in the wilderness, but Robinson Crusoe would bring Friday to Christ. That's what this real estate development was all about, after all. A small group of Methodist families had pitched their tents on this beach the summer before. "The great world we did not seek," explained one of the founders, "but rather shunned, following the Savior's invitation, 'Come apart into a desert [or quiet] place and rest awhile.'" The savagery of the shorefront had scared them, at first. Then, as the story goes, two of the founders were walking along the beach and found an old Spanish silver dollar washed up in the sand. The ministers took this as a divine omen. Thirteen Methodist clergymen and thirteen laymen founded the Methodist Camp Meeting Association, committing an initial fifty dollars to buy eleven barren, inhospitable, and virtually inaccessible acres. According to the preamble of their charter, they'd made the investment "with a single eye to the Divine glory [and] to provide for the holding of camp meetings, for the promotion of Christian holiness, rigidly excluding all forms of speculation." They eventually bought 266 acres, including a small grove set back from the beach, and decided to call the holy city Ocean Grove.

In a way, it's only apt that the sign God gave these pilgrims was a piece of money. As an early guidebook put it, Ocean Grove was "essentially a faith undertaking, aided, however, by business shrewdness." Despite their moral position against speculation, simple math shows that the church did all right. As the first to sign up, Bradley got a deal, paying eighty-five dollars for each of his lots. That was certainly a bargain, but, after all, the Camp Meeting Association had only spent fifty dollars on the first eleven acres. Plus, the Association didn't actually grant Bradley—or anyone else—ownership. To assure that the town stayed devout, its bylaws stipulated that lots would be leased rather than sold. That way, if the town fathers suspected drinking, dancing, or any other deviation from the Methodist discipline, the transgressor could be asked to leave. Ocean Grove became a tent city, the real estate staying in the Association's hands.

But there was no city in 1870. Bradley and Baker were mostly alone, occasionally seeing workmen or taking part in tent services on the Sabbath. Periodically, Bradley would ride to Long Branch and, from there, make the two-and-a-half-hour commute into New

York City, where he'd check on his business and see his wife. During one of those trips away, the summer's second revelation occurred. As usual, Baker met Bradley at the Long Branch railroad station, but this time before Bradley could climb up into his carriage, Baker raised his hand and testified:

"Bless de Lord! Mr. Bradley, de light has come into my soul!"

That's how Bradley reported it. It seems Baker had heard a preacher at Ocean Grove over the weekend and been converted. The atmosphere of this wilderness place had succeeded, had "let the light in." The brush manufacturer must have been even more convinced that this stretch of shore was, if not sacred, special.

The question became how to keep it that way. From the beginning, John Wesley had cautioned against "worldly delights." In Bradley's day, the convention of the Methodist Church reiterated their founder's warning against "a tendency to worldliness—to vain and demoralizing amusements." Young people were particularly susceptible, especially when dancing. On the dance floor, one Methodist paper pointed out, "many a fair maiden and noble youth have betrayed the Savior." The trouble wasn't so much the music, as where it led: to "emotional action, the expression of emotion by rhythmic, choric movement."

The charter of the new city of Ocean Grove was filled with prohibitions not only against music and dance, but liquor, tobacco, Sunday bathing, card playing, bicycle riding, peddlers, theater, cursing, and "the practice of the sexes in assuming attitudes on the sand that would be immoral at their city homes." By the turn of the century, Ocean Grove's government would be called "autocratic [and] the most rigid on the continent."

All the rules were to protect the church not only from the world, but from its own success. By 1871, there were a million and a half Methodists. The membership base had long since shifted from Wesley's "submerged classes" to small-business owners and even the robber barons of the day. Daniel Drew, for example, had made millions through railroad monopolies, insider trading, and other stock manipulations. "He holds the honest people of the world to be a pack of fools," wrote one of Drew's contemporaries, "[because] when he has been unusually lucky in his trade of fleecing other men, he settles accounts with his conscience by subscribing toward a new chapel or attending a prayer meeting." Two years before Ocean Grove was founded, Drew had given his note for a quarter of a million dollars to start the Drew Theological Seminary in Madison, New Jersey.

Not only had the nature of its membership changed, but the church itself had become big business. By the turn of the century, its book-publishing concern alone would have a budget of $6 million. The chance to make money produced "glaring frauds": family members granting each other exclusive contracts to sell the church its ink, binding leather, paper. Eventually, the Methodist hierarchy had to bring in lay members to monitor the finances. All around him, Bradley saw men "whose nerves were shattered by too close application to their profession, studies, or their chase of the 'almighty dollar.'" As he knew too well, even the church couldn't protect them.

Which is why the founders designed Ocean Grove to grow in isolation. And why, in the summer of 1870 when the city was little more than a few construction sites, they were already worried about their Eden. They had Fletcher Lake to the south and the ocean to the east, both acting as natural barriers. And inland, on the west, Ocean Grove's founding fathers would build a high fence to make sure that only believers entered. The entrance would be locked from Saturday evening till Monday (the only exception being made for the undertaker). But to the north, up the coast, there was no buffer between their unfinished paradise and the town of Long Branch except the stretch of undeveloped beachfront. And that was hardly enough protection, given the kind of intoxicating corruption that thrived in The Branch.

Satan's amusements had existed in Long Branch for decades now. Back in the fall of 1809, Bishop Asbury himself had preached there, taking as his subject Acts 3: "Repent ye therefore, and be converted that your sins may be blotted out." In his log, Asbury noted that it was "given to me to speak in strong words, words of God and from God." The bishop had helped Long Branch establish one of the earliest Methodist gatherings in America. Still, sin not only took hold but prospered.

Even in its early days, when there was no railroad service and Long Branch was its own outpost in the wilderness, the town was known for its uproarious hunting and fishing parties. There may have been only six buildings along the narrow wagon track they called Ocean Avenue, but it was still "Flirtation Way" with visitors promenading up and down in their vacation best. Adventurous visitors stayed in farmhouses that offered all the oysters you could eat and late-night barn dancing. Women sported the latest fashion of dyed starfish dangling from satin ribbons. According to one contemporary account, there was "grace at each meal, hymns in the evening, [and] regular prayer meetings." But, after one particularly wild night, a farmer found his favorite cow stranded on the third floor of a downtown hotel.

The entertainment quickly became more sophisticated. In 1846, the largest, most exclusive hotel of the time, the Allegheny House, opened. Two years later, Monmouth House followed. Mrs. Abraham Lincoln visited the year the Civil War started. New Jersey had voted against her husband (the only free state to do so) and was, in the words of one expert, "profoundly pro-Southern and openly hostile to talk of general emancipation." But Long Branch was mainly interested in attracting people of wealth and prestige, never mind their politics. In 1869, President Grant was given a house by the influential men of the city. The president was drawn not only by the hunting and riding but by the gambling. The Pennsylvania Club, which he frequented, had plush Victorian furnishings, gold weather vanes, and marble-topped gaming tables featuring roulette, faro, cards, and dice.

In the summer of 1870, when Bradley pitched his tent on the shore, Long Branch had "probably the liveliest thoroughfare in the United States." Arriving at the train station, a contemporary writes, "The depot is crowded with splendid equipage . . . The ladies are attired in the most charming of Summer costumes [and] bands of music are playing on the cliffs." It was a "sea-shore cosmopolis" that drew the most elegant urban vacationers. On July 4, 1870, what Bradley and the other Ocean Grove pioneers would call the debauchery reached new heights. Three miles outside town, the Monmouth Park racetrack opened. Built on 128 acres of land, Monmouth Park featured the largest grandstand of any racecourse in the country. Its total opening-day purse was a mind-boggling $31,000 and lured gamblers from New York, Philadelphia, and beyond. With the blessing of Tammany Hall and Boss Tweed, senators, congressmen, judges, and fire commissioners showed up, and the newspapers reported that the chief owner and proprietor of Long Branch, Diamond Jim Fisk, arrived in his "gorgeous six-in-hand turn-out, and was accompanied by his two inimitable blondes." Methodists might campaign against The Branch—its loose women, liquor, and crude dance bands—but as the *New York Times* correspondent wrote that summer, "The truth is that few men who are engaged in the active business of life can withdraw themselves all at once . . . The sudden change from the bustle and excitement of business pursuits to complete solitude very rarely does the hard-worked man any good . . . 'Perfect seclusion' may have its uses, but . . ."

Ocean Grove tried. As one observer wrote, "I cannot think of the lake and bridges by which one enters the [Grove] otherwise than the moat and drawbridges of some medieval fortified town." But the town gates couldn't always be locked. The holy city's police chief ended up issuing numerous warnings to no less than President Grant, who kept racing his horses up and down the Grove's main street. No, the only real way to protect Ocean Grove from The Branch was to secure the undeveloped land in between.

One day that August, Bradley decided to take a look. Starting from his lot, he and one of the reverends crossed Wesley Lake and immediately hit a thicket of briars. They risked, Bradley wrote, "having our clothes torn from our bodies." Struggling on, they fought the brush, the heat, and the bugs for about a half mile, till they came to another inland lake with a number of small islands in its midst. They may have been "mere sloughs," as one reporter would later describe them, "covered with rushes, wild lilies, and huge bunches of the marshmallow plant," but to Bradley this was "as beautiful a sheet of water, as can be found anywhere." In his mind, the half-mile walk into the bush had been a passage of discovery. Here was an untouched place, an opportunity, a promised land.

At first, he tried to get other Ocean Grove members to buy it with him. But his fellow pioneers had barely begun building one model community and weren't keen on starting another. Even the man who'd first sold Bradley on the Jersey shore declined: "I think we have enough land, now." Plus, the asking price of $90,000 seemed much too steep. So, the Association opted out. But Bradley couldn't get the empty acreage off his mind. He had started a successful business from scratch; times were good; now he hungered for something more challenging than making brushes. He finally decided to go it alone, borrowing the $90,000 against his business and home to buy five hundred acres of scrub oaks and sand dunes.

According to one observer, among the reasons Bradley took this chance, "money making was secondary." The founder of Asbury Park had "a vision of a community not only, but of a particular kind of community, a wholesome community, a moral community." He would dedicate the community to Bishop Asbury. It would hold to the same principles as Ocean Grove except . . . except that Asbury Park would be owned and operated by one man. And while moneymaking might be secondary, it did have to be part of the equation. To make back his investment, Bradley would not only sell building lots, but he'd become a tireless public relations man. His new city would need to attract paying visitors. Even as it buffered Ocean Grove from sin, Bradley's dream city was inevitably going to end up a tourist town in competition with Long Branch.

In the spring of 1871, Bradley had what he called "the jungle" clear-cut from Wesley Lake to the northern border at Deal Lake. The sand dunes were leveled and carted off as fill. Then, all that summer, he walked the sandy desolation, pacing off the streets, deciding where the parks and the churches would be, measuring out the future. Main Street would run from lake to lake, extending the road that ran outside Ocean Grove's fenced perimeter. That's as far inland as his city would go. From Main Street to the shore, he drew broad avenues, guaranteeing vistas to the sea. At the beachfront, he outlined a promenade that would run next to the surf. That would be called Ocean Avenue, and the next avenue back would be Kingsley, named after a recently deceased Methodist bishop. Then there'd be Heck Street, for a family of pre-Revolutionary War Methodists, and Webb Street after an early, charismatic minister.

The beachfront would be kept open for visitors. Hotels would be set back from that, with the first homeowners nestling to the south as close as they could to Ocean Grove. The business district would be there, too, off Main, and Bradley named the avenue Cookman after one of the ministers who'd helped purchase Ocean Grove. At the corner of Cookman and Main Street, Bradley would build Park Hall, a two-and-a-half-story frame building that housed not only the frontier town's general store but its drugstore, tin and stove store, carriage house, post and telegraph office, and a meeting hall for clubs and churches. It would become the police station, court, and jail, polling place, and Asbury's first library and school. Overall, the city was designed to be a (religious) model for urban reform. As one historian put it, "Bradley viewed landscape as theology."

But all of this was to come. In the summer of 1870, it was still just Bradley and his man, Baker, and that first season of solitude seems to have created the strongest impression on Asbury Park's founding father. During those long days and nights when the two men were often the only people on the shore, an incident took place that, for whatever reasons, had particular importance to Bradley.

It occurred some time after their arrival in June but before the August day when Bradley pushed through the briars and "discovered" Asbury Park. We'll pretend it happens on the Fourth of July; it's certainly a kind of Independence Day.

On this evening, in their solitude, Bradley suggests to Baker that they go "bathing" in the ocean. Though Bradley had come to the shore for his health—and though the Gilded Age considered salt water a restorative, and though Bradley had bought oceanfront lots and was about to buy a whole town site on the shore—the idea of actually getting into the Atlantic swells had, until this moment, proved too much. When Bradley suggests the idea, Baker smiles at his boss, then politely declines. Jump into that pounding, roaring blue-black that came crashing against the empty shore? No, thank you.

"Remember, John," Bradley insists, "cleanliness is next to god-liness."

In the darkness, with the foam shining at each hissing crest, the white man strips down. Then, standing naked, he loses his nerve: "It *is* somewhat lonely to trust yourself in the great ocean in the twilight and alone."

Baker watches, fully clothed and a safe distance inland. Finally, the founding father of Asbury Park reaches a compromise. He won't actually give his body up to the surf. Instead, he lies down where he is, in the wet sand, at the place where the last force of the wave is spent in a gentle push. He "allowed the water," as he would write later, "to just touch my body."

For a moment, he lies there, savoring the sensation and making sure he's safe. Then, some movement catching his eye, he glances to the side. Baker has stripped down, too. Imitating his boss, he's lying at the edge of the water, the ocean lapping his body. "His dusky skin," Bradley would write, "was somewhat in contrast with the white sand."

Nothing obviously important has happened. Two men lie side by side in the dark as the ocean crashes before them. But something about the moment so burnt itself into the white man's consciousness that fifteen years later, when Asbury Park is a prosperous tourist town and Bradley decides to write a short history of it, this bathing incident takes up one of only thirteen paragraphs. And Bradley reprints the story weekly for years in the local paper he owns.

"The whole scene," Bradley writes, "forcibly reminded me of Robinson Crusoe and his man Friday." What exactly that meant, we never learn. We know that later, John Baker would leave Bradley's employ, marry, and move to Washington, where he became a carman, hauling freight with a horse and cart. One day, loading some boxes, he had a stroke and was paralyzed. He lived long enough for Bradley to visit him on his deathbed. But the image we're left with, the last image of the summer of 1870 before Bradley begins to build his "moral community," is of the two naked men—one white, one black—lying side by side at the edge of the dark sea.

FOURTH OF JULY, 1885

By 1885, THE dream was a reality. Parts of it, anyway. "The growth of towns along the Atlantic shore for the past ten years," James Bradley wrote, "has been something wonderful." A nearly continuous stretch of resorts had sprung up along the thirty miles of Monmouth County's coast. People mobbed the place, packing the beaches, the summer population of the area estimated at two hundred thousand. Bradley had been a key promoter and developer. And yet . . . and yet . . . "I fear," he wrote, "we have built too fast and too carelessly."

Since the day Bradley had bushwhacked north from Wesley Lake, his acres of briar and sand had grown into a resort worth $2 million. The city of Asbury Park featured two hundred hotels and boardinghouses that offered some eleven thousand rooms: more than double Long Branch's capacity and three thousand more than Atlantic City. While its summer population sometimes reached fifty thousand, Asbury Park also had three thousand year-round residents. There were two public halls (Bradley had moved one in its entirety from the Centennial Exposition Grounds in Philadelphia and plunked it down on Grand Avenue in 1877), an opera house that seated twelve hundred, some eight hundred "cottages," seven church buildings, and fifteen miles of storm drains and pipes, making it, Bradley boasted, "the first seaside resort on the American Continent to adopt a perfect system of drainage." New Jersey had legislated compulsory school in 1874, and Asbury's original single classroom, which Bradley's niece had run, was now a $10,000 brick building with seven hundred students.

In 1883, the summer season had drawn an astonishing total of six hundred thousand visitors. The New York and Long Branch railroad, which had been extended to Asbury in 1875, provided thirty trains daily from New York City and Newark. The "Pleasure Guide" to Asbury Park highlighted fishing, crabbing, sailing on "handsome yachts for hire," driving the shore in rented rigs (available with or without liveried footmen), and walking the boardwalk. The last had been installed the length of the beach from Wesley Lake to Deal Lake in 1877. At first only wide enough for two people to walk side by side, it was removed at the end of each season. By 1880, the boardwalk had been raised, widened, and made permanent, with elevated pavilions built at the foot of the cross-streets Asbury and Fifth. The next year, wooden piers were constructed, so the ladies in their long dresses and the men in their top hats could walk out and catch an offshore ocean breeze or watch the local fishermen try their luck with schools of late-summer bluefish.

In the winter, Asbury's businesses drew shoppers from all over Monmouth County. When the Steinbach brothers' little store had first opened in 1874, it had sold everything from clothing to home furnishings, averaging a gross of "a few thousand a year." Ten years later, Steinbachs was housed in a majestic brick building called The Ocean Palace. It anchored Asbury's commercial center on Cookman Avenue, employing twenty to thirty clerks, plus milliners and tailors, and had sales in "the hundred thousands." In 1885, Henry Steinbach had electric lights installed, and he also put in a "package railway" with miniature tracks. The little trains would carry purchases and money to the back of the store and reemerge with wrapped parcels and change.

But Asbury lived for the summer, and its main attraction wasn't man-made. "The tonic saltwater," wrote a visitor in the 1870s, "the stimulus of breasting the big waves, or the delicious relaxation of floating, face up, on the buoyant, upbearing element, furnishes the chief refreshment of a seashore holiday." Under the watchful supervision of "bathing masters," the ladies in their flannel or woolen dresses waded into the surf, careful never to go in past their waists. Their regulation nine-piece bathing suits included blouse, vest, pantaloons, stockings, kerchief, shoes, and a bonnet: a total of seven square yards of cold, clammy cloth. Males wore full suits of the same blue flannel, with loose pants, jackets, and sun hats. As a character in an 1890s short story complained, "It ain't a bathing suit. It's an auditorium, a ballroom, or something. It ain't a bathing suit."

You could cover up the human body and dictate proper etiquette, but by the Fourth of July, 1885, the contradictions of a religious resort town were obvious. And Asbury's main attraction turned out to be a big part of the problem. Bathing might be a healthy, even medicinal pursuit, but there was no denying that it encouraged venal thoughts and actions. "The surf lubricates the joints like oil," wrote a nineteenth-century observer, "grave men fling out their limbs like colts in pastures; dignified women . . . sport like girls at recess." As to youth, "Young men and maidens forget how far society keeps them apart and together dash in, in entire forgetfulness of all society may think." The *New York Times* reported that one of the resort's most admired ladies wore thick makeup, bleached reddish yellow hair, and a dress "cut so low in the neck it left very little to the imagination." On the male side, an Ocean Avenue dandy paraded in white duck trousers and waistcoat with a green necktie and a straw hat turned up in back.

Bradley did his best to stem the tide of sinfulness. He personally patrolled the beach and the lakes, catching couples spooning in rented rowboats or lying too close together in the sand. On Sunday, he'd make sure the beaches closed at eight in the morning and the barbershops by ten thirty. He even had a series of handwritten signs put up around town: by the bathing houses, on the fences, painted on Asbury's curbstones. The signs forbade peddling and cursing, quoted from Scripture, and gave general advice on how a good Christian ought to behave. Modesty, visitors were reminded, was more to be prized than silks and riches. "Jesus," one read without benefit of punctuation, "saves from hell praise him." The city was famous for its churches—"as thick as clouds in the sky," the *Times* observed. "Puritanism broods over the place," the reporter went on, "and blue laws of the bluest kind make a modern human being almost afraid to smile."

At the same time Bradley was following the Methodist stricture against amusement, he knew his city needed to draw visitors. And his ideas of how to do that even his admirers called "queer and extraordinary." He'd taken to strewing the beach with all kinds of junk: "old boats and animal cages, funny benches and see-saws and spars, old stoves and pieces of statuary . . . massive marble bathtubs, great wooden umbrellas" Bradley's childhood neighborhood of Lower Manhattan was being torn down for the new "skyscraping office buildings," and he haunted the demolition sites. He bought stone ornaments dating back to when the Dutch had controlled New York and plunked them down in one of Asbury's parks. He set up a dilapidated fire engine, "Old Washington," at the end of Sixth Avenue. There was a beached whaling boat from Newfoundland, complete with harpoon and rope, and a "monster stone cat's head." One summer, he had tanks built at the foot of the fishing pier and displayed a pair of sea lions. The attraction was so popular he had to install grandstands, and when the sea lions died, he replaced them with giant turtles.

"Not a person to be easily understood," as his contemporaries wrote, the self-made man built a city that reflected his enormous contradictions. The sole owner and developer of a thriving resort, he was a fervent "anti-monopolist." A land speculator, he supported a limit to how much property an individual could own. A millionaire, he was for reining in the powers of the rich. He republished a favorite sermon, which argued that "this is not a government of the people, by the people, for the people, but of the corporations, by the corporations." Yet, he opposed socialism as a spreading evil and, the son of two immigrants, wanted a quota on the number of people allowed into the country, believing that Europe was making the United States into "the world's penitentiary."

Bradley blamed some of the shore's problems on growth. "I give it as my opinion that if not another house should be erected during the next two years from Sandy Hook to Barnegat Inlet it will be of great advantage." The shore was no longer a desert where a man could rest awhile. It was overbuilt and underdesigned. Ocean Avenue, also known as the Golden Road, followed the boardwalk down through Long Branch past mansions and estates till it became Asbury's promenade. But periodically, the sea would simply take it back: the Long Branch stretch had to be rebuilt three times before 1862. And Long Branch's spectacular eight-hundred-foot-long iron pier, completed in 1879, was washed away just a few years later.

But the sea, Bradley reasoned, could be controlled. Sin was

another matter. As an 1880s editorial in the *Asbury Park Journal* put it, while "the history of the town has been one of unexampled prosperity throughout the long years since 1869 . . . in this pleasant place, as its popularity increased, Satan came in his worst form." Asbury's religious overtones had become, to the *New York Times* anyway, a "hypocritical cloak to hide all kinds of iniquity. They do say," it reported, "that this is one of the wickedest places in the world."

One major concern was liquor. Bradley included a clause in each lease that prevented the sale of alcohol, but a growing number of "pharmacists" had found a loophole: medicinal alcohol. "A man has nothing to do but walk in a drug store and ask for a soda with a stick in it," wrote the *Times*, "to get a whole telegraph pole if he wants it." Hotels, catering to Gilded Age patrons, became bootleggers, and hard cider was sold openly. "In spite of the utmost precaution," Asbury's *Daily Journal* concluded, "rum got an underground but firm hold in Asbury Park in the first decade of its existence." The impressive row of churches that stretched down Grand Avenue did nothing to stop it. "Six days in the week," a contemporary account tells us, Asbury "does enough mischief to condemn any ordinary, unhallowed resort like Long Branch."

Bradley wrote and distributed thousands of copies of an anti-alcohol paper called *The Artesian*, lobbied to get tougher anti-drinking laws passed, and personally supervised raids. It became a common sight to see him racing down the city's streets after illegal beer wagons. The chief of police hired Pinkerton men to help patrol. But a local judge fought the law, and a firm of liquor dealers from Red Bank set up shop in one of Asbury's premier hotels. By 1885, Asbury Park had nearly a hundred illegal saloons.

It was, in short, a party town. While Bradley opposed all of this, some citizens were willing to look the other way when it came to the more genteel visitors—the ones who came down with their families and rented a suite of rooms or a cottage for the season. But on peak summer days, fifty-five hundred visitors would pay a dollar each to take special excursion trains out of New York and Philadelphia. Disembarking at Asbury's Main Street station, these day-trippers would set out to find as much sun and good times as they could squeeze in before night. The railroad companies provided their own destinations: "excursion houses" with dance halls, skating rinks, and billiard rooms. Asbury's small business-men supplemented those with restaurants, bathing pavilions, and other diversions. The Surf Palace roller-skating rink, at the corner of Lake Avenue and Kingsley, featured a 100-by-190-foot floor that looked across Wesley Lake to the ocean, a restaurant, and an ice cream parlor. Nearby, the Epicycloidal Wheel was actually four huge wheels that carried sixteen people at a time in eight dangling gondolas.

At least this honky-tonk aspect closed down at night. But then there were the menials. Granted, someone had to do the laundry, work in the shops, sweep the beaches, and generally maintain the infrastructure of the booming city. But some of these laborers, instead of leaving when the season was over, became permanent residents. Not in Asbury Park proper, but in a second city that had grown up in the shadow of Bradley's promised land.

The way Asbury had been designed, the beach itself was for visitors. Other shore towns had mansions on their beachfront, but Bradley owned Asbury Park's and operated it as a business. Merchants could lease space to sell saltwater taffy or rent beach umbrellas or run changing rooms, but Bradley kept control of the real estate. The grand hotels and boardinghouses were set back from the beach. Then came the residential area where Victorian homes with mansard roofs and shady porches sat on relatively small building lots. Here, topsoil was brought in so roses could bloom, and carriage houses were added with the servant quarters up above. This is where the architects, doctors, and lawyers lived. Then came the commercial district. Bradley's dream was carefully sectioned off, controlled.

It ended at Main Street, where the railroad tracks ran. But there was a city beyond that. Once you crossed the tracks, heading away from the shore, you entered what felt like a different country. Here, on unpaved streets, workers had thrown up what many had first thought of as temporary dwellings. It wasn't officially Asbury Park, and there was no sewage system or garbage pickup. The center of this shadow city was a broad avenue at the very south: a wilder, ethnic version of Cookman Avenue. Here, many of the Jewish merchants had their small shops. And here is where the Negro population lived, drawn up North by jobs as chambermaids, porters, and dishwashers in the big hotels. By 1883, there were enough children on this—what locals called the West Side—for a separate Colored Free School.

In the summer of 1885, a Morristown lawyer named Frederick Burnham bought 135 acres on the wrong side of Asbury's tracks and started a development called West Park. Burnham was a staunch Republican and devout Christian and, like Bradley, wanted to help establish moral order. A year later, he'd donate land in upstate New York as a refuge for "wayward boys." But his Asbury purchase was pure investment. On the Fourth of July, 1885, there was every indication that Asbury would keep growing. Which meant its shadow city would, too, creating economic opportunities and, as it turned out, a national sensation.

Independence Day was still pastoral in Asbury Park. Farm wagons rolled into town, and there was a bicycle race at Wesley Lake with Henry Steinbach donating "a fine Jersey Bicycle Shirt" as a prize. Elegant dances were scheduled at most of the shore hotels. And as a reporter for the *Shore Press* captured the scene,

"Everybody felt happy. The beach was crowded with bathers and sightseers. The ice cream saloons and soda water dispensaries enjoyed a lively trade; the Auditorium, Ocean Grove, resounded with patriotic singing and orations; the small boy was happy with his torpedoes and firecrackers." That evening, an overflow crowd gathered to watch fireworks over the beach. "Rockets, Roman candles, Greek fires, and Chinese bombs filled the air with their variegated brilliancy, and illuminated the ocean to a considerable distance from the shore." It was a long way from two men lying naked on a stretch of empty beach.

The problem, as outlined a few days later in the lead editorial of the *Daily Journal*, was a group of "impudent and unmannerly men and boys." They had taken to standing around the pavilion every evening, smoking "vile cigars and cigarettes," and staring at the passing ladies. What's more, wrote the *Journal*, the typical ruffian seemed to expect each woman to take "as much notice of him as he aims to do of her." In some ways all this was harmless: an extension of the surf-romping flirtation that took place during the day. The difference—according to the editorial—came down to class. "The average specimen . . . apes the manners and fashions of those better able to afford them." The chief of police should clear out these loiterers, who (the local paper made clear) were "white as well as black."

A week later, however, the focus had narrowed.

The headline of the *Journal*'s July 17 editorial made it clear enough: "Too Many Colored People." While it was "a disagreeable thing to say," and while the editors wanted "to give the colored people their full rights and privileges," the fact of the matter was that "the colored people are becoming a nuisance in Asbury Park . . . We allow them to vote, to have full standing and protection in law," the editorial went on, "but when it comes to social inter-mingling then we object most seriously and emphatically." After all, Asbury Park was a "white people's resort and it derives its entire support from white people." Colored people followed, as servants, but then they began "intruding themselves in places designed only for guests." Specific mention was made of the pavilion, the promenade, and the seats along the boardwalk. To top it off, excursion trains were bringing in Negro day-trippers. "Some days," the editors concluded in disgust, "the whole beach seems given up to them."

The solution was clear. The promenade, the pavilion, the entire beach from Ocean Avenue to the low-water mark, were private property. Unless the number of "colored monopolists" became smaller, the paper was going to urge the owner—James Bradley himself—to bar them.

This was a little misleading. The *Journal* was Bradley's paper: he had almost certainly okayed these editorials and may have helped write them. When the paper reported, "The matter has been talked over thoroughly by local property owners," it was probably Bradley talking to himself. And when the editorial concluded, "It was thought best to see what a little agitation would do before adopting more radical measures," it's the town's founding father warning his children to get in line . . . or else.

Both the *New York Evening Post* and the *New York Times* gave the issue prominent coverage. In a front-page piece, the *Times* claimed that what had brought the problem to a climax was "a big colored picnic" thrown by a group that had come in on the excursion train from Newark. Having "taken possession" of the beach, the picnickers "strewed it with peanut shells." Which may not have sounded so awful but was part, the *Times* explained, of a larger pattern:

"White people from the cities felt offended because as soon as the day's work was done colored women flocked by the hundreds to Bradley's beach, jostled for room on the plank walk, and said impudent things to persons who resented any effort at familiarity. By 9 o'clock every evening the negro waiters from the hotels would join them, and by giving full play to the spirits natural to the race, drive white persons back to the cottages and hotels long before Mr. Bradley's 10:30 limitation was reached."

This was not supposed to be in the dream.

"The colored folk indignantly deny the charges," the *Times* pointed out. They weren't "impudent" but good Christians; many of them good Methodists, in fact. There was nothing wrong with the behavior of colored people, the Reverend A. J. Chambers of the local Bethel Methodist Church asserted. Three thousand African Methodists had attended a jubilee meeting in Ocean Grove just the Thursday before, and their behavior had been so exemplary that Ocean Grove had invited them back. If they were good enough for Ocean Grove, why weren't they good enough for Asbury Park?

Because in the one case they stayed to themselves, and in the other they were an "intrusion" on the white beach. This distinction, as with many of Bradley's beliefs, was drawn from his religion. At a Methodist conference Bishop Asbury himself had organized in Baltimore back in 1780, preachers had declared that the institution of slavery was "contrary to divine and human justice." But the split in Methodism had begun just seven years later. At St. George's Church in Philadelphia, five free African-American congregants were asked to please stop praying on the main floor and move up to the gallery. They'd refused and, after being forcibly removed, vowed never to return to the Church. One—Richard Allen from New Jersey—founded and became bishop of the African Methodist Episcopal Church.

The second racial split in the Methodist Church occurred fifty years later. During the general conference of 1844, a group of white Methodists formally rejected founder John Wesley's belief that slavery was an "evil." Ordered to free his slaves, a bishop from Georgia refused, declaring that manumission was illegal in his state. The result was the establishment of the Methodist Episcopal Church, North, and the Methodist Episcopal Church, South. This "snapping of the ecclesiastical cords binding North and South together" helped lead the way to the Civil War. During that war, two thirds of the Negroes who were still members of the southern Methodist Church left it. The resulting African Methodist churches became organizing centers in the era of Reconstruction—and targets of the Ku Klux Klan.

Six years after Bradley founded Asbury Park, the northern and southern branches of white Methodism had met down the shore in Cape May and reunited under a "Declaration and Basis of Fraternity." But Asbury's roots were in the abolitionist northern wing, and that, according to the *New York Post*, made the city more liberal on the "color question [than] any other place along the coast." In Asbury, the *Post* declared, the "negro population," estimated at two thousand, "mingled freely with the white promenaders on the beach, skated in the rinks, and listened to the music in the pavilion." But that liberal tradition drew the line at "large parties of negroes gathering upon it day after day." The fact is, the *Post* went on, "that the overwhelming majority of white people prefer not to come into contact with black people on anything like terms of social equality. Everybody knows this is true of the South, and Asbury Park shows that it is also to some extent true of the North."

Bradley's moral community had been built to set an example. Now, the *Post* argued, Asbury Park offered a case lesson in how difficult integration really was—and how unrealistic the North had been in believing that an "off-hand act of Congress" could solve the colored question. Asbury's racial politics on this Fourth of July, 1885, were part of a larger debate on the limits of both the

Emancipation Proclamation and the recently abandoned experiment of Reconstruction.

Asbury's *Daily Journal* reprinted this editorial approvingly and suggested "a thoughtful consideration of the facts." Then, it restoked the fire by declaring that their resort town was in danger of gaining the reputation of being "run by the colored people, and white people are not wanted."

By the end of July, the controversy had spread nationwide. The Galveston, Texas, *Daily News* carried an article that described the Asbury and Ocean Grove population as "good people who like to mix a little summer religion, camp meeting, and Bible instruction with their surf bathing." The Texas paper sarcastically attributed the area's liberal racial attitude to high religious morals and then got to the heart of its criticism. These same "sentimental religionists of the Jersey coast," who frequently and loudly criticized the South for its treatment of blacks, panicked at the thought of prolonged integration. Especially inflammatory, it argued, were boardwalk flirtations across the color line, as "colored beaux . . . laid siege to the hearts of . . . pale-faced damsels. If the affair had come in the South," the Galveston paper concluded, "it would have raised tempests of denunciation . . . Now, Ocean Grove and Asbury Park are taking their own medicine, and both are very sick indeed."

Bradley went to Europe during the summer of 1885. According to the *New York Times*, this supported the assumption that he was behind Asbury's segregation campaign: "Bradley always goes off on a little trip after breaking out with one of these assertions." But as founding father, he had yet to weigh in publicly. According to a columnist in the *Shore Press*, Asbury had long since been divided into "two distinct factions," with Bradley representing the old anti-liquor, anti-gambling fundamentalist school while the hotel owners and other merchants fought to modernize. When Bradley returned to the shore that fall, the welcome-home dinner in his honor at Educational Hall was something of a peace offering. The evening began with a rendition of "Old Folks at Home," that "good old plantation song." Then, everyone from a member of the electric-light company to town commissioners lauded the fifty-five-year-old Bradley. In his remarks, Bradley professed amazement at the town's prosperity and wondered aloud, "What will be the outcome of all this?" The question—which, by implication, included the city's racial problems—remained unanswered all winter.

That spring, eight miles north of Asbury, an African-American in his sixties was accused of attacking a twenty-four-year-old white woman. Samuel Johnston was a stable hand in Eatontown, where Monmouth Park was located. Most people knew him as Mingo Jack. He was arrested around seven on the evening of March 5, 1886. The local constable checked his cell at ten, then went home to bed. Early the next morning, Mingo Jack was found hanging by his neck in the jailhouse doorway, his hands tied, his face so badly beaten that one eye had burst its socket. According to the *New York Times*, it was the first lynching in New Jersey since the Revolutionary War.

Most of the local people, including the constable, immediately declared that this was a crime that would never be solved. An editorial in the *Eatontown Advertiser* even called on the prosecutor and the coroner to stop any investigation, "as the people of Eatontown didn't want the identity of the lynchers discovered in the court." Witnesses would later say they saw two wagons, each carrying six men, heading toward the jail after a rowdy gathering at the local saloon. But when the coroner was asked if he'd gotten testimony from the alleged victim's father and brothers—who'd been parading around town vowing there'd be a lynching—he replied, "Why should I subpoena them?" When, three weeks later, the constable was arrested on manslaughter charges for leaving the prisoner unguarded, there was public outrage. The district attorney called the investigation "uphill work" and added, "not a single person in the community had in any way assisted in securing evidence."

A few months later and a dozen miles down the shore, the *Daily Journal* reopened the issue of colored people being allowed on Asbury's beaches. The lead editorial of July 29, 1886, began by quoting "a man who has been very prominently identified with this place." The thinly disguised Bradley stated, in convoluted prose, that "the people who make their living out of Asbury Park have no rights that our visitors are bound to respect." Elaborating on the theme, the editors explained that if it were a crowd of white workers monopolizing the pavilion every evening, they'd have to be censored, too. But it happened to be "crowds of negroes who nightly swarm in the vicinity of Asbury Avenue." The paper didn't want "to stir the matter as was done last year, but the evil must be abated or our place will suffer." Having begun the piece by implying that Bradley supported them, the editors concluded that hotel and cottage owners might be "compelled for self preservation to cease to employ colored help."

That was the first threat. The next day, a letter to the editor signed simply "Citizen" applauded the *Journal*'s position and argued that "nine-tenths of our people would be inclined to use much stronger language" on the subject of "crowds of Africans infesting every promenade and public place, day and evening." As its follow-up editorial, the *Daily Journal* printed a letter from a writer who had been visiting Asbury for the last decade. He wondered if Mr. Bradley couldn't be persuaded to build a separate pavilion down the beach for colored people, who, the writer felt sure, "would be glad to know they had at last a place of their own." The same issue noted that Asbury Park's Opera House was presenting the Wilson & Rankin minstrel show, featuring the "burnt-cork acts" of George Wilson, whose "drollery is irresistible, natural and infectious."

In mid-August, under the headline "A Colored Man's View," another voice was heard. William H. Dickerson described the entire issue as one of the "relics of America's barbarous institution of slavery." Why not enforce the law for anyone, black or white, who acted as a public nuisance? Wasn't that the principle of our republican form of government? "For whites and blacks to sit in the same pavilion and bathe in the same ocean does not make the white man any blacker nor the black man any whiter . . . As long as both are well-behaved, neither suffers from unavoidable juxtaposition." Finally, Dickerson pointed out that he'd had several conversations with Mr. Bradley and did not believe "he can be induced to change his broad and liberal views for a narrow and discriminating prejudice."

That Saturday, the *Journal* went back on the offensive, interviewing an unnamed hotel man who, again, suggested that "one way out of it" was for businesses to stop hiring colored people. "Then the annoyance will be at an end, and the cure will be accomplished without any damaging publicity and without any trouble."

The Bradleys were back in Europe during the summer of 1886. But this time, in a letter from Wiesbaden, Germany, the founder of Asbury Park finally made his opinion public. Wiesbaden had been a successful resort since Roman emperors had come for its mineral waters and hot baths. While the waters were free to all, Bradley wrote, one side of the stream was set apart for townspeople so they wouldn't interfere with the pleasure of the tourists. That's how a resort town *should* behave, where "every person in the town, whether landlord, storekeeper, servant, car driver, or railroad employee seems to do their best to impress the stranger with the fact that he is a welcome guest."

This was, Bradley wrote, "in strong contrast" to Asbury Park, where millions of dollars in capital had been invested (much of it, he didn't have to say, his own) "and a like care must be shown by us, as is shown by the frugal and clear-headed Germans." Then, just in case anyone missed the parallel, Bradley drove his point home:

"The best seats on the board walk and the pavilions must not be monopolized by colored servants, who in addition to the fact that they intrude themselves into places that belong by right to others, are often *impudently intrusive* [his emphasis]. The time is coming, indeed may have arrived, when some decided action must be taken to show our colored friends that the board walk and pavilions are private property." All this, Bradley concludes, "for the permanency of the town and the protection of the capital invested."

Bradley's promised land had its limitations. They were realistic and necessary ones. The country itself had begun with a Declaration of Independence, but did that mean all men, or women, had equal rights? No. That was impractical. A poor man might want to be rich, the same way a rich man might want to be king, but that had never been part of the promise.

By the time Bradley's letter appeared, it was late in the season, and the matter rested through a second winter. Bradley, meanwhile, focused on the temperance issue. In a letter to the *Asbury Park Journal*, he accused Asbury's drugstores of being "dens of iniquity, containing private rooms where young girls were taken, drugged, and ruined."

But in its first issue of 1887, the *Daily Journal* devoted a large part of the editorial page to reprinting Bradley's letter from Germany. It was the third summer in a row that the local papers had featured the racial issue, and this time, the minority population organized. On the last Sunday of June, 1887, it was announced from the pulpit of the A.M.E. Zion Church, across the tracks on Lake

Avenue, that there would be an indignation meeting held the next evening.

Bradley wrote an open letter he distributed throughout Asbury. While he encouraged the idea of a public meeting, the founding father asked that if there was one, his entire article (the letter from Germany) be read aloud "in a distinct and clear voice," because he could only conclude that some "wrong deductions" or inference had been drawn.

Monday evening, the church was filled with over 250 people, many of them women. Tubs of flowers covered the altar, and kerosene lamps flickered dimly (the town had run electricity to light the boardwalk, but not apparently to the colored part of town). After "America" was sung and following an opening prayer, the pastor of the church, the Reverend James Frances Robinson, denounced Bradley in what the *Journal* would later call the "most offensive and incendiary language."

"We will take no dictation from James A. Bradley or any other white man on the face of the earth," the Reverend Robinson began to general applause. "We are seven million five hundred thousand strong. We own land; we raise the wheat, the corn, the cotton, and we helped save the Union . . . Mr. Bradley and the white people object to the negroes on the beach, where the free air of heaven blows, and yet in the dining room they are willing to have the negro sweat right over them."

The congregation interrupted with applause and laughter.

"In the barbershop the white people are willing to have our black hands upon their faces, and yet they object to our presence on the beach. What an intelligent man this Bradley is!"

Again, the crowd laughed.

"Shall we sit and bear it?" the reverend called, and the crowd answered, "No!"

"We will go on the beach, and, however bitter the pill for Mr. Bradley," the speaker concluded, "he shall be made to swallow it."

After the applause, public-school teacher Moses Newsome followed with a much more mild-mannered resolution. Since Bradley's article was "unwholesome to the tastes of cultivated and respectable colored citizens," from now on Bradley and his colleagues should "specify more definitely the class to whom they refer." Respectable colored people, the resolution concluded, were just as eager to censure troublemakers as the man they called the Boss. What were unacceptable were "the slurs hurled at us as a nation."

That might sound reasonable, but what Asbury's colored people were forgetting, according to the *Shore Press*, was that whether they were "respectable" or not, whether they lived on the West Side or took a train in for the day, they were all merely visitors. The New York City papers had it wrong in declaring that Asbury had colored residents who owned property worth $200,000. They were assuming the shadow city was in Asbury. "The fact is that there is not a foot of land in the borough owned by a colored person." Then the *Shore Press* reprinted with its approval an editorial from the *Newark Evening News* that reminded colored people that Bradley, as owner of the beach, had a "legal and moral right" to decide who could come on his beach "as long as private ownership of land is recognized."

And that was tolerant compared to the *Daily Journal*. Its lead editorial began by denouncing radical colored "agitators" like the Reverend Robinson. These sorts weren't satisfied with the Negroes' progress from slave to citizen. They wanted to be "treated not only as well but even better than the whites." As an example, the paper quoted Robinson's statement that "if there was a sign up over the gates of hell, 'no colored people allowed,' we would go right in, because we've a right there." An amusing flight of fancy, but the concept went against all rules of law, including and especially property rights. "Respect and equality can never be gained by such a course," the *Journal* declared, "and our colored brethren surely must have reasoning power enough to understand it." And if they didn't? How to deal with those who couldn't or wouldn't understand? "Whether their skin is black or white," the editorial concluded, "they should be effectually extinguished."

There was no mistaking that. Especially just down the shore and barely a year after the lynching of Mingo Jack.

The evening after Independence Day, 1887, the Reverend Robinson took the issue to St. Mark's Church on West Thirty-fifth Street in New York City. There, the church pastor started things off by objecting to the "ante-war spirit of race distinction that still prevailed" in Asbury. "They have resurrected the old ku-klux idea in the North," he declared, "and there ought to be as much indignation against it as when it was south of Mason and Dixon's line."

When it came the Reverend Robinson's turn to speak, he was introduced as the only one of the town's four colored pastors "who had dared to cry out against Mr. Bradley." Now, the Reverend Robinson announced that he understood the language of the *Daily Journal* editorial perfectly well. It was enough, he said, "to make one think it was edited in Georgia."

"Boycott it!" someone shouted, and the church applauded.

"The fact is," the reverend continued, "that neither the paper nor Mr. Bradley can keep us all off the beach. I went down there last night and saw some elegant colored ladies. There were China-men there, too, and Italians. Mr. Bradley himself is an Irishman." There was more applause, and the reverend concluded, "Mr. Bradley might as well try to hang his handkerchief on the horns of the moon as to keep the colored people off God's beach."

The next day the *Daily Journal* insisted that this had nothing to do with race. The paper was against "all nuisances white or black." Bradley repeated this position in a statement to the *Shore Press*. "I am free to admit that I wish to discourage the great number of colored people coming here," he told a reporter, "not because I have any feeling against them as a race, but because I find that the patrons of the Park object to their great number." He declared that he was "and always have been a firm friend of the race, but I would not be doing justice to the vast amount of capital that is invested in every way in Asbury Park if I allowed my sentimental feelings to assert themselves."

It was a fine turn of phrase, this doing justice to capital. It implied that money had its own rights. Maybe all men were created equal, but that was a "sentimental feeling" next to the basic freedom to turn a profit. (Add this to the list of Bradley's contradictions. Because when it came to selling booze, the founding father believed a man's right to make a living was trumped by the higher moral truth of temperance.)

Still, Bradley insisted, this was not about skin color. As an example, he brought up the Italian workers who were in Asbury that summer installing an electric railway. "Now if they would stay on after their work is done there would be nothing for them to do, and the same principle will hold good in regard to the colored people, and any impecunious class."

By the following Fourth of July, Bradley had instituted what he called "commission hours." During those identified times only, colored people would be allowed to swim at the Asbury Park beach. He didn't "feel it would be right to shut the colored people out entirely," so he was trying this experiment. "Personally," the Boss concluded with a smile, "I have esteem for a respectable person whether his skin is white or black." But he couldn't afford to offend his paying (white) guests.

Bradley may have thought this solved the problem. But the

Asbury Park Journal news piece describing that Fourth of July, 1888, suggested otherwise. And does so without mentioning race or class.

"Before sunset the promenade was thronged," the piece began, "by 8 o'clock it was almost impossible to move. Baby carriages made confusion; babies made noise; likewise the torpedoes and fire-crackers, rockets, candles and toy pistols. The small boy had his innings, and a happier collection of juvenile humanity it would be hard to find anywhere. Some had been on the sand all day and showed burned fingers, scorched clothing, sunburned and dirty faces, but the merry twinkling eyes gave evidence that these misfortunes didn't count. The stereoptician show was looked at by an immense crowd that packed every inch of space clear back to the lawn. Both floors of the pavilion showed a mass of heads above the railing. From one end to the other, the Pier was alive with people."

Nowhere does this unsigned piece mention Bradley's distinctions between white and black, respectable or not. But the sheer exuberance of the description and its clear sympathy with the mass of celebrating people argue against the founding father. These are the democratic throngs, and they—not Bradley—are what bring the pier to life.

The author of the piece might have been Townley Crane, a well-known local reporter. Or conceivably his mother, Mary Helen Crane, who also wrote occasionally for the Asbury papers. But the most likely suspect is Townley's youngest brother, sixteen-year-old Stephen Crane. Whether Asbury Park knew it or not, an observer with a conscience, a predilection to sympathize with the "mass of humanity," and a wicked sense of humor had already focused in on the city. Soon enough, the social realism he championed would stand in opposition to this idea of doing justice to capital—and to the founding father himself.

AMERICAN DAY, 1892

STEVIE CRANE WOULDN'T have struck James Bradley as much of an opponent—if the founding father even noticed the kid.

Thin, with almond-shaped, gray eyes and dirty-blond hair, he had a hacking cough fed with a constant string of cigarettes. Though he came from a respectable Methodist family, by the time he was a teenager Crane was hanging around the beach with the local riffraff. He worked part-time as a reporter and spent the rest of his day walking in the dunes, playing baseball, or shooting his pistol at nothing in particular. He was, in short, exactly the moral type that Bradley's handwritten signs warned against: sarcastic, sensual, happy to give in to whatever temptations the boardwalk life offered. He was a tramp in the sense Springsteen would use the word nearly a century later: an outcast, a renegade, "tramps like us."

Stephen was born in Newark, New Jersey, the winter after Bradley bought his oceanfront jungle. He came from high Methodist stock. His father, the Reverend Doctor Jonathan Townley

Crane, was the presiding elder of the Methodist churches in Newark. His mother, Mary Helen Peck, was the daughter of the Reverend George C. Peck—editor of the *Methodist Quarterly Review*—and the niece of the Methodist bishop, Jesse Truesdell Peck. Crane would later write that everybody on his mother's side of the family "as soon as he could walk became a Methodist clergyman of the old ambling nag, saddle bag exhorting kind." Not quite. Whether or not he wanted to admit it, the beach tramp came from the aristocracy of American Methodism.

Stephen's father outlined his brand of Methodism in a series of tracts: "An Essay on Dancing" (1849), "Popular Amusements" (1869), and "Arts of Intoxication" (1870). Contact with any of these, from whiskey to waltzing, exposed the soul to "inexpressible evil." According to the reverend doctor, something as seemingly innocent as the popular parlor music of the day could lead a man so far astray that he might end up "guilty, condemned, corrupt, helpless, the wrath of God resting on him, and hell waiting his coming, with its eternal darkness and despair."

This was post–Civil War orthodox Methodism and shows just how far the church had moved since the days of John Wesley. The part of the population Wesley had reached out to—"the poor and less educated"—weren't going to find much comfort here. Instead, by the late nineteenth century, they were often turning to new Holiness sects that promised the kind of immediate, ecstatic experience that had once been part of the Love Feast: talking in tongues and visions. Like James Bradley, the Reverend Doctor Crane opposed this born-again revivalism. Stephen grew up in a church and a family that fought the wickedness of sensual pleasure. It verged on a sin to be glad you were alive.

If anything, Stephen's mother may have been even more judgmental. At forty-five, she had already given birth to thirteen children when he was born. Like Bradley, she'd had alcoholism in her family: a brother who died of drink. As the daughter and wife of clergymen, Helen would have been pro-temperance anyway, but she was passionate on the subject. She was often out on the lecture circuit, where her specialty was a graphic demonstration of the physical effects of alcohol. She'd drop the white of an egg into a glass of liquor and show the audience how it hardened into a solid mass "much resembling the state of being cooked."

Despite his ferocious beliefs and his wife's family connections, the Reverend Doctor Crane doesn't seem to have had a very successful church career. Starting in Newark, the family moved three times before Stephen was ten, ending up in the sticks: Port Jervis, New York, out by the Delaware River. Stephen's father tried to make the best of it, but it's hard not to hear a hint of disappointment when he writes, "I am much more concerned that we should live truthfully and kindly here than that we should be busy in condemning the luxuries and sins of New York."

The family didn't suffer financially (Mrs. Crane had inherited money), and the children prospered. Stephen's brother William became a judge in the next town over. Another brother, Townley Crane, worked as the Associated Press reporter in Asbury Park and doubled as the Long Branch stringer for the *New York Daily Tribune*. In Port Jervis, Mrs. Crane helped organize an industrial school "to supply the lack of early training . . . by instruction in the use of the needle . . . [to] colored women and children." But despite the reverend doctor's efforts to be optimistic, his disappointments included a fundamental spiritual one. He had never felt the kind of revelation that had struck James Bradley. "Much encouragement in my work," he wrote. "Still, thus far, no wave of power has come sweeping all before it, as we sometimes see. Perhaps it will, if we hold on our way, doing our duty."

He did his duty, but the wave never broke. In February 1880, age sixty, Dr. Crane died of a heart attack. Stephen was eight. For the next few years, the Cranes remained near William in Port Jervis, visiting Townley on the Jersey shore in the summer. There, the old-fashioned Methodist values of Ocean Grove and Asbury Park appealed to Mrs. Crane, especially the active local temperance society. In June of 1883, when Townley was named editor of the *Asbury Park Shore Press*, Mrs. Crane, eleven-year-old Stephen, and his twenty-eight-year-old unmarried sister, Agnes, moved to 508 Fourth Avenue in Asbury Park. Their home, Arbutus Cottage, was a proper two-story place in the good part of town. It cost Mrs. Crane $7,000. As Stephen later described the neighborhood, "There is square after square of cottages, trees and little terraces, little terraces, trees and cottages, while the wide avenues funnel toward a distant gray sky."

The Cranes moved to Asbury during boom times. The Coleman House Hotel had gone up on the beachfront in 1879, with the Madison Hotel just to its west; a year later, the new "promenade boardwalk" drew thousands of couples, strolling to see and be seen; two years after the Cranes arrived, the massive Grand Avenue Hotel was completed. Mrs. Crane was soon elected president of the Women's Christian Temperance Union of Ocean Grove and Asbury Park. In Asbury's morals debate, she supported James Bradley's brand of old-fashioned Methodism (with Mrs. Bradley playing the melodeon at local Methodist services). In a piece Mrs. Crane wrote for the *Ocean Grove Record*, she weighed in against "the growing taste for worldly amusements which keeps the young from the house of God." That included card playing, dancing, and theatergoing, all of which Stephen's mother described as "devices to 'kill time,' which means to waste the precious hours given us for holier uses."

Stephen, meanwhile, was killing time as often as he could. He'd later write that he spent his childhood riding his pony, playing baseball, swimming, and fishing. These were not "holier uses."

Plus, he tried smoking and drinking early on. Some of this may have been because his mother wasn't around that much. According to Stephen, she had "lived in and for religion," and much of his rearing was left to sister Agnes, a teacher at Asbury's intermediate school.

Almost immediately after their move to the shore, the family's fortunes began to fail. The panic of 1884 led to massive strikes in the Pennsylvania coal mines, which, in turn, cut Mrs. Crane's dividends. ("Strikes," she would later write in a letter to the local paper, "were fomented by the idle and the vicious." The true problem, in her opinion, was not low wages or bad working conditions but "the drinking habits of the working classes.") Starting that second summer in Asbury, she was forced to rent their cottage to tourists.

One misfortune followed another. That June, with Stephen not yet thirteen, his surrogate mother, Agnes, died of meningitis. A quiet, unwed schoolteacher, she'd encouraged Stephen to enjoy life and speak out instead of succumbing to what she called their "oyster-like family." After her death, Stephen's mother packed him off to boarding school, and when he'd come home on vacation or for the summer, it was his brother Townley who took care of him. Before Stephen had turned fifteen, the *Asbury Park Shore Press* was reporting that Mrs. Crane was "extremely ill . . . with mental troubles." Townley was his own kind of eccentric. A *New York Daily Tribune* columnist, he was described as a "physical derelict" who—even in the hottest weather—walked the shore in a long coat, no shirt, and a muffler. As an added blow to the family, another brother, Luther, having survived an overdose, fell in front of a train on the Asbury tracks.

So, by the time he was a teenager, Stephen was mostly on his own. It isn't surprising that he rebelled against the values of his disintegrating family. There's the story that when he was seven, he bought a mug of beer and drank it down in one, long gulp. When a friend, astonished, asked how he could do such a thing, Stephen reportedly answered, "Beer ain't nothing at all . . . How was I going to know what it tasted like less'n I tasted it? How you going to know about things at all less'n you do 'em?"

The incident sounds a little too pat to be true, a perfect precursor to his career as a realist writer. But Crane encouraged stories like this, adding on tales of sea rescues and playing soldier, all of which fed the image of a daring rebel. Growing up in a particularly moralistic city and raised by religious crusaders, Stephen Crane ended up, in the words of Teddy Roosevelt, "a man of bad character." It was a reputation the son of the reverend doctor seemed proud of and had worked hard for.

His first newspaper piece may have been an 1887 *Philadelphia Press* sketch of young lovers at the shore. Crane's characters deliberately flaunt the social conventions of a town a lot like Asbury Park. Crane set them on the beach, where "they were partly protected from the sun's rays by a very loud striped parasol, but shielded from the gaze of the beach throng by nothing." So in love were the two as they sat together that "the whole world was but a myth to them." Enter a puritanical beach censor. The lovers had broken that restriction described in the Ocean Grove charter as "assuming attitudes on the sand that would be immoral at their city homes." When the censor, pretty clearly modeled on Bradley, descends upon them, the sixteen-year-old Crane sides with the "tender seaside doves" and against the old and narrow-minded.

The young writer would return often to this subject matter: the battle not so much of good versus evil as morality versus sensuality. And Bradley's promised land offered a perfect battlefield. In the hot sun, with the Epicycloidal Wheel ringing in the distance, the nineteenth century was ending. Some new, liberated time was coming. Even in this early story, Crane heard the boardwalk's promise of excitement, pleasure, desire.

Stephen's unwell mother continued to lecture against drinking, now using a small distillery to demonstrate the "presence of alcohol in many things of common use." Meanwhile, her son took to satirizing the hypocrisies of Asbury Park and Ocean Grove. In an 1890 *New York Daily Tribune* column, he has a newcomer ask, "Don't the people go to meeting all the time, and don't the constant singing and praying make one nervous?" If the question is irreverent, Crane's answer verges on the blasphemous: "Many ministers and other Christian workers come here to get away from the responsibility of conducting meetings to be in a place where they need not preach or even attend." If you go down to the beach, he wrote, you'll see "the entire population is disporting itself in the surf or lying in the sand." And he dismissed one of Bradley's most successful publicity schemes—the annual Baby Parade, where infants dressed as adults competed for prizes— by keeping his coverage of the "dimpled youngsters" to a single sentence.

These jabs apparently landed close enough to the mark for another *Tribune* writer (some commentators think it may have been brother Townley) to answer with a long, laudatory profile of the "great religious summer resort." Ocean Grove was easy to make fun of, the author says, and "a certain class of newspaper writers expend a great deal of energy and ink every year in denouncing the officers of the association and what they call 'their Puritanical laws.'" The best rebuttal was Ocean Grove's prosperity. It now boasted an open-air auditorium with a capacity of ten thousand, a tabernacle, a young people's temple, a chapel, and a summer population of over twenty-five thousand devout Christians.

Stephen didn't answer directly. As a cub reporter, he probably couldn't. Instead, he used the weapon of description, sprinkling his newspaper columns with the kind of realistic detail that flew in the face of these ideal communities. In the opening of an 1891 column, he evokes "great train-loads of pleasure-seekers and religious worshippers . . . arriving at the huge double railway station of Ocean Grove and Asbury Park." He goes on to describe "the rapacity of the hackmen," "the huge pile of trunks," and "the wriggling, howling mass of humanity." In other reports, he pauses lovingly over the foolish glory of the seaside amusements: a machine called a "razzle-dazzle," the big Wheel "to tumble-bumble the soul and gain possession of nickels," the steam organs, which made "weird music eternally." Were these, as his parents preached, "devices to kill time?" Absolutely. He calls them "enlarged toys." And what exactly is wrong with that? "Humanity only needs to be provided for ten minutes with a few whirligigs and things of that sort," he writes, "and it can forget at least four centuries of misery."

In the Methodist war against amusement, Crane's deadpan satire always came down on the same side. The next summer, he carefully dissected the average summer visitor to Asbury as "a rather portly man, with a good watch-chain and a business suit of clothes, a wife, and about three children. He stands in his two shoes with American self-reliance and, playing with his watch-chain, looks at the world with a clear eye." Here was Asbury's ideal visitor. In contrast, Crane reports that an attraction for the day-trippers—the big, steam-driven Observation Wheel on Lake Avenue—was getting into "a great lot of trouble" with hotel owners, who were complaining about its sparks and ashes. "Also," Crane adds, "residents of Ocean Grove came and said that the steam organ disturbed their pious meditations on the evils of the world."

Crane can barely contain his disgust with the pious middle class. At the same time, he begins to explore and empathize with the misery of the urban poor. During the summer of 1891, in what was supposedly little more than a seaside gossip column, Crane discussed the new documentary trend of social realism. "Muckraking" journalists were starting to expose the dark side of the Gilded Age, and Crane joined them. He had taken to spending time in New York City, particularly down in the Bowery, where Bradley had come from and where he still ran his brush factory. Walking the tenement streets, drinking in the bars, Crane was collecting material for his first novel, *Maggie: A Girl of the Streets*. A groundbreaking piece of fiction, it would describe a young factory worker "gradually and surely shriveling" from hopelessness. Describing Maggie's job in a typical sweatshop factory, Crane writes how "the begrimed windows rattled incessantly from the passing of elevated trains," and the "grizzled women in the room" were little more than "mechanical contrivances sewing seams."

Crane had completed an early draft of *Maggie* when his mother died in the winter of 1891. Still legally a minor, he was placed under the guardianship of yet another brother, Edmund. By this time, Townley may have been too eccentric to take charge. Meanwhile, brother William, the judge, bought out the siblings' remaining shares in the coalfields at a bargain price. Stephen spent the early part of 1892 working for a mercantile company and beginning his Civil War novel, *The Red Badge of Courage*.

The next summer, Crane returned to Asbury Park as a stringer for the *New York Daily Tribune*. In one column, he described an illustrated lecture by the early documentarian and activist Jacob Riis. Riis's groundbreaking book, *How the Other Half Lives*, had come out two winters before and created a sensation. In it, Riis had focused on the nearly half a million tenement dwellers living below New York City's Fourteenth Street, insisting that America couldn't forget the poverty, disease, and near starvation found there. The book had helped inspire and was, in a way, the nonfiction version of *Maggie*.

During his Asbury lecture, Riis made the point that writers who continued to produce inspirational, Horatio Alger stories were duping their public. By focusing on the few shining examples—self-made men like James Bradley—these writers supported the illusion that anyone with perseverance could escape tenement life. "We know now that there is no way out" is how Riis put it in his book. "The 'system' that was the evil offspring of public neglect and greed has come to stay."

It was a radical analysis, certainly in Asbury Park. Bradley's rags-to-riches story was a false model, implicitly attacking poor people for not working hard enough or having high enough morals. What's more, Riis implied that a resort like Asbury was at best just a release valve. It allowed its middle-class vacationers to look the other way (out to sea) instead of facing the disturbing facts. Stephen Crane found some hope in the large audience that showed up to hear Riis: "The thousands of summer visitors who have fled the hot, stifling air of the cities to enjoy the cool sea breezes are not entirely forgetful of the unfortunates who have to stay in their crowded tenements."

Crane, meanwhile, haunted the shore. A description by his girlfriend of the time paints a picture of a loner in the midst of the "tumble-bumble" of a beach town. "He was abjectly poor and undernourished—ate little and seemed to resent others eating heartily." With a cigarette hanging off his lower lip and his battered, unkempt clothes, Crane would walk the boardwalk, observing life, stopping for a Day's ice cream (though he could barely afford it), and taking his lover on the new sensation, the Kingsley Avenue merry-go-round. Not far from the big Observation Wheel, right about where the briars had first torn into Bradley's clothes, the Carousel House had gone up in 1888. The glittering machine spun in a special four-sided pavilion with multicolored sliding doors and brilliant murals of boardwalk scenes. Its array of elegantly carved, shiny wooden horses could carry seventy-eight passengers at a time. Mirrors reflected their speeding images, and there was the added excitement of leaning out into the wind and reaching for the brass ring that guaranteed a free ride. It was pointless, of course, this spinning in circles: a diversion from Jacob Riis's social crusade. But Crane and his girl rode it over and over, then would walk together along the shore. "Steve particularly enjoyed watching the surf," his lover remembered. He would tell her that "whenever she saw the ocean she would think of him."

This portrait of an artist as a young man had a flip side: an anger as strong as the romantic streak. Judging by one of his columns from that summer, Crane defined himself in opposition to Asbury Park's values and to James Bradley in particular. He started with the hand-painted moral warnings that dotted the beach and moved on from there:

"There is probably no man in the world that can beat 'Founder' Bradley in writing signs. His work has an air of philosophic thought about it which is very taking to anyone of a literary turn of mind. He usually starts off with an abstract truth, an axiom, not foreign nor irrelevant, but bearing somewhat upon a hidden meaning in the sign—'Keep off the grass,' or something of that sort . . . He is no mere bungler or trivial paint-slinger. He has the powers of condensation which are so much admired at this day. For instance: 'Modesty of apparel is as becoming to a lady in a bathing suit as to a lady dressed in silks and satins.' There are some very sweet thoughts in that declaration. It is really a beautiful expression of sentiment . . . A thoughtless man might have been guilty of some . . . unnecessary uncouthness. But to 'Founder' Bradley it would be impossible. He is not merely a man. He is an artist."

Through the thick fog of irony, you can hear Stephen Crane

dismissing the idea of moral uplift and trying to figure out what a real artist might be. And later that summer, he'd make clear that he wasn't limiting his attack to just the founding father. "Asbury Park," Crane wrote in 1892, "creates nothing. It does not make; it merely amuses. There is a factory where nightshirts are manufactured, but it is some miles from town. This is a resort of wealth and leisure, of women and considerable wine." The occasion for this outburst was an American Day parade held in mid-August by the Junior Order of United American Mechanics. Here were people who made their living with their hands walking right in the midst of the "cool sea breezes," and Crane dug into the contrasts with a vengeance:

"The throng along the line of march was composed of summer gowns, lace parasols, tennis trousers, straw hats and indifferent smiles. The procession was composed of men, bronzed, slope-shouldered, uncouth and begrimed with dust. Their clothes fitted them illy, for the most part, and they had no ideas of marching. They merely plodded along, not seeming quite to understand, stolid, unconcerned and, in a certain sense, dignified—a pace and a bearing emblematic of their lives. They smiled occasionally and from time to time greeted friends in the crowd on the sidewalk. Such an assemblage of the spraddle-legged men of the middle class, whose hands were bent and shoulders stooped from delving and constructing, had never appeared to an Asbury Park summer crowd, and the latter was vaguely amused."

Almost a century later, Bruce Springsteen would write the music that fit this scene: the heavy, dragging beat of his song "Factory." For Crane, as for Springsteen, if these workingmen are heroes, they're confused, very human heroes, plodding forward through what Springsteen would call "the mansions of fear . . . the mansions of pain." Crane, who had spent the previous year writing *Maggie*, recognized that these guys weren't Riis's starving masses.

Compared to the folks in the Bowery, they were well-off. At the same time, they're distinctly *not* the summer crowd in their tennis trousers. Partly because he insisted on describing the scene in all its contradictory detail, the American Day march became known as "the parade that made Stevie Crane famous."

First off, he lost his job. Asbury's *Daily Journal* attacked Crane's reporting as "slanderous," and the *Tribune* agreed. His assignment as the resort-town stringer was to boost tourism, not make fun of it. Typical shore reports were full of who was dining with whom and which visitor had the fanciest horse and buggy. How dare the twenty-one-year-old say that Asbury Park made nothing? It made people happy. To attack wealth and leisure was to attack the basis of the city's economy.

At the same time, Crane had managed to offend the working-man. The Junior Order of United American Mechanics resented his description as an "uncalled-for and un-American criticism" of their appearance and parading abilities. If he thought calling them "stolid" and "dignified" made the artist and the worker allies, he had another thing coming. They were patriotic Americans, the mechanics declared, dedicated to restricting immigration, teaching the Holy Bible in public school, and protecting business from "the depressing effect of foreign competition."

But the reason the article made Stevie Crane famous was that it came out just as his boss, the *Tribune*'s owner and editor, was running for vice president on the Republican ticket. A gleeful opposition jumped on the column as evidence that the owner/candidate was an enemy of the workingman. In the resulting scandal, the article was reprinted and discussed nationwide, and Crane (who was still a year away from self-publishing *Maggie*) had the beginning of the bad-boy reputation he would ride to fame.

"I seemed to have forgotten for the moment that my boss on the *Tribune* was running for Vice-President," he would write, years later. "You'd hardly think a little innocent chap like me could have stirred up such a row in American politics. It shows what innocence can do if it has the opportunity!" Crane's piece is a complicated mix of criticism, provocation, satire, and admiration—but the element it does not show is innocence. He isn't innocent about Asbury Park's class distinctions—which he describes from a street-smart perspective—and there's nothing innocent about his choice of subject matter. Crane may not have known how big a stink he was going to make, but this is a calculated piece of, among other things, self-promotion.

What he hadn't gone after was the town's racial politics. Back in a July 1890 dispatch, he had mentioned, "There is considerable feeling here against the running of excursion trains to Asbury Park and Ocean Grove, loaded with colored people." But it was Townley Crane who took on this issue. A piece by Townley in the *New York Times* ends with a pointed scene where a black man describes the awful singing and proselytizing of a Salvation Army band, "containing a noisy dwarf and some young women with tambourines." Townley quotes the colored citizen of Asbury as saying that *his* race would never "disgrace God or man in such a manner." The barb is aimed at Bradley's contention that Asbury only segregated against vulgar behavior.

Stephen was certainly aware of racial issues. A couple of months before the mechanics parade, he'd been back visiting Port Jervis when a drunken mob had come marching up East Main Street. Behind them, at the end of a length of rope, they were dragging a Negro. Like the Mingo Jack incident six years earlier and others across the country, this was about a white man accusing a colored man of attacking a white girl. As the mob pulled Robert Lewis through downtown Port Jervis, townspeople came out to watch. Women threw garbage at the colored man, and men snapped riding whips. On the corner of Ferguson Avenue, a rope was thrown over the branch of a tree. According to an article called "Depravity not Justice," which Townley Crane wrote for the *Tribune*, lightning and thunder lit the sky "as if God was trying to say something." Stephen and his brother Judge William Crane reportedly fought to pull Lewis down, but the mob won out. Later, Lewis's white accuser turned out to have beaten the woman himself. But instead of shame, Port Jervis commemorated the 1892 lynching with pride, displaying Lewis's shoes and the rope in a local museum.

Crane never wrote about the incident, although his short story "The Monster" describes a small town's "accustomed road of thought" with children reciting rhymes of "Nigger, nigger" and adults referring to "coons." Did Asbury Park's segregation offend him? The closest he comes to revealing his racial attitudes is in a private letter written to an old friend from boarding school. The friend has apparently complained that his sex life in Norfolk, Virginia, is miserable to nonexistent. Crane, six months shy of turning twenty-one, writes back:

"So you lack females of the white persuasion, do you? How unfortunate! And how extraordinary! I never thought that the world could come to such a pass that you would lack females, Thomas! You indeed must be in a God forsaken country. Just read these next few lines in a whisper:-I-I think black is quite good-if-if it's yellow and young."

"Black"—not a human being at all, just a color—"is quite good"; it's like a master describing his slaves. No more than a tossed-off sentence in a private letter and obviously meant to shock, it still reveals a lot about the values of the time and about Crane himself. It's written as a kind of joke, complete with mock stutter, as if to say, "Is this really so terrible?" If there's any truth to the boast, Crane is exactly what Bradley feared: the kind of tramp who hung around the boardwalk and "intermingled." The founding father's values made that morally repulsive *and* bad for business. Crane seems to have found the idea exciting and somewhat amusing: another chance to thumb his nose at middle-class convention.

Those conventions were Stephen Crane's real target. He didn't challenge Bradley by writing about racial issues. Maybe segregation didn't bother the young Crane. ("The Monster" was written six years later.) Maybe he suspected he'd get more attention if he focused on the slope-shouldered workingmen. For Crane, the mechanics parade was the perfect opportunity to throw the town's hypocrisy into hilarious, gruesome relief. And that middle-class moral hypocrisy was an issue he never quite shook. As late as 1896, after *The Red Badge of Courage* had become a best seller and *Maggie* had cemented his literary reputation, the twenty-five-year-old Crane looked back on his hometown in a *New York Journal* piece. By that time, the merry-go-round pavilion on Kingsley was known as The Palace. Next door, the owner had cashed in on the craze that had begun at the Chicago Exposition by installing a modern Ferris wheel.

"Coney Island is profane," Crane wrote. "Newport is proper with a vehemence that is some degrees more tiresome than Coney's profanity. If a man should be goaded into defining Asbury Park, he might state that the distinguishing feature of the town is its singular and elementary sanity."

So far, the town fathers must have thought, so good. "Distinctly American, reflecting all our best habits and manners," Crane writes, Asbury is a town of "restrictions," with "an ordinance whenever one wishes for novelty or excitement" and a "deep feeling of isolation." If this is distinctly American, then the country is about control. And the city's "elementary and singular sanity" begins to sound like a national tradition of repression.

The living embodiment of these values, of course, is James Bradley, whom Crane describes as the founder of "the greatest

Summer resort in America—the vacation abode of the mighty middle classes." Bradley at age sixty-six is "the one star in the sky over Asbury Park," and, according to Crane, a laughable, out-dated figure who "invariably walks under a white cotton sun umbrella," while "red whiskers of the Icelandic lichen pattern grow fretfully upon his chin. [He] carries his sublimity," Crane goes on, "with the calmness of a man out of debt . . . [and] for purposes too mystic, too exaltedly opaque for the common mind . . . placed a marble bathtub in the middle of a public park." Crane has this demigod moaning about how his will is not being done: "I own the pavilions and the bath houses, and the fishing pier and the beach and the pneumatic sea lion, and what I say ought to go."

For all Crane's bile, the native son clearly loves the place. He ends his piece looking out beyond the fishing piers to where "the incoming waves are shot with copper beams and the sea becomes a green opalescence." Bradley and his ilk—men who "define virtue as physical inertia and a mental death"—can enact all the ingeniously silly restrictions they want, but in the end, "the brave sea breeze blows cool on the shore, and the far little ships sink." Before he died of tuberculosis, aged twenty-eight, Stephen Crane proudly described himself as "about as much a Jerseyman as you could find."

But it wasn't love of the place that kept bringing him back to writing about Asbury Park. And it wasn't just his fight with Bradley, or even with the ghost of his father, the reverend doctor. For Crane, Asbury Park was a battleground in a national struggle. He saw the work of "extraordinarily optimistic architects" in the fun houses, the bathing pavilions, the domes and wheels. They reminded him of "youthful dreams." It wasn't just Asbury's rules and regulations that were distinctly American, but also the raunchy, unquenchable honky-tonk idealism. The brass bands, the barkers calling to the crowd, the calliope music drifting out of the merry-go-round, were Crane's pop culture: the product of that "wiggling, howling mass of humanity." Sure, the pleasure was fleeting, no more permanent than saltwater taffy. But the best part of Asbury Park didn't try to hide that. In the off-season, Crane wrote, "There is a mighty pathos in these gaunt and hollow buildings, impossibly and stolidly suffering from an enormous hunger for the public."

That was it! There was a hunger at the very heart of the thing. Crane's definitive take on Asbury is an 1893 story about a summer romance on the shore, "The Pace of Youth." It takes place mostly at Stimson's Mammoth Merry-Go-Round. Stimson is a man of "granite will" who believes he reduces those who oppose him to "quick and abject submission." Is he a stand-in for the founding father, James Bradley? No more than the merry-go-round stands for Asbury Park.

Stimson makes his living by selling wholesome "fun": the controlled pleasure of riding the wooden horses and stretching for the brass ring. None of this allows for any real passion. So when his daughter starts to fall for one of his employees, Stimson orders it to stop. Otherwise, the boy's fired. Crane has the two continuing to exchange glances around the cashier sign that hangs in their way. Finally, they arrange to take a walk along the shore.

"The electric lights on the beach made a broad band of tremoring light, extending parallel to the sea, and upon the wide walk there slowly paraded a great crowd, intermingling, intertwining, sometimes colliding." Despite all the censor's attempts to stop it, the crowd pushes the lovers closer and closer, until they make contact. It's then that the paper lanterns out on Wesley Lake, "flashing, fleeting, and careening, sang to them, sang a chorus of red and violet, and green and gold; a song of mystic bands of the future."

Call that chorus what you will—the American Dream, or just an enormous hunger—it was the great possibility that Crane felt rising out of Asbury Park. If it sounds like something Springsteen would write one day, both men were, after all, looking at the same city. And beneath Asbury's honky-tonk promise of getting away, of having fun, Crane saw a real dream of freedom. Once the crowd pushes them together, and they touch, Crane's lovers realize they have to get out from under. They jump into a horse and buggy and start driving. At the climax of the story, when Stimson sees he's not going to be able to catch them, the owner is struck by "the power of their young blood, the power to fly strongly into the future and feel and hope again."

But Crane's story doesn't end there. As a student of Jacob Riis, Crane knew there was no escaping the system. The "elementary sanity" would try to control you wherever you went. So, at the end of his story, as the lovers race down the highway, the dusty beach road "vanished far away in a point with a suggestion of intolerable length." As if that flashing, fleeting, careening song was somehow always in the future. As if being born to run was both a blessing and a curse. As if Asbury Park were forever.

FOURTH OF JULY, 1903

THE *EVENING NEWS* called July 4, 1903, Asbury Park's "greatest patriotic celebration." More accurately, it was its greatest celebration of independence. Because on this Fourth of July, for the first time ever, Asbury Park's beachfront belonged not to James Bradley, but to the elected government. The colony had broken from the king.

Maybe not completely. New Jersey governor Franklin Murphy came to Asbury to celebrate its newfound freedom. "You are trying to outdo Atlantic City," the governor shouted over applause, "and I hope you will succeed. You are leaving off the old to put on the new, but let me tell you that this city owes its greatness to James A. Bradley, who was a good man—better than any of us. He builded for the future. He believed in the right. He was a good senator, and I hope you will place his statue on the new boardwalk."

It was a glorious obituary except that James Bradley—the founding father, the man whom Stephen Crane called the "one star in the sky over Asbury Park"—wasn't dead. He had merely been eclipsed.

Sixteen years earlier, when Crane was publishing his first newspaper piece, Asbury Park had officially incorporated under a city council system of government. That hadn't affected Bradley's power. "In reality he was the government," the local papers admitted. "He owned the beachfront and the riparian rights," not to mention most of the other real estate in town. Some of the king's subjects had been trying to rebel for years, but always within gentlemanly bounds and always without success. Even in this year of independence, 1903, the council had no intention of altering Asbury in any radical sense. There was no move to change the basic economy, for example, or somehow embrace Stephen Crane's vision of a sensual, democratic future.

But the city's growing business class did agree with Crane that Bradley's restrictions were "ingeniously silly" and amounted to an economic stranglehold. As one leading property owner wrote in the fall of 1902, "With the number of wideawake merchants and hotel men in our community there is no reason in the wide world why Asbury Park should not lead the summer and winter resorts. We cannot do it, however, unless we own the beach and make a number of needed improvements at once."

Bradley, at seventy-two, had been managing every detail of the city for over thirty years. His vision was widely acknowledged. Many praised how he'd laid out a city both functional and forward-looking; how he'd tried to set a high moral tone; how his boardwalk, pavilions, and fishing piers were—in the words of Dr. Bruce S. Keator, president of Asbury's Board of Trade—"well made and in keeping with the earlier days of this place." But by the fall of 1902, the pavilions had become "dingy by day and poorly lighted by night" and the beachfront "old and dilapidated." The metaphor Keator used was that "the child

Asbury Park has matured to manhood and should be clothed as a man."

For years, the founding father had listened to such talk, often nodding his agreement, even writing letters full of promises to change things, but nothing had happened. The last time the council had asked him to improve the boardwalk, Bradley had smiled and replied that the walk "suited him very well and his next walk would be to the Golden Gate." He was an old man. He'd accomplished a lot. Couldn't his children respect him during the brief time remaining?

In the past, this benevolence—and the old-fashioned values behind it—had carried Bradley through. A decade earlier, in the fall of 1893—even as Stephen Crane had been making fun of his values—Bradley's antidrinking, antigambling position had gotten him elected to the state Senate. He'd run as a member of the Prohibitionist Party, touring Monmouth County in an elegant carriage with a brass band and an old tree stump. Crowds would gather as his immaculately liveried coachman drove him into town. Then, Bradley would have the stump pulled out of the back, mount it, and exhort the audience to join him in cleaning up the morals of their beloved but corrupt state of New Jersey. He'd finish by handing out free scrub brushes (from his Pearl Street factory) bearing the slogan "Brush Up."

His opponents accused him of trying to bribe voters with handouts. They also claimed that Bradley was prejudiced: Asbury's beaches were still segregated. But Monmouth County supported Bradley's Methodist values and wrote off the rest as eccentricities. He was elected to the Senate and immediately set to work to clean up the state, starting with what Bradley called "the Mecca of gamblers": the racetrack at Monmouth Park. Recently renovated, with a new monumental iron grandstand, Monmouth was setting national records for daily and monthly grosses. To cynics, the founding father was out to close one of Asbury's closest competitors. But the bill on which Senator Bradley cast the deciding vote, March 21, 1894, prohibited gambling in the entire state. Monmouth Park wouldn't reopen for another fifty-three years.

Less successful was Senator Bradley's bill to have city governments take over all the riparian rights on the Jersey shore. In fact, the proposal was the butt of statewide ridicule: understandable, since even as the founding father stumped for his bill, he refused to give up his own beachfront holdings. The shore was the key to how Bradley controlled not only Asbury's economy but its morals. During the summer of 1902, for example, the city council had passed a resolution licensing the use of slot machines on the city sidewalks. It had stipulated that there would be no gambling involved, that these were merely pleasure machines where a gentleman could win his lady a souvenir. But Bradley disapproved so vehemently that the city council had to pass a second resolution requesting that he stop harassing this licensed and legal business.

For the founding father, Asbury Park was still an island of Christian values—and he its Robinson Crusoe. But as well as losing the battle against amusements, he hadn't solved the problem of the shadow resort on the West Side. The quarter-mile square neighborhood was officially in Neptune township, but its economy depended totally on Asbury's. And vice versa. The city's tourist trade functioned thanks to Southern blacks drawn North by the relatively well-paid and dignified jobs. Lenora Walker McKay, author of *The Blacks of Monmouth County*, recalls how "in May or June, many students from Black colleges converged on the seashore seeking resort related work." McKay herself had a regular summer job in an Ocean Grove hotel, where she earned a dollar a day plus tips.

Bradley had set up his city to function a lot like its hotels. The illusion was that service simply happened: you went out on your morning promenade along the boardwalk, and when you got back, your room was miraculously clean. In the same way, Bradley had assumed that the porters, maids, and ditchdiggers would live invisibly. By 1903, the African-American population had grown enough to establish the Second Baptist Church, the Mt. Pisgah Baptist Temple, the St. Stephen A.M.E. Zion Church, and St. Augustine's Episcopal Church. But all remained on the West Side. (Legally so: the 1896 decision of *Plessy v. Ferguson* had made separate-but-equal the law of the land.) Colored people were allowed on Asbury's beaches, but only in the section known as the Mud Hole, where the city's sewers dumped into the sea.

When the colored population overstepped its bounds, measures were taken. This Fourth of July, 1903, as the governor congratulated Asbury Park on its freedom and its future, there was a traffic accident involving two colored men from the West Side and a white woman from Eatontown. The police arrested the men on the fifth, and that evening, as the woman lay in the hospital, word reached the Asbury police station that a mob was forming. At four thirty in the morning, the city's police chief had to hurry the suspects over to the county jail in Freehold "to escape lynching."

Asbury's workforce wasn't entirely made up of blacks, and neither was the West Side. McKay remembers playing as a child with all kinds of kids including "Mulatoe" and "Gypsy." In 1894, the *Shore Press* described the neighborhood as home to "Italians, Turks, Germans, and several varieties of the genus tramp." The city of Asbury Park excluded them all. Back in the 1880s, when Bradley had set up his beach segregation, he'd argued that if Italians decided to settle in town, they'd be kept out, too. At the time, the idea had seemed far-fetched, but twenty years later there were enough Italians in Asbury for them to organize their first annual parade.

Bradley was perfectly benevolent about the West Side. He served as the honorary "patrino" of the Italian festivities, which included a dance and a musical concert of the Lega Operaia Corpo S. Benigro. According to the *Shore Press*, the music, the wine, and the bright clothing proved that "the warm impulsive heart of the American Italian clings closely to the scenes of sunny Italy, that his bosom pulsates and swells under the rhythm of the dance." It was the kind of description that might apply to a minstrel show. Bradley and his city looked at the West Side with bemused condescension, willing to accept the new, Mediterranean immigrants as long as they stayed with the other tramps on their side of the tracks.

The trouble was that the West Side proved contagious. Officially, Lake Avenue stopped at Main Street, but its continuation—called Springwood Avenue—was home to a thriving mixed economy of kosher butchers, discount haberdashers, and itinerant peddlers. What the paper called the general "uncleanliness" included bars, betting parlors, and whorehouses. There still wasn't an effective sewer system west of Main, and Asbury considered the neighborhood an incubator for flu and smallpox. Not the least of it—in fact, maybe the most contagious—was the music.

The Negro bellhops from Georgia, the Sicilian ditchdiggers, and the other gypsies and tramps forced to live in the same crowded neighborhood had found more in common than just poverty. Musical styles mixed over an infectious, syncopated beat. The result was turn-of-the-century dance music that not only shocked Asbury's grown-ups but threatened to infect their kids. By this Fourth of July, 1903, ragtime was a national and international craze. The year before, the King of Ragtime—Scott Joplin—had followed up the astonishing success of "Maple Leaf Rag" by publishing another hit, "The Entertainer." Thousands upon thousands of copies of the sheet music were sold, and Joplin, a black man, saw no limits to the new sound. As Asbury Park celebrated its freedom, Joplin was writing his first ragtime opera, *A Guest of Honor*. With a cast of thirty-two, the two-act drama celebrated the day when the Negro leader Booker T. Washington had been invited to dine at Teddy Roosevelt's White House.

Joplin, who had attended a Methodist-run college in Missouri, saw his music in elegant, danceable opposition to both organized religion and the stranglehold of "serious" classical music. With the left hand pumping a stride beat and the right syncopating over the top, Joplin (and other ragtime piano masters like Jelly Roll Morton) could get a crowd of hundreds up on their feet and dancing. To match this intoxicating music, new steps appeared: the Turkey Trot, the Grizzly Bear, the Cakewalk.

The infection spread everywhere. Between 1890 and 1909, piano production in the United States would more than triple. The dignified European instrument became a centerpiece in every well-appointed parlor. It also became a carrier, as ragtime managed to slip in the side door and get its sheet music onto the stand. To the musical establishment, this was the national equivalent of the West Side coming over and using Asbury's beachfront. Ragtime was "a popular wave in the wrong direction," bred and born in the whorehouse, and designed to encourage physical contact, loose clothing, and looser morals. Mainstream magazines such as *Metronome* tried to convince their readers that it was a passing fad, its "days numbered." In 1900, the American Federation of Musicians ordered all its union members to stop playing the stuff. "Musicians know what is good," the union proclaimed, "and if people don't, we will have to teach them."

According to this view, good music was played by military bands, like the one James Bradley had taken out on the campaign trail. These brass bands had grown out of the European tradition but were considered patriotically American, evoking the village

green and the gazebo, a country of simple and democratic plea-
sures. Many of them were big enough to qualify as orchestras, with
cornets, trombones, flutes, clarinets, and even string sections.
Their repertoire tended toward marches. And the musicians
dressed in dignified quasi-military uniforms. Even a town as firmly
against frivolous amusement as Ocean Grove allowed marine
bands—although acceptance hadn't always come easily. As *The
Music Man* would reflect, years later, small-town America heard
sin in the sound of seventy-six trombones. That play's main
character, Professor Harold Hill, was based on a member of the
era's most popular band, led by John Philip Sousa.

Sousa was to band music what Bradley was to Asbury Park. By
the summer of 1903, the man known as the March King had
reigned supreme for nearly a decade. He'd started with the
United States Marine Band. Then, in 1892, Sousa had launched
his own unit, first appearing in Plainfield, New Jersey. The
country, in the midst of a severe five-year depression, had gone
crazy for his brand of proud and vivid nostalgia. Eventually, the
band would go on to make annual summer tours up and down
the Jersey shore as well as massively popular trips to Europe.
Sousa not only led a crack unit with some of the era's most
famous soloists, but he wrote a string of stirring patriotic
marches, including "Stars and Stripes Forever."

In its first year, Sousa's band had established a national
reputation by playing the Chicago World Exposition. Also performing there were the greatest ragtime musicians of the day,
including Scott Joplin. Sousa may not have appreciated their
music much—the syncopated beat existed outside both his skills
and his tastes—but he quickly recognized its popularity. He'd have
to give his audience at least a taste. For that, he turned to his
young trombone player who, unlike Sousa, had a feel for these
"ethnic rhythms." After helping Sousa modernize his sound, the

trombone player—Arthur Pryor—would go on to establish argu-
ably the most popular band in Asbury Park's history.

Pryor was born in one of the country's ragtime centers, St.
Joseph, Missouri, in 1870. His early musical training came from his
father, a bandleader, and his mother, a pianist. By the time he was
eleven, Pryor was being billed as the "boy wonder" of the valve
trombone, an instrument with keys like a cornet, popular in
German and Italian bands. Around this time, one of his father's
students couldn't pay for lessons and, instead, gave the family a
slide trombone. On the slide, you didn't have keys. It was a more
slippery, adjustable instrument where you had to feel your way to
the notes. Pryor described the man who left it as a "tramp."

His parents couldn't help with the slide. The only people in St.
Joe who played this kind of horn lived across the tracks. Pryor
began heading over there to the local pool hall. Soon, he'd picked
up the basic positions and the beginnings of his incredibly fast,
slurred-note technique. The world of formal marine bands had
never heard anything like it, and at the age of twenty-two, Pryor
was invited East to audition for Sousa.

At first, the March King was skeptical: "This young fellow may
be just a flash." But Pryor won him over with his clean tone, four-
octave range, and his stunning speed. When he took his first
public solo (at the Chicago Exposition), the papers reported that
the crowds threw their hats in the air and cheered. Within two
years, he was not only Sousa's best-known soloist but his assistant
conductor, one of his main jobs being to lead the band through
ragtime tunes. Experts called Sousa's attempts at the new music
"ponderous echoes of the Negroes' light-footed syncopation."
Sousa couldn't hear it, they criticized, and neither could most
of his musicians: "The stiff-backed old fellows felt it was beneath
their dignity, and they couldn't or wouldn't give in to it."

So, the March King left ragtime to Pryor, who produced hit after hit, among them "At Georgia Campmeeting," "Whistling Rufus," and "Smokey Mokes." Though Sousa became famous for bringing ragtime and the cakewalk craze to Europe, Pryor deserves much of the credit. On top of his musicianship, the trombone player also composed, and his own hits included "Razzazza Mazzazza" and "A Coon Band Contest."

The titles tell the story. Pryor may have been fifteen years younger than John Philip Sousa and a lot hipper to syncopation, but calling his piece "A Coon Band Contest" sent the same message as "Smokey Mokes." Both men were making clear to their public that though ragtime was colored, they weren't. (Meanwhile, Scott Joplin's rags had titles like "Elegant Syncopations.") The distinction was crucial to getting work. If a marine band was going to succeed, it had to be able to play resort towns like Asbury Park. There, James Bradley had stipulated that any band hired to play the beachfront couldn't employ "ethnics." "I don't want a band on my beach," he had announced, "that has musicians who in appearance are distinguished from others." He insisted on what he called an "Americanized band." In that, he appears to have reflected the views of the city. When Mayor Frank L. TenBroeck had tried to change this stipulation, in 1888, the council had voted 6 to 1 to support Bradley.

On July 4, 1903—as the governor spoke in Asbury Park—Pryor was in the process of leaving Sousa's band to start his own. The unit he put together carefully modified the March King's sound without changing it too radically. Pryor's band would swing a little more, dare to invoke modern times, even incorporate a little of what was percolating over on the West Side. All of which pushed at the limits of Bradley's ethnic restrictions without breaking them. Pryor was leaving the March King in much the same way that Asbury Park had risen against its own royalty.

The city's reason was simple enough: Bradley's old-fashioned values were no longer doing justice to capital. The town couldn't blame Bradley for the collapse of the First National Bank in the winter of 1903. That had been the result of false-entry bookkeeping and the board of directors' misuse of funds. But the news "fell like a thunderbolt on the business community," and it came in the midst of tough economic times. One businessman spoke of having lost $6,000 during the 1902 summer season, and this he did blame on the founding father's refusal to change with the times. "If the beach is Bradley's," the outraged citizen complained, "let him put it in order and let us live. We are not living now." The proprietor of one of the big hotels agreed. "I must say," he wrote, "that the boardwalk and pavilions, in their present conditions, do not warrant a greater investment on my part."

After more than a decade of trying to either buy the waterfront or get Bradley to modernize it, the city now made a last desperate move. Lawyers were hired to prove that the founding father had never actually owned the beach. Nervous about the power and popularity of the seventy-two-year-old, opponents waited till Mr. and Mrs. Bradley were on their annual late-summer tour of Europe. Then, the Board of Trade, led by Councilman Keator, announced that early maps and surveys showed the beachfront, lakes, and parks as *public* property. Bradley himself, they claimed, had used public access as part of his pitch to sell building lots. The beach, they declared, was now and always had been the "people's."

When Asbury Park's attorney presented this case, he took it a step further. First, he made sure to praise Bradley for all "he had done for this place." But then he argued, "If we cannot claim the property, let's buy it, and if we can't do that, then begin condemnation proceedings." A resolution to that effect passed the Board of Trade September 17, 1902, and was followed by similar actions from the Association of Hotel Keepers and the city council itself.

The Bradleys returned in early October. A reporter from the *Asbury Park Journal* came to the brush factory, and the founding father was happy to chat about increasing wages for the city's policemen and about a recent local Republican convention. But when asked about ownership of the beach, he tore a scrap from the roll of wrapping paper that lay on his Pearl Street desk and wrote on it, "Silence Is Golden."

For a month, Bradley wouldn't respond. November 7, the front-page headline in the *Journal* read, CITY PROCEEDS AGAINST MAYOR. A committee headed by Councilman Keator had concluded that the beachfront, lakes, and parks were, in fact, public property. Bradley was given five days to hand the real estate over or have it confiscated.

Not everyone supported the revolution. A young councilman, T. Frank Appleby, led the city's conservative wing. That group felt this confrontational approach "ill advised" and "lacking diplomacy." Appleby was a local boy made good, a realtor who had been partners in the construction of the 150-room Hotel Bristol and the Appleby Building, the first in the city to have an elevator. At thirty-eight, he was the young hope for the old-timers who wanted to keep Asbury Park true to Bradley's vision.

The founding father wrote the city council that while he would "prefer to remain silent," his "shock [and] regret" prompted him to reply. In his letter, Bradley described himself as a man who didn't like antagonism and whose role as town censor derived from the "paternal character" of his relationship to the city. He described the movement to claim the beachfront for the city as "the efforts of sons and daughters to realize on the estate before the head of the house has shuffled off his mortal coil." Still, to avoid tying the city up in years of litigation, he would be willing to sell the beachfront, the parks, and the sewage system for $150,000.

Councilman Kinmouth came right out and called the offer "a

farce." They'd heard all this before, he said. "Mr. Bradley doesn't intend and never will sell the beach to the city until he is forced to do so." Bradley's next move seemed to confirm that. He filed papers to sue his children, the city council.

In the past, this had always been the point where city officials had backed down. They'd push just so hard, then concede that the founder probably really did own the beach and meekly request some shorefront improvements. Oh, and would Mr. Bradley please leave the slot machines alone? But this time was different. The economics were too bleak, the beachfront too dingy, and the town falling too far behind the times. The city council answered Bradley by calling for a public meeting to be held on November 21 in Educational Hall.

The setting itself was a reminder of all Bradley had done for the city. This was the hall that he'd had moved from Philadelphia's Centennial Exposition back in 1877. On the night of the twenty-first, the place was packed. The *Asbury Park Journal* remarked with some surprise on how a third of the audience was female, "many of whom are tax-payers and deeply interested." There was also a sizable group from outside the city limits who were convinced the future of the whole area hinged on this question of who owned Asbury's beachfront. There was no mention of anyone attending from the West Side. And Bradley passed, too, sending his regrets and adding that he hoped "your deliberation may be productive for the good of our city."

The two-hour debate that followed—sometimes angry, sometimes apologetic, occasionally disruptive—underlined the divisions that ran through town. On the one side, there was Council President Appleby, who joined with many of the city's original landowners in championing Bradley and advocating a cautious, nonconfrontational approach. "What has built up Asbury Park," one of the city's original businessmen declared, "is its reputation for morality." That's what made it special, and that morality stemmed directly from the founding father. Another old-timer stood to proclaim that he would "take Mr. Bradley's word as being as good as his bond, and his bond was as good as any man's in this place tonight." For these citizens, trying to take the beachfront from Bradley wasn't just a waste of time and taxpayers' money; it was a kind of blasphemy.

On the other side was the group of merchants and councilmen led by Councilman Keator. The beachfront didn't belong to Bradley, and as ex-mayor TenBroeck put it, "If it belongs to us, why should we pay for it?" He doubted that Bradley meant his offer to sell and dared to go even further. "That man has not kept faith with us for fourteen years, why should he keep faith with us tonight?"

That was too much for Educational Hall. Appleby had to gavel the meeting back to order. But before TenBroeck sat down, he pointed out that if—*if* Bradley owned the beachfront, the city had another case. The founding father had never paid a dollar in taxes. He owed the city a fortune. "We tax the widows and orphans," as one irate citizen declared, "and let the most valuable property go untaxed . . . Where is the backbone of the common council?"

Between the conservative and the confrontational lay a middle ground. Citizens like Dr. Henry Mitchell felt a city lawsuit against Bradley would take too long and cost too much and, finally, who cared? The beach was being offered at a bargain price; Asbury Park should snap it up. Bradley's figure of $150,000, Mitchell argued, was "simply to reimburse himself for certain expenditures with no idea of being fully paid." And the city would make its investment back in just a few years. "The capitalists would flock in," Captain Jonathan Minot told the crowd, "and invest their millions."

In the end, this argument won the day. It was, after all, the era of John D. Rockefeller and J. P. Morgan. The twentieth century was leaving the dock; America was positioned to reap incredible profits; and their little beach town was on the verge of being left behind. "Asbury," one citizen declared, "has reached a crisis." At the end of the evening, when the chairman asked how many were in favor of accepting Bradley's offer, an "overwhelming majority" rose from their seats. A resolution passed calling for the city council to stop its legal action and okay the expenditure. Then the audience filed out into the cold November night to the sound of the Monmouth concert band. They were still playing old-fashioned oompah music.

That Monday afternoon, James Bradley tendered his resignation as mayor. In the evening, with Appleby presiding, the council agreed to pay the $150,000. In addition, it set two mid-January elections. At the first, the council would decide on a new mayor. A week later, all the eligible citizens of Asbury would vote on a bond to purchase and improve the waterfront. What the elections were really deciding was whether to redraw the promised land: where the city was headed, what role democracy would play, how the dream would change.

The mayoral election was the test. Bradley's supporters ran Appleby against Councilman Keator, leader of the rebel forces. The night of the election, as Keator climbed the stairs to enter the council room, a group calling itself the Taxpayers Association handed him a letter. The signatories denounced Keator's "injudicious and conspicuous action" against Bradley and implied that, if he was elected, the council would lose the support of the business community. It was one thing to buy the beach: that only made economic sense. But to attack the founding father's good word, these taxpayers argued, was to question the moral underpinnings of their Christian city.

In the end, the council supported Keator over Appleby, 4 to 3. It wasn't just a vote against Bradley's legacy. It also swung the city toward the merchants' vision. "The beach, with its future development," said Mayor Keator in his victory speech, "will be the key of success to this city, as a health and pleasure resort, for all time to come." A week later, the bond passed easily.

The following April, when Bradley arrived in town, the *Shore Press* reported that "the founder looked sadly on his old possessions but . . . then he thought of the $150,000 check and if there were any unbidden tears nobody saw them." As soon as the sale was final, the council approved funds to build a new boardwalk from Fifth Avenue south to the Pavilion, to install "beautiful lamp posts" and "artistic galvanized iron railing," to give everything on the waterfront from the pier to the benches a fresh coat of beige paint, and to remove the "old lion cages, etc."—those last reminders of the king's eccentricities.

In May, the council accepted a $20,000 bid from a local businessman to run the various boardwalk concessions and amusements: the bootblack stands, the stereopticon booth, the tackle shop. For the first time, the boardwalk income would come to the city. Over at the Palace Amusement center, the owner was doing his bit to modernize by constructing something he called The Crystal Maze: a two-story, hundred-foot-long building featuring a hall of mirrors that thrilled tourists by distorting their images and encouraging them to lose their way.

But there were some Asbury Park values that the merchants had no intention of changing. The beach would still be divided into clearly marked sections: season renters, transients, and colored. A glance at the July schedule for the auditorium shows the city's bread and butter was still respectable middle-class organizations. First, New Jersey's Sunday School Association would hold its convention, followed by the state Dental Society and then the American Food Exhibition. No less than Frederick Law Olmsted, the founder of American landscape architecture and codesigner of

New York City's Central Park, confirmed this conservative approach. "Asbury Park," Olmsted wrote in a report that the council commissioned that spring, "has developed a character different from that of many of the beach resorts and appealing to a different class of people." What the city had avoided, according to Olmsted, was "vulgarity," and his advice was to "hold such clientele" while increasing profits by extending the tourist season.

Walking the boardwalk that Fourth of July, 1903, you could *hear* this cautious, traditional approach. The council had hired Dr. G. E. Conterno's band to play the boardwalk, and his military unit was modeled on Sousa's right down to the conductor's white suit shining with medals. Toward the end of that year, Arthur Pryor's band premiered at the Majestic Theater in New York City, and Asbury's merchants recognized that this was the sound that matched the city's new direction. Pryor wrote songs that reflected the old values, including regional boosterism ("On the Jersey Shore") and patriotism ("Triumph of Old Glory"). At the same time, he was a modern man, forward thinking. Where Sousa saw the invention of the phonograph record as a threat to his concert income (he called the result "canned music"), Pryor embraced it. In its first three years, his band recorded 168 tracks at RCA Victor's Camden, New Jersey, studio. Pryor would eventually cut some twenty-five hundred selections and become, according to some historians, the first musician to live off record sales.

Asbury Park hired Arthur Pryor's band for the 1904 season, and he was an instant hit. That first summer, he played 269 concerts and drew more than three hundred thousand listeners. Within a couple of years, the city was paying him $17,000 a season. Within five years, Pryor would quit touring elsewhere and buy a house in Asbury. Over the next quarter of a century, he became such a fixture that the city eventually dedicated the Arthur Pryor Bandstand on its boardwalk.

If there was a turn-of-the-century music that *meant* beachfront and boardwalk—a shore sound—it was Arthur Pryor's. By carefully marketing "ethnic" music without ethnic musicians, he produced arrangements that were modern only in comparison to Sousa's. A Pryor concert was a semiformal event. The audience got dressed up for the occasion and then responded not with anything like the wild ragtime dances, but with toe tapping and applause. It was, in short, merchant's music. For decades, Arthur Pryor's sound embodied Asbury Park's definition of what it meant to be born in the USA.

The merchants fully expected a new era of prosperity. In 1903, the city spent $60,000 to replace the open-air Bradley Pavilion, which jutted out over the ocean at the end of Asbury Avenue, with the two-story Casino: a state-of-the-art hall that could seat seven thousand visiting conventioneers. Two years later, the city invested nearly $400,000 in improvements and modernizations, a budget six times greater than ever before. But it quickly became obvious that income from the boardwalk alone would never cover all the expenses. Asbury's service economy ran at a deficit (Bradley often said he lost $10,000 a year), and the promised flood of capitalists hadn't materialized.

Suddenly, the city found itself discussing an issue that had only been whispered about before: the possibility of annexing the West Side for the additional tax revenue. Estimates put the worth of the shadow city at more than a million dollars; the taxes would bring in around $20,000. When the idea of annexation was broached, Bradley wrote to the citizens of what he still considered his city that he would "stand aside and in a fatherly way watch." He had just one proviso: Asbury Park must not include the Springwood Avenue section. If the city felt it needed to absorb the northern part of the West Side, where many of the Jewish merchants lived, fine. According to the local paper, these neighbors shared basic

Asbury Park values such as "thrift." But bring the ragtime, discount, ethnic center of Springwood Avenue into his promised land? Bradley announced he would "most certainly oppose [that] because of its class of voters."

The city council's first instinct was to agree with their founding father. But soon a countermovement sprang up. Led by the town tax collector and the head of the Ocean Grove church, the Reverend A. E. Ballard, this group argued that the council had both a fiscal and a *moral* obligation to include Springwood. It would certainly increase revenue. And as a group of leading merchants pointed out, if this section stayed outside the city, deliverymen and others might have to buy extra, expensive licenses to do business there.

In addition, the Reverend Ballard argued, "with [the] Springwood Avenue section outside of the new city's jurisdiction it would always be a menace." Only by annexation could the good people of Asbury Park institute "a complete house-cleaning of the 'red-light' district." That included getting rid of smallpox and other diseases: with an estimated seventy-five percent of Asbury's hotel workers living on or near Springwood, the area posed the threat of an epidemic that would ruin the tourist business. But the real menace was moral. As one editorial argued, if Springwood wasn't incorporated, the city would have to "suffer from the evils that breed there without having the power to apply corrective or punitary treatment." Councilman Keator described it as "a festering cancer." Supporters appealed to the ethics of old Methodist Asbury, arguing that the city had to root out the hookers, the gin joints, the ragtime infection.

None of this convinced Bradley. For days, he used a section of the front page of the newspaper to declare his view that annexing Springwood would "place Asbury Park in the hands of the people of the west side, many, very many of whom are not imbued with the old established American ideas, especially as to beer and liquors." If Springwood became part of the city, "their representation would be equal to ours." Power would shift; morals would fall. The founding father telegraphed his state senator that for Asbury Park to include Springwood Avenue was "to commit hari-kari." He was "not prejudiced against colored people" and offered as proof the time more than thirty years before when he and his colored man had stretched out together on the empty beach. But if Springwood Avenue was annexed, "our city will have the largest pro-rata colored voters of any city in New Jersey." That would lead to a "great depreciation of property." Justice would not be done to capital. What's more, democracy would not be served because, in the founder's opinion, "the majority of the colored vote of Monmouth county is a purchasable article."

To this last, the Reverend Ballard replied that if the colored vote was for sale, "Mr. Bradley had the longest purse." (The reverend quickly explained he meant that as a joke.) On the other side, Councilman Appleby lined up firmly behind Bradley, saying there were 350 empty lots still available in Asbury: plenty of room for expansion and more taxes without taking over the West Side. But an investigation by the local paper couldn't locate those lots. And having done the math, the editors assured their readers that between the old city and the northern section of West Park, the majority of voters would still share Asbury's "old established American ideas."

In the midst of the debate, Booker T. Washington (Joplin's "Guest of Honor") was invited to speak in town. "I am proud of my race," Washington began before a crowd of five hundred gathered at Asbury High School. He then went on, "Our people, however, have got to learn one thing: the value of a dollar . . . I ask the ministers and the people of the community to get after the hanger-on, the shiftless, lazy colored man." Hearing this in the midst of the raging argument over annexing the West Side must have reassured Asbury Park. There were some good Negroes. According to the Asbury paper, "Race prejudice was swept away by forceful argument." It did note, however, that only a small percentage of Washington's audience was colored.

The city council ended up proposing the annexation of the entire West Side, including Springwood Avenue. On May 16, 1906, the resolution passed by a more than two-to-one margin. The front page of the next day's paper featured a sailor groom and his young bride: the shore linked to the shadow city. The caption to the cartoon read, "Now you're married you must obey . . ."

The vote was Bradley's final defeat. A few days beforehand, at a rally of his supporters, the founding father had announced that this would probably be his last appearance on a public platform in Asbury Park. It wasn't, but over the remaining fifteen years of his life, the king's influence continued to decline. At age eighty, he would say, "I want to look down on Asbury Park, and I want to be pleased with the view." But eventually, he lost hope that he would ever see his promised land. He denied what he called his "early enthusiasm" and talked about the founding of Asbury as if it had been a simple economic investment all along. Even that hadn't worked out. "Had I put my money out at interest," he said not long before he died, "I would be a richer man today, and I would not have had the cares and worry . . . No, summing it all up, Asbury Park to me was a financial failure. I would have been much happier in my old age had I never heard of the place."

FOURTH OF JULY, 1924

To UNDERSTAND THE fourth of July, 1924, you have to go back to the Business Men's Show of that spring and what came to be known as the Merchants Orgy. To understand the Fourth of July, 1924, you have to get to know the Ku Klux Klan.

Twenty years had passed since Asbury Park had gained control over its own beachfront. While the city still depended primarily on the one hundred thousand visitors who came to the beach each summer, it was now home to over five hundred businesses and had emerged as the shopping hub of the north Jersey shore. The fourth annual Business Men's Show celebrated what Bradley's dream had turned into: the merchants' vision.

The trade show was held in the Casino, down on the board-walk. The decorations committee had hung the place with laven-der bunting and freshly cut greens: tasteful, sober, modern. Ads for the show promised "a liberal education . . . in what to buy for the home and for personal use." Okay, there would be a bathing-suit contest. And a display of fancy roller-skating. And an appearance by Madame Guida, the Danish "toe dancer." After all, Asbury was still a resort town, and its businessmen knew how to draw a crowd. But they advertised not for the thrill-seeking steeplechase riders but for the new, progressive consumers who "plan the home budget scientifically and economically."

Every booth was rented. A hundred city businesses took part, from the Monmouth Ice Cream Company to the local auto dealers, from Isaac Berger's women's apparel store to Walter Tindall's print shop. The Chamber of Commerce boasted that $100,000 worth of merchandise was on display. An estimated sixty thousand people would eventually pass through the six-day show.

By 1924, Sinclair Lewis's *Main Street* had revealed the underside of small-town America, and some may have recognized a similar provincialism and self-righteousness at the Business Men's Show. Those were the types who might have taken offense at the Consolidated Gas Company's booth, where free waffles were handed out by a "living reproduction" of Aunt Jemima. But most who came seemed to agree that the city's merchants were pointing the way to both a sensible and prosperous future. As Isaac Berger, chairman of the event, proudly told the papers, "It would have been possible for us to fill a building twice the size of the Casino." The city council had recently addressed that problem by passing a resolution to build a new Convention Hall. The four-thousand-seat structure would expand Asbury's tourist capacity and make it the envy of the shore towns.

No wonder, then, if the merchants decided to celebrate their success. Thursday night after the Business Men's Show had closed, over a hundred shop owners, politicians, and city leaders showed up at an invitation-only affair out at the Deal Inn. According to one witness, the inn's windows were shuttered, its doors locked, and city policemen guarded the entrances. That same witness testified that, inside, Asbury Park's leading citizens got so drunk "that they could not get off their chairs."

There was more. The affidavit by the local printer, Walter C. Tindall, went on to state that he saw "semi-nude women." In particular, Tindall accused Asbury's mayor, Clarence E. F. Hetrick, of having "caressed a half-nude dancing girl sitting on his knees" and of handing Chairman Berger a packet that contained "$1,000 of his [the mayor's] unpaid bills" from Berger's downtown clothing store. Berger accepted the envelope "too drunk to describe its contents."

That's what Tindall reported, anyway, to Asbury Park's Civic-Church League two days later. The Civic-Church League, along with its ally the Anti-Saloon League, stood for the old Asbury Park—James Bradley's Asbury Park—a city with a conscience and a Christian mission. Twenty years ago, these forces had sided with Bradley against the annexation of the West Side, against vulgar amusements, against drinking. This Saturday morning, as the League gathered in Tindall's First Baptist Church, its members had their own victories to celebrate. Prohibition had become national law four years earlier. It was Asbury Park's antiliquor statutes written on a grand scale, the result of untiring lobbying by various religious groups. In fact, one historian writes that "the temperance movement was in many respects the *characteristic* Methodist battle of the century" (emphasis in original). Which didn't mean the war was over. The same way Asbury's "dry" laws had turned the city's drugstores into under-the-counter gin mills, the Eighteenth Amendment had produced a nationwide black market. In 1924 alone, the Department of Commerce estimated some $40 million of illegal booze was entering the United States. Monmouth County's newspapers were referring to the Jersey shore as "The Rum Coast," with bootleggers arriving nightly to unload their speedboats.

Walter Tindall's testimony that Saturday evening confirmed what the Civic-Church League had long believed: sin flourished in

Asbury Park, the leading members of the merchant class were among the worst offenders, and the city government was deeply involved. The party at the Deal Inn was dubbed the Merchants Orgy, and the city's preachers hurried home to rewrite their Sunday sermons.

At the First Methodist Episcopal Church, the Reverend Furman A. DeMaris told his congregation he wouldn't read Tindall's affidavit aloud—it was too disgusting—but they should know it was a document "the like of which I never dreamed could be written in the twentieth century." The reverend demanded that the Deal Inn be padlocked and that the accused officials resign immediately. The Reverend Shaw at the Presbyterian church agreed. So did Rabbi Davidson at the Temple Beth-El.

Walter Tindall's own minister, the Reverend David A. Mac-Murray, was a leader of the Civic-Church League, and he called down a full quota of fire and brimstone. The Reverend MacMurray opened his sermon by quoting from the twelfth psalm: "Sinners walk on every side and the vilest men are exalted." That was just a warm-up. "No matter how beautiful the town," the Reverend MacMurray told his congregation, "the soul of the community is determined by the soul of the people. Unless we are honest, moral and clean, we shall wake up and find ourselves the cynosure of the entire world. They will think of Asbury Park as hell."

James Bradley had died three years earlier, age ninety-one, resigned to the fact that his promised land was never to be. But the Merchants Orgy proved something worse: that Asbury Park had become the devil's playground. That Sunday, as news spread across the city, the ministers had what amounted to an exclusive. On Monday morning, the *New York Times* front-page headline read ASBURY PARK MAYOR ACCUSED IN PULPITS. Local papers reported that a number of the accused had already filed affidavits claiming Tindall made the whole thing up. Some offered proof that they hadn't even been at the Deal Inn that night. "There was no lewdness, no vulgarity and no drunkenness," Mayor Hetrick declared. "I had no liquor and saw no liquor. The charge that a nude woman sat in my lap is a damnable lie. In the first place," he spluttered, "there were no nude women, and in the second place nobody sat in my lap."

The agitated mayor was backed up by, among others, Isaac Berger. Berger, a founding member of Asbury's conservative synagogue, explained that he couldn't have been drunk because he didn't drink. "Of course we didn't have any booze, and I didn't see anyone sitting on the mayor's lap," he added. "Everybody said that it was a rotten party. By that I mean they thought it was too tame and that the girls were not lively enough."

Berger, a Jew, taunting the Christian moralists? Suggesting that their crusade against drink was as old-fashioned as button-down spats? Implying that not just the party, but the city was too tame? To the Civic-Church League this must have seemed like clear evidence that Berger and the merchant class had taken over the city and now felt themselves invulnerable.

For his part, Mayor Hetrick saw "a political aspect" to the charges. Hetrick had been mayor since 1915, elected as part of a citywide reform movement. After Bradley had sold the beachfront to the city and the West Side was annexed, there had been an upwelling of optimism. The city was going to run in a progressive, businesslike way; profits were bound to follow. But the first decade of democracy had been laced with corruption. Asbury's council members were accused of renting prime boardwalk real estate to their friends and cronies, who were often the lowest bidders. Income on the Casino—once $4,000 to $6,000 a season—had mysteriously dropped to nothing. Finally, in 1915, the city had voted to switch from a seven-person council to a five-person commission, hoping to clean house and end "the old partisan politics."

The entire city government had resigned, and fifty-seven candidates had announced for the five new openings. There were "dry" candidates and pro-business candidates, even colored candidates. Straw polls had showed Clarence Hetrick as, at best, a squeak-in fifth commissioner. But on election day, he pulled in the most votes, 1,091 out of 2,007, making him the new mayor.

The day before the election, James Bradley himself had taken out a full-page ad under the headline SOUND THE ALARM. The founding father had warned his children that, with the annexation of the West Side, Asbury's tramps threatened to play a decisive role in a city election. Now, Bradley called on the city to follow his advice by "voting down the colored man." And it did, electing Hetrick instead. Which began what the Civic-Church League saw as their city's slide toward hell.

Clarence Hetrick was born in Ohio in 1873 and had come to Asbury when he was fourteen. While Stevie Crane was hanging around the boardwalk, Hetrick had been working at his father's real estate office. He eventually ran the place. At age thirty-one, he became tax receiver for the town of Neptune, which borders Asbury on the inland side. Through (he claimed) his "financial acumen and business ability," Hetrick had reduced the town's debt from $45,000 to $1,500. That gave him credibility as a fiscal reformer, and he had gone on to serve for two years as Asbury Park's treasurer. But it was his next job, as sheriff of Monmouth County, that made Clarence Hetrick's political career. Which is to say that Asbury's future evolved out of a sensational, racially charged murder case.

On November 9, 1910, a ten-year-old white girl, Marie Smith, disappeared on her way home from school on Asbury's West Side. A search of the area turned up nothing. It was front-page news, and the *Asbury Evening Press* coverage included a list of likely suspects. A band of gypsies had camped in the area the week before. An Italian "had been in the habit of selling whiskey" to Marie's mother. One witness came forward to say she'd seen Marie standing in front of Kruschka's nursery on Asbury Avenue while a German worker, Frank Heidemann, watched from behind a hedge. Finally, there was Thomas Williams, a colored man who worked for Marie's aunt. According to reports, the day after the girl's disappearance, Williams, "better known as 'Black Diamond,'" had been drinking heavily. The papers announced that the police were looking for him.

Two days later, Marie Smith was found in some sandy woods near Asbury Avenue. She had been raped, strangled, and beaten to death. "Strong evidence is hourly being produced," the *Asbury Press* declared, "to show that Williams is the man." Black Diamond had been found. A detective brought him to the city morgue, showed the colored man the corpse, and thundered, "Swear that you did not murder this child!" To which Williams replied, "I swear to God I didn't touch the girl." But by then, it was almost too late.

It didn't matter to Asbury that Williams denied the murder, or that there was no evidence linking him to it. To the contrary. According to a front-page story, "Everything points to the negro [*sic*] as the slayer, and the fearless attitude he has assumed seems to bear out the contention of the police that he could be guilty of the murder and still show no sign of shrinking." A lead editorial entitled SWIFT JUSTICE claimed, "The honor of Asbury Park is at stake." And a front-page news story (that read like an editorial) laid out the self-fulfilling logic behind the city's rush to judgment. "Criminal assault plainly was the motive of the crime. This is a negro crime. 'Black Diamond' was the only negro known to have been near the scene at the time the murder was committed."

It was an old equation with an equally old solution. The night of Williams's arrest, a surging mob of would-be lynchers arrived at the jail with sledgehammers, axes, and crowbars. The paper reported that the mob was made up of citizens from all over Monmouth County, many of them bragging they'd been part of the Mingo Jack lynching years before. Black Diamond was smuggled out of the city and rushed to the county seat in Freehold.

In all of Asbury Park, only three citizens seemed to have had any doubt about the colored man's guilt: the city coroner, the man who employed Marie Smith's father as his chauffeur, and Sheriff Clarence Hetrick. Because Asbury Park's detectives were "positive" about William's guilt the three men went outside the city and hired the nationally known Burns Detective Agency. The head of its New York City bureau was brought to the shore and, with the quiet help of Sheriff Hetrick, investigated the various witnesses and theories. Suspicions returned to Frank Heidemann, the German-born employee of Kruschka's nursery.

Heidemann had since left Asbury Park, but the Burns Agency sent a German-speaking detective to befriend the man. Two weeks after Marie Smith's body was found, with Black Diamond still in the Freehold jail, the *Asbury Press* announced that Heidemann had been arrested and held on two thousand dollars' bail. Having discovered that Heidemann had left Germany after molesting a young girl, the Burns detective had worked out an elaborate scheme to prove his guilt, including a faked second murder and a bogus newspaper. Finally, he'd employed the then revolutionary technique of taking fingerprints off Marie Smith's clothes and comparing them to the suspect's.

Asbury Park was unimpressed. In jail, Heidemann continued to deny his guilt, and the front-page headline in the local paper read SUPREME EFFORT TO GET CONFESSION FROM NEGRO. The paper went on to accuse the Burns Agency of conducting an expensive and unnecessary investigation that had created "an open breach" between the city's coroner and its police force. But in the end, Heidemann confessed. On his way to the electric chair, he would declare death "no more than I deserve." So, four years later, when Hetrick ran for city office, he didn't have to woo the key West Side vote. He was the progressive candidate who had saved Black Diamond's life and uncovered Marie Smith's real murderer.

The hero of the West Side had (inevitably?) become the enemy of the Anti-Saloon League. Hetrick shunned its endorsement, and when he ran for reelection, the League issued an eighteen-page pamphlet, "Why Prohibition Did Not Prohibit." It came right out and accused Hetrick of taking graft from bootleggers and gamblers. The mayor had denied it, a grand jury had refused to indict, and Hetrick had ended up trouncing the League's candidate, attorney Joseph Turner. Now, in 1924, the mayor saw the same forces at work. This Merchants Orgy was just a way to get the old "dry" Bradley forces back in power. What's more, Hetrick didn't believe Walter Tindall could have come up with the affidavit on his own. Tindall was, in the mayor's words, "weak-minded but . . . harmless." Hetrick suspected that the lawyer Turner was behind the whole thing.

When the papers interviewed Turner, he not only admitted having advised Tindall but confessed that he "knew before the 'party' was held that an exposé was slated." Still, that didn't mean the orgy hadn't happened. Turner denied he was out to get anybody. "Of course everyone knows that I am Mayor Hetrick's bitter political enemy," he explained, "but outside of that I am not opposed to him. It's just the administration I am opposed to." The next day, Turner took back even this concession when he told a reporter he'd been misquoted: "I *am* opposed to Mayor Hetrick personally."

Hetrick was a Republican in good standing. He publicly supported Prohibition and opposed gambling. But as the leader of a resort town, as the merchants' ally, as a politician who needed the West Side's vote, he refused to toe the strict Methodist line. Back in 1919, he'd introduced a resolution to allow Asbury Park theaters to show movies on the Sabbath. That kind of permissiveness drove the Civic-Church League crazy. Less confrontational than Isaac Berger, Hetrick had a similar, relaxed view of sin and sinners. "Asbury Park," he would say in the fall of 1924, "is not the worst place in existence. Nor do I contend that it is the best place in existence. It is a city made up of a great number of human beings subject to human foibles in which there is no more immorality than in any other town its size."

You could almost hear the Civic-Church League's response. Asbury Park is not just "any other town." It was never meant to be. It's the city James Bradley founded as a moral community. When the League met again the Monday evening after the Merchants Orgy, it declared it was "determined to continue its fight for good government" and, specifically, to "clean-up" Asbury Park. The New Jersey Anti-Saloon League pledged its support. So did a number of other organizations, including one that vehemently announced it was "back of the Civic-Church League in this move" and would "do everything within our power to aid it." That power was considerable. The organization was the Ku Klux Klan.

By 1924, the Klan was no longer the largely Southern, rural phenomenon of the post–Civil War era, but "the most powerful fraternal and nationalistic organization in American history" with four and a half million members nationwide. Of those, New Jersey could claim sixty thousand—more than Alabama, or Louisiana, and just behind the state of Georgia. And within New Jersey, as one researcher noted, the Klan "felt most at home among the Methodists of Asbury Park."

The original "Invisible Empire" had peaked during Reconstruction when hooded night riders had fought equality with arson, torture, and lynching. That manifestation of the Klan had eventually dissolved, partly because it was outlawed but also because it had won its fight to "save the South." With the Hayes-Tilden "compromise" of 1876, former slave owners regained control. Twenty years later, *Plessy v. Ferguson* made segregation a national law, and leading historians such as Professor Woodrow Wilson of Princeton University would go on to characterize Reconstruction as a period of corruption, carpetbaggers, and laughable colored politicians.

The rebirth of the Klan came about thanks to two modern inventions: the motion picture and the public relations firm. In January 1915—as Hetrick was winning his first mayoral election and President Wilson was finishing his first term in the White House—D. W. Griffith released *The Clansman*, soon to be retitled *Birth of a Nation*. The movie presented Klansmen as heroic freedom fighters and immediately raised protests from the NAACP and others. Threatened by a boycott, D. W. Griffith arranged private screenings for both President Wilson and for the chief justice of the Supreme Court, Edward White, himself an ex-Klansman. With their endorsements, the movie went on to become the first blockbuster, grossing an estimated $18 million.

Among those *Birth of a Nation* inspired was one William Joseph Simmons. Simmons had been a Methodist circuit preacher in Alabama and Florida: what Stephen Crane called a "clergyman of the old ambling nag, saddle bag exhorting kind." In October 1915, Simmons chartered the new Ku Klux Klan, memorializing the event by climbing Stone Mountain in Georgia and burning a cross. (This symbol of the new Klan, "the fiery cross," hadn't existed during Reconstruction; it was popularized through Griffith's movie.) Four years later, despite massive post–World War I race riots and a national "Red scare," the KKK was still a tiny fraternal group of fewer than five thousand members. Then in 1919, Simmons hired the Southern Publicity Association. The firm agreed to take over recruitment with the understanding that it would receive eight out of every ten dollars in membership fees. "If you are a Native Born, White, Gentile, Protestant, American citizen," the association proclaimed, "eventually you will be a Klansman and proud of that title."

The publicity campaign worked. Within fifteen months, the Klan grew to almost one hundred thousand members with fully half coming from urban areas. In 1921, a lawyer named Arthur H. Bell of Bloomfield, New Jersey, established a klavern near Asbury Park and made himself district kleagle. That fall, the *New York World* published a two-week-long exposé, listing 152 "Klan outrages," including four murders. Imperial Wizard Simmons was called to testify before a congressional investigation. Instead of slowing the spread of the organization, "Congress," according to Simmons, "gave us the best advertising we ever got. Congress *made* us."

Asbury Park's weak-minded printer Walter Tindall was a perfect fit for the new Klan. As the operator of a small business, he was having an increasingly hard time making a go of it. Construction on the Jersey shore was at an all-time high, as were rental fees, especially, the *New York Times* reported, "the larger and more pretentious places." But the expanding economy wasn't reaching all people equally. Across the country, the top one-tenth of one percent of the rich were receiving as much income as the bottom forty-two percent of American wage earners. Tindall was in that bottom group. Three days before the Merchants Orgy, he'd bounced a seven-dollar check at the cigar store down on Cookman Avenue. He was due in court for failing to pay $197 to the grocer Shoendorff, who was one of the men he'd accused of being at the lewd party. And he even owed Joseph Turner, the lawyer for the

Civic-Church League. "It is my opinion," Turner candidly told the press, "that Tindall is broke."

As soon as the Merchants Orgy story had gone public, reporters had rushed to Tindall's home in Ocean Grove. He was nowhere to be found. Instead, two young men met them at the door and explained they were there to protect Tindall's "considerably disturbed" wife. They wouldn't say who had hired them, but as the newspapermen were leaving, one of the guards whispered a phone number. It turned out to be District Kleagle Bell's. Bell insisted that he had nothing to do with the orgy affidavit and didn't know where Tindall was. But the next day, when the printer reappeared at his Asbury shop, he was riding in Bell's touring car.

The story of the Merchants Orgy quickly began to disintegrate. Within a few days, the *Asbury Park Evening Press* was calling it "a more or less unsubstantiated charge." Within a week, front-page headlines had shifted to the upcoming bond vote to build a new high school. And within the month, a grand jury had officially exonerated Mayor Hetrick and the others, calling Tindall's affidavit a fabrication that had "irrevocably damaged . . . the fair name of Asbury Park." Hetrick had now added to his reputation by becoming the man who had saved Asbury Park from the Klan.

Which didn't mean that his government championed equality— or was even very tolerant. Colored men looking to work for the city's fire department watched their applications get marked with a red C and rejected. Negro children weren't allowed on the Casino's merry-go-round, and the only African-Americans permitted to attend Arthur Pryor's band-shell concerts were nannies accompanying white children. The week of the orgy, when a city resident named J. Bently Mulford proposed erecting a memorial to the recently deceased Lenin, a member of the American Legion publicly offered what he called a tip: "If you know what is good for you, you will not linger in Asbury Park." When Mulford turned to the Asbury Park police for protection, he got a response that sounded a lot like the KKK. "If Mulford is a Bolshevik," the city's police commissioner told the paper, "he ought not to be permitted to stay."

Despite the collapse of the Merchants Orgy accusations, the Klan continued to recruit among the Methodists of the Jersey shore. In 1924, the new imperial wizard, H. W. Evans, proudly declared, "The Klan is Protestantism personified." Protestantism and what the KKK called "one-hundred percent Americanism," Evans explained, "spring from the same racial qualities, and each is part of our group mind." One historian estimates that during this period as many as forty thousand fundamentalist ministers joined the Klan.

The Jersey shore was no exception. A month after the grand jury had dismissed the orgy accusations, the senior bishop and president of the Ocean Grove Camp Meeting invited District Kleagle Bell and his wife to speak at Sunday school. According to the paper, an "exceptionally large audience" came out to the Grove's famous auditorium, listened to the Bells speak on the goals and values of the KKK, and responded with "frequent applause."

The Klan appealed to the religious in Asbury, but it recruited more broadly than that. People wanted someone to blame for the hard times—and the KKK had an enemies list. Of course, colored people and their amoral, intoxicating music were part of the problem. The now seventy-year-old John Philip Sousa had preceded the Bells into Ocean Grove's auditorium, and the March King was still railing against those "primitive rhythms" that appealed to "the basic human impulse." People said that ragtime had died with Scott Joplin in 1917, but there was this new syncopated sound called jazz, and as far as Sousa was concerned, it was more of the same: a symptom of the decline of social standards. The March King declared jazz would soon disappear, "unwept, unhonored and unsung." This time, Asbury's own Arthur Pryor agreed. Ragtime had been one thing, but improvised jazz, Pryor announced, was "the parasite of music." There was something un-American about it and its dances: the Shimmy, the Toddle, the Black Bottom. Both bandleaders were on the side of the *Ladies' Home Journal* in its 1921 crusade against "the abominable jazz orchestra with its voodoo-born minors and its direct appeal to the sensory center."

One of those minors was the nineteen-year-old William Basie, raised in Red Bank but hanging out that summer of 1924 in Asbury Park's jazz scene. Basie loved ragtime and the even faster stride piano style that had followed it. His father, a caretaker for the white-owned mansions in Red Bank, and his mother, who took in laundry, had managed to pay for piano lessons. Basie had won a piano contest down in Asbury and played at some dances there. Despite the city's promise of a "complete house-cleaning" after annexation, Springwood Avenue had flourished, especially as a musical breeding ground. The Ellington family had vacationed in the area back in 1913, and it was here that the fourteen-year-old Duke Ellington had got wind of a ragtime sound that gave him his first "real yearning to play." So when Bill Basie decided it was time to leave home and make it as a musician, Springwood Avenue was a logical destination.

Basie took to hanging out around Brown's poolroom. "That was like the main stem," he recalled, "and it was also where you found out about gigs." That spring, he got a job at the Hong Kong Inn, a roadhouse on the outskirts of town. His quartet—piano, horn, drum, and violin—played rags and speeded-up parlor music and tunes they'd learned off piano rolls: anything that got the crowd moving. In the dawn hours, when the joint finally closed, he'd go back to what he called "a very big house with a lot of rooms" in another part of Asbury. "I won't say exactly what kind of business Uncle Ralph was in," Basie writes of his host, "but there was always a lot of very good-looking and very, very friendly female companions." The great stride piano player Willie Gant stayed in a place next door, and one day Basie got to witness a cutting contest between Gant and the equally talented Don Lambert. Even the great Fats Waller performed in the area.

Major players like these came out to the shore to cash in on the tourist money. During the winter, they mostly stayed in Harlem, which is where Basie wound up. After studying there with Waller, the Red Bank kid hit the road, landing in Kansas City, where he eventually acquired his own band and nickname. But Count Basie's stay in Asbury gives some idea not only of what a fertile musical town it was, but how its "primitive rhythms" were hooked into a nationwide culture. No wonder Arthur Pryor and others denounced the jazz influence. It was the tip of a renaissance that had a political aspect, too. That winter of 1924, Marcus Garvey, billed as "the greatest living Negro leader and orator," spoke at Springwood Avenue's Roseland Hall. Garvey's black separatism grew out of what he called the "hopeless economic and industrial state" of his people. "It is time for the Negro to be radical," Garvey declared in 1924, "and let the world know what he wants."

The dangers of all this were obvious to the Klan—but worth repeating. District Kleagle Bell announced that he had personally "learned of eighty-seven thousand cases of white girls living with Negroes and men of the yellow race." But the white folks of Asbury Park had long ago figured out how to contain the "negro question." It wasn't a threat, and it wasn't the basis of the Klan's appeal on the shore. A failing, small-time businessman like Walter Tindall might dislike the coloreds, but as the Klan's imperial wizard declared in 1924, "The Negro is not a menace to Americanism in the sense that the Jew or Roman Catholic is." As a Klan speaker explained it during a rally down the shore at the Pt. Pleasant First Methodist Episcopal Church, "Foreign people have it on the Klansmen because they come to this country with clothes on, and Klan members did not."

Asbury Park could narrow the menace down even further. Certainly the city's Jews were a threat and a target of the Merchant Orgy accusation. But these "foreigners" had been part of the city's makeup since the turn of the century when they'd held services over Meyer Sharfstein's butcher shop on Springwood Avenue— and then at Morrow's Hall, a "black entertainment center." By 1905, James Bradley was donating land for Asbury's first official synagogue on the white side of the tracks, near the business district on Cookman Avenue. And by the 1920s, most of the big stores along Cookman were Jewish-owned, including Steinbachs. The Klan didn't like the wise guy Isaac Berger and his alliance with Mayor Hetrick, but the Jews—like the colored—weren't the real issue.

No, for men like Walter Tindall, the direct threat was foreigners willing to work long hours cheap. And according to the Klan, Roman Catholics were "the most dangerous of all invaders." Back when Asbury Park was founded, only fourty-four thousand Italians lived in all the United States. By now, that figure had jumped to nearly five million. In New Jersey, one out of five white people was now foreign-born.

Tindall's church knew what to do about it. The Reverend MacMurray brought in guest speakers, like the one from the YMCA who assured the congregation, "Any nation has an inherent right to decide who shall compose its citizenship." Afterward, the reverend urged his congregation to go to the rear of the church and sign the petition supporting an anti-immigration bill. And it wasn't just the Civic-Church League that felt this way. President Warren Harding might not have gone as far as the Klan, which called for a five-year national ban on all immigration, but he had supported an Immigration Restriction Act. Hadn't he won the 1920 election on the backward-looking, fundamentalist theme of a "return to normalcy"? The threat was everywhere. According to District Kleagle Bell, Catholics were "extending their power over the armed services." And anyone with eyes could see that Italians were deep into bootlegging. What Asbury had once looked upon as the "warm impulsive heart of the Italian" was now seen as part of the city's slide toward hell.

That Fourth of July, 1924, Asbury Park did its best to cover up these deep streams of hate. They weren't, after all, good for business. Tourists came to forget their cares. It was the Roaring Twenties, the era F. Scott Fitzgerald called a "borrowed time" between World War I and the Great Depression. "Flappers danced merrily along" is how the paper reported the city's Fourth, "would-be flappers pranced with more or less grace; [and] floppers—the male specie—in squadrons studded." Women wore their hair short with long, swinging strands of pearls and favored yellow that season. The men dressed in white linen suits and snappy straw boaters.

Asbury needed their business. James Bradley had lost money on the beachfront. His successors hadn't produced the flood of revenue people had expected, leading to Hetrick's election as mayor. And even now, with the Business Men's Show bragging about prosperity, the local newspaper noted that this was "the first time in many seasons that the bathing pavilions from one end of the boardwalk to the other were jammed to capacity on the Fourth of July." A "monster crowd" attended the free concert at the Arcade, and another danced through the heat at the Casino. According to the *Asbury Park Evening Press*, under the spell of the boardwalk even "old maids and stern businessmen forgot the cares of life and agreed that it was great to be living."

Inland, Springwood Avenue celebrated apart from the tourists. At sophisticated jazz clubs like Joe Mikes, patrons drank black-berry wine and smoked cigarettes in holders. At spots like the Smile-A-While and the Two-Door Tavern, the music was louder, the dancing raunchier. You couldn't hear jazz on the radio because the American Society of Composers, Authors and Publishers (ASCAP) had banned the broadcast of its "primitive rhythms" the year before. But live bands like Bill Basie's quartet made up for that. And by now, record companies had targeted the Negro audience with "race records." Asbury's West Side jumped to Bessie Smith's latest, "Jailhouse Blues," and Jelly Roll Morton's own "Jelly Roll Blues." If the Civic-Church League needed proof of the tramp conspiracy, they didn't have to look any further than the first jazz record, laid down seven years earlier. It had been cut by The Original Dixieland Jazz Band, an all-white group led by an Italian-American who had grown up in a New Orleans neighborhood not that different from the mixed-race cultural breeding ground of Springwood Avenue.

Asbury Park's Fourth passed with the city managing to keep its separate Americas separate and its tensions hidden. Not so up the shore in Long Branch. There, the Independence Day parade consisted of four thousand men, women, and children—all dressed in white robes, all hooded—led by a man (also hooded) riding a white horse and carrying an enormous American flag. According to the promotional literature, it was the largest Ku Klux Klan gathering ever held in the United States. Twenty-five thousand people lined Long Branch's streets to watch. Men in black bowlers stood by their Model T's. A Boy Scout held up a sign that read, WE WANT THE HOLY BIBLE IN OUR SCHOOLS.

The parade highlighted a daylong celebration that took place out at the old Monmouth Park site. With horse racing still banned, the KKK had been able to purchase 175 acres for its new Imperial

Palace. The Klan's daylong, all-American affair included a mid-morning baseball game between the Pennsylvania and New Jersey klaverns, a christening, an egg-and-spoon race, and a "Minister's Race." In the evening, fireworks were shot off and the Lakewood Klan Orchestra played. The Fourth of July souvenir program featured an etching of a Klansman pointing to a flaming cross, and inside, portraits of local supporters, including Kompany A of the Asbury Park Kavaliers. "Amid the bluffs, dunes and beaches of Monmouth County," as one historian put it, "the Klan was king." Imperial Wizard Evans had to send his regrets to Long Branch, but the day's speakers echoed Evans's position that hardworking men like Walter Tindall were being driven out of business by "cosmopolitans . . . assailing the foundations of our civilization." The dangers were Communism, Socialism, Anarchism, Judaism, and "especially" Roman Catholicism. American civilization, Imperial Wizard Evans declared in 1924, was based on the principle "that each race to be worthwhile must be kept pure."

When one of the speakers in Long Branch specifically promised the crowd that "no one but a Protestant will ever sit in the White House," everyone knew he was referring to the Democratic National Convention taking place up the coast in New York City's sweltering Madison Square Garden. There, under what the Associated Press called "the cloud of the Ku Klux Klan," the Democrats were hung up in a brutal, two-week-long political deadlock. Their most charismatic and potentially their most popular presidential candidate was Governor Al Smith, but Smith hailed from what the Imperial Wizard called "the most un-American city of the American continent," New York. The Klan and its allies saw him as being soft on Prohibition. Most importantly, Smith was Catholic. And according to the Imperial Wizard, a Catholic's "first allegiance is to a foreign temporal sovereign." Outside of Long Branch that Fourth of July, the Klan set up a booth where a nickel got you three chances to throw hardballs at a poster of Smith. By day's end, the governor's face was in tatters.

Asbury Park didn't have a Ku Klux Klan parade, but the city didn't denounce the organization, either. Instead, the next day's lead editorial in the *Asbury Park Evening News* declared that the major threat to 1924 America was "the multitudes of new-comers of lower quality and alien cultures." Congress should enact quotas, the paper went on, to limit immigration to those "of the stock built into the original fabric of the nation." (Which Congress soon did, passing a law that reduced the number of Italians who could enter the United States to fewer than four thousand a year—ten percent of the number of British and Germans allowed.) The *Asbury Park Evening News* position was the Klan's, just without the hoods.

After their show of force on the Fourth, the Monmouth County KKK announced it was going to concentrate on the upcoming elections. It would support only those candidates who promised to "protect the public and close some of the notorious places that exist [in Asbury Park] today." Missing from the statement was how the Klan would deal with those it didn't support. That summer, Frederick W. Vanderpool—a professional songwriter (" 'Neath the Autumn Moon")—decided to campaign for the Republican nomination for assemblyman. Vanderpool declared he was anti-Prohibition and anti-Klan. A few weeks after the start of his campaign, he appeared at the Asbury Park police station seeking protection and a permit to carry a handgun. He'd gotten anonymous phone calls whispering that he had "only a short time to live" and been mailed death threats "marked with a fiery cross."

But the Klan's main focus was the congressional primary. T. Frank Appleby was running for the Republican nomination against Major Stanley Washburn. Appleby's support of Bradley's old American ideas had helped get him elected to Congress once before. He had long been "one of the most earnest workers of the

First Methodist Episcopal Church." But now Appleby was facing a tough challenge from Major Washburn, a war veteran and a personal friend of President Coolidge's.

Washburn's platform included a plank that called for revising Prohibition "to a point where public opinion will back its endorsement." As if that weren't heresy enough, the major's personal secretary was a Roman Catholic. Five days before the primary, a delegation of Klansmen visited Washburn and demanded that he fire the secretary. Washburn refused. According to the *New York Times*, the KKK immediately endorsed Appleby.

The political maneuvering that followed underlines just how powerful the Klan was on the Jersey shore. Appleby didn't want to be labeled an extremist and quickly declared the rumor that he was a member of the KKK "absolutely false." At the same time, he didn't decline the Klan's endorsement: it meant too many votes for that. Major Washburn, meanwhile, announced that he had never sought the KKK's endorsement—and then proceeded to cozy up to its membership. He predicted that "80 percent of the Klansmen" would support him because they shared the same essential values. (Despite this supposed sympathy, the major spent his last days on the campaign trail traveling with a security force of twenty bodyguards.) District Kleagle Bell, responding to this elaborate courtship, issued a statement from the Imperial Palace. "The Klan is not a political machine," he told the press. "It doesn't take upon itself the authority to tell its members how they should vote."

That was a lie. On the day before the primary, a full-page ad appeared in the *Asbury Park Evening Press*. Under its headline SHALL THE KLAN RULE? two letters were reprinted. One, signed by Kleagle Bell, was addressed to "Faithful and Esteemed" Klansmen. It recommended that they study an enclosed, confidential voting card that named the Klan's "Preferred List" of candidates. The other letter was much the same, except it went to Klanswomen and was signed by Mrs. Bell. In an added flourish, she reminded female voters "the Klan has been raised up to save America."

The ad was taken out not by the KKK but by a private citizen who wanted to reveal the Klan's strategy. He urged voters to exhibit their "TRUE PATRIOTISM" by defying this "un-American organization." Caught in the act, the Klan argued that the letters had never actually been sent. In fact, Walter Tindall (in whose shop the voter cards had been printed) called the Asbury Park police to report that someone had stolen the mailing.

The next day, T. Frank Appleby defeated Major Washburn by sixteen thousand votes. In Asbury Park, he won by an overwhelming fifteen hundred votes. The *New York Times* announced Appleby's victory under a subheadline: KU KLUX BEAT WASHBURN. "It is clear that my refusal to dismiss my Catholic secretary has lost me many votes throughout the district," said the major in his concession speech, "but I would far rather be defeated on so fundamental an issue than be elected by any compromise whatsoever." Statewide, some moderate Republicans won nominations, which the *Times* described as a "crushing blow to the Anti-Saloon League and to the efforts of the Ku Klux Klan." But approaching the general election, the power of the Klan, if anything, seemed to be growing.

Just before the November vote, concerned citizens formed the Monmouth County Equal Rights Association to "combat the political influence of the Ku Klux Klan." The umbrella group combined the efforts of the Klan's various "invaders," drawing from the Long Branch Hebrew Political Club, the Italian Tammany Club, the Irish Catholic Monmouth League, and the Tiger Club, "a colored organization." According to the *Asbury Evening Press*, the Fourth of July parade in Long Branch had been the main "impulse" for forming the association. The Equal Rights Association saw the spectacle of the Klan marching down Main Street not only as a "direct insult" but a terrible business decision. One leading Jewish merchant said he'd spoken to more than three hundred "members of his race" who were threatening to cancel their summer reservations because of the Klan presence.

But that fall's election made clear which America the majority of Monmouth County's voters preferred. They elected Appleby to Congress by a margin of more than twenty thousand votes. The two Klan-backed candidates for Assembly also won. And nationally, gubernatorial and senatorial elections featured, as the *New York Times* front-page headline put it, VICTORIES BY KLAN. KKK-endorsed candidates won in Indiana, Kansas, Colorado, and Oklahoma.

T. Frank Appleby never got to occupy his congressional seat: he died of an intestinal tumor that December 1924. Overt demonstrations of Klan power soon faded in Asbury Park and across the country. Locally, Mayor Hetrick got the reputation as the man who had saved the city from the KKK. That, along with certain favors he handed out, solidified his power base on the West Side. Dedicating a new two-story Child Welfare home, Hetrick declared he was "in closer touch with those in need . . . than the general run of people."

But whom had he saved the city for? The West Side still didn't receive basic services. The city government still didn't represent Negroes or Italians. Beneath Asbury's benign Fourth of July celebration, the Klan's doctrine of "one-hundred percent Americanism" hadn't so much disappeared as been absorbed into the system. In the broadest terms, Mayor Hetrick had sided with the merchants and against the Civic-Church League. But the two sides were in basic agreement on Asbury Park's future.

The Civic-Church League, the Klan, the businessmen, and Mayor Hetrick all supported the same vision of their city: the Merchants' Vision. Asbury Park depended on tourists. Tourists would be attracted by modern accommodations, exciting amusements, and, of course, the beach. But they would only come if it was safe. And everyone knew what that meant. Segregation was one of the foundations of the Merchants' Vision, the underpinning that allowed the attractions to attract.

When a disastrous fire destroyed four shoreside hotels in 1923, private investors led by the Steinbachs rushed to the rescue, replacing the lost rental units with the eight-story, brick Berkeley-Carteret Hotel. And Mayor Hetrick took his reelection victory as a mandate to push forward on a major beachfront renewal that included the new Convention Hall. The architects responsible for New York City's Grand Central Station would design it, and the result would be a huge beaux arts building housing a theater, arcade, and exhibition space and studded with glittering copper sculptures and carved stone relief. Fourth of July, 1924, marked Clarence Hetrick's lock on power. He became the city's new boss, taking over where Bradley had left off, and reigning for a quarter of a century. Convention Hall was the embodiment of *his* Asbury: the high church of the Merchants' Vision.

According to those who planned "scientifically and economically," by the time the hall was completed—around the Fourth of July, 1930—the business climate would be reaching new heights. Never mind that this model hadn't worked for Bradley or his successors. So committed were the city fathers to their vision of the promised land that when, instead, the stock market crashed, and Asbury entered a deep economic spiral, they kept right on course. They rebuilt the Casino that had burnt down in early 1928, and they filled their new Convention Hall with the finest big bands of the day: Tommy Dorsey, Benny Goodman, Paul Whiteman. The finest white-led bands, that is. It would be years before Duke Ellington or Count Basie would play Convention Hall. The music drew segregated crowds, but it wasn't enough to keep the city afloat. The scene on the boardwalk was like some exquisitely designed, perfectly white engine, spinning ineffectively onward. "I pressed my nose against the door," an African-American resident recalled. "We were not permitted in [Convention] hall. Our amusement was watching the whites dance."

FOURTH OF JULY, 1941

IT RAINED ON the Fourth. Independence Day in 1941 was supposed to feature a "gigantic patriotic parade and rally" sponsored by the Veterans of Foreign Wars. It was going to include a long list of fraternal organizations, high school bands, even blimps flying over Main Street. Soldiers and rolling equipment were scheduled to come down from Fort Hancock, Fort Monmouth, and Fort Dix. The local papers hoped for some twenty thousand marchers and crowds "matching those of the old palmy days of the city's famed baby parade." Asbury had even lured the seventy-one-year-old Arthur Pryor out of retirement to kick off the festivities on the third.

It was a typical mix of patriotism and nostalgia, cranked up to new heights because war was right around the corner. Nazi forces were invading the Soviet Union. On July 3, after a day of stifling ninety-eight-degree weather, the citizens of Asbury Park opened their papers to read of the Germans capturing one hundred thousand Russian troops and Stalin calling for a scorched-earth policy. The editorial cartoon was of a nervous Uncle Sam watching a bomb-bursting "pyrotechnic display," while over his head the thought bubble read, "1942?"

Over at the St. James movie house, Robert Taylor was starring in *Billy the Kid*, to be followed by the Marx Brothers in *The Big Store*. There was roller-skating at the arena, and Tepper's Department Store was holding a holiday sale of bathing suits as low as $2.95, complete with "floating bras." Out Springwood, on the West Side, the great boogie-woogie piano player Meade Lux Lewis was playing Jackie's Cotton Club, and Cuba's was offering three floor shows nightly that included "Congo Dancers," the comedian Spo Dee-O Dee, and an all-black swing band. The white equivalent would be down in Sea Girt, where the Harry James band was appearing. His singer, Dick Haymes, had replaced James's discovery and 1941's most popular vocalist, Frank Sinatra.

According to the local papers, some 250,000 people swarmed into Asbury Park over that weekend, filling the hotels and the boardwalk, ending the shore's "patient" wait to "feel the full impact of the nation-wide boom."

Except it rained on the Fourth. Some indoor celebrations went on. Springwood Avenue residents complained about the loud, late partying at the clubs.

And then it rained again on the fifth.

So, it wasn't until Sunday that the parade finally set off down Main Street. The Asbury police force strode in front. Behind them, according to the *Evening Press*, "members of Holy Name societies marched side by side with Jewish war veterans in a great outpouring which would be possible only in democratic America."

The paper's point was that, compared to the fascism overseas, here Jews were coming down Main Street side by side with Catholics. Which was certainly a shift from the height of Klan power in the 1920s. But if this Fourth of July parade was about democratic America, the main evidence was in the lead car. There, waving to the crowds, rode the city's newly elected mayor and councilmen. Never mind who they were; it's who they weren't that mattered. After more than a quarter of a century, Asbury Park was no longer led by Clarence Hetrick.

Democracy—if that's what it was—had certainly taken its time.

After Hetrick's 1924 mandate, his government had floated some $8 million in municipal bonds, almost all of it going to the massive overhaul of the beachfront. As well as the spectacular Convention Hall, new buildings included a pool, bathhouse, heating plant, and two solariums. Hetrick also put money toward the endless fight to hold on to Asbury's beaches. Old maps showed the city's shoreline had receded 180 feet between 1839 and 1920. In 1925, an eight-hundred-foot-long, $100,000 stone jetty was completed at the northern border, and two others followed. The overall investment was huge. By the end of the decade, the city's bonded indebtedness had jumped from $2.75 to $15 million. But Asbury believed in this future. "Tremendous revenue" was bound to follow. That's how the city's promotional brochure put it. "No one who has knowledge of business enterprises doubts."

And then the Depression hit.

Asbury Park reacted slowly. Maybe its capital-spending spree temporarily floated the local economy. For a year or so after the crash of 1929, while the rest of the country suffered through bank failures and unemployment lines, the promised land almost seemed immune. And even when the situation began to fall apart—tourist income dropping, taxes rising—the city stuck doggedly to its vision. Surely, this was a hitch, not a major flaw? Surely, the gleaming new beachfront would prime the pump? Surely, their mayor—a corporate executive with offices in Washington, D.C., and a mansion in upstate New York—would lead them through the darkness?

Given how long Clarence Hetrick had run the city, Asbury knew surprisingly little about him. The local papers called him "an enigma." Childless, he was rarely seen on the streets. He seemed to spend most of his time out of town on unspecified and slightly mysterious business. Even at election time, the mayor stayed "remote from the crowds," delegating responsibility and often speech making to his "henchmen." He was as unassuming as James Bradley had been extroverted. And when Hetrick was in Asbury, he mostly holed up in a suite of offices in the Electric Building, where, as the papers would write, he was "ostensibly operating a real estate business."

It turns out that Hetrick's employer was actually a complex, interstate holding company called Utilities Power & Light. With its corporate center in Chicago, UP&L held investments in 366 towns and cities across the nation. Because it operated in so many states under so many different names, its business was almost impossible to decipher—or regulate. Utilities like this faced accusations of price fixing and hiding profits, of shifting money from state to state to avoid taxes, of milking consumers through regional monopolies. In 1927, UP&L's octopus-like corporation had shown an annual net income of over $2.5 million. That year, it sank some of its profits into construction of the eleven-story Electric Building in Asbury's business district. The city boasted that it was "the tallest office building on the entire Jersey coast." The first three floors were occupied by UP&L's Asbury subsidiary, Eastern New Jersey Power Company: a mini-conglomerate that included electric transmission lines serving over five thousand customers, gas plants, and even a yellow cab company. In 1930, as the Depression was swallowing the rest of the country, UP&L's profits climbed to over $15 million.

Through the end of President Hoover's term, the Depression only got deeper. Part of the blame, candidate Franklin Roosevelt maintained, had to fall on unregulated, undemocratic monopolies, especially large utilities like UP&L. One of the first acts of Roosevelt's New Deal was to force such holding companies to operate in a single state and answer to federal regulation. UP&L was soon denouncing the "radical nature . . . of political attacks on the electric utilities." Meanwhile, the *Asbury Park Evening News* hailed FDR as "the savior of the capitalistic system of government."

It's a phrase worth examining. According to the textbooks in the Asbury school system, America had a *democratic* system of government. But by this time, in Asbury Park anyway, the Merchants' Vision had ruled decision-making for a long time. Democracy and capitalism had strolled the beach hand in hand. Now, like thousands of communities across the country, Asbury was trying to figure out why its prosperous future—scientifically formulated—still seemed so far off. Was there something wrong with capitalism itself? With democracy? Both? The gleaming new Convention Hall jutted out from Asbury's boardwalk, pointing the way to . . . what?

In his inaugural speech, President Roosevelt tried to reassure the country. The only thing to fear was fear itself. And, the new president added, "We do not distrust the future of essential democracy." It was a sign of the times that there was even a need to say such a thing. Roosevelt's New Deal promised to restore the capitalist economy and save democracy. The fault wasn't in the system; it simply needed to be reformed. As cities and towns across the country took a hard look at their elected representatives, Asbury Park launched its own version of the New Deal.

Asbury's faith in capitalism remained unshaken; its city's central article of faith was that the beachfront made money. Never mind that James Bradley had claimed for years that the boardwalk cost him more than it brought in. That was because he was an eccentric and unrealistic businessman. Never mind that in 1926, two decades after the city had taken it over, the beachfront was running a $42,000 annual deficit. That was because the boardwalk needed to be revitalized. And never mind that in 1932, *after* revitalization, the beachfront was losing even more money: over $600,000 a year. That, a newly organized reform group argued, wasn't because of the Depression or the "capitalistic system of government." It was because Hetrick's administration was corrupt. He had saved the city from the Klan in order to sell it to the Mob.

Asbury's reformers—calling themselves the Citizens and Tax-payers Association—called on the governor of New Jersey to investigate "close connections existing between public officials, both city and local, and certain undesirable individuals." Page-one headlines revealed that Mayor Hetrick's police chief had endorsed gun permits for three well-known gangsters, amongst them Irving Wexler, "known throughout the state as the 'big boss' in the beer racket." Wexler, aka Waxey Gordon, was a junior partner of mobster Arnold Rothstein and ran an East Coast beer distribution network out of northern Jersey. His Asbury Park gun permit listed his residence as the newly built Berkeley-Carteret Hotel. The Citizens Association suspected more ties between these "undesirable individuals" and Mayor Hetrick's political machine.

During his more than fifteen years in office, Hetrick had survived numerous attacks on his character. These had all been in the James Bradley/"merchant orgy" tradition of purging the city of sin. The attacks hadn't worked because the majority of the city's voters profited from Hetrick's laissez-faire attitude toward the underground economy. As one commentator put it, the core of his support had always been "south of Asbury Avenue and west of the railroad tracks." His coalition of beachfront concessionaires, Jewish merchants, Italians, Negroes, and others made their living off the "undesirables." And that voting bloc handed Hetrick victory after victory. But now the two-thousand-member Citizens Association threatened the mayor not on moral as much as fiscal grounds. Among other things, corruption equaled bad management. Asbury needed new leadership to survive the Depression. The *Asbury Evening Press* called the reform movement "a city-wide upheaval."

First, the Association initiated a referendum that called for a city manager, rather than elected representatives, to run Asbury's finances. Towns across the nation were switching to this system, hiring outside fiscal experts as a way of guaranteeing more efficiency and honesty. When the referendum carried, the Association smelled blood. It launched a campaign to unseat the mayor, with its star witness Hetrick's former Casino manager, John Osgoodby.

Osgoodby claimed that, in 1930, the Casino had regularly drawn between twenty-five hundred and five thousand people a night. He had personally deposited over $50,000 in its account. Yet at the end of the year, the city government had reported a $32,000 loss. The reason, according to Osgoodby, was that Hetrick's machine skimmed profits at any and every opportunity. For example, in 1931 and 1932, the beachfront commission had budgeted $1,550 a week for a dance orchestra to play the Casino. But the musicians never received more than $1,100 in pay. "The difference for those 22 weeks," Osgoodby stated, "was more than $9,000. Where did that go?" When he tried to report the situation to his superiors, Osgoodby was told, "It's none of your damn business." Nor was it any of his damn business that his workers were hired because they were friends of the Hetrick machine. When Osgoodby caught one stealing admission tickets (and selling them on the side at half price), he was ordered to keep the man on the payroll.

Asbury Park had suspected this kind of corruption for a while, but the details had never been made public before. Now, Osgoodby went on to outline the cushy deal set up for his boss, Thomas Burley. Burley was made beach director with a salary of $3,000 a year, plus additional fees for any special events he organized. He received another $5,000 to be secretary of the Chamber of Commerce, "when any merchant can tell you," Osgoodby declared, "there isn't any such body in the city." But the beach director's real money came through WCAP, the local radio station. The "Chamber of Commerce" had transferred ownership of the AM outlet to Burley, and then Hetrick's government paid WCAP $25,000 a year to broadcast city-sponsored music programs. The broadcasts originated from two storefronts in the Convention Hall complex: storefronts that the city advertised for rent at $6,000 a year but let Burley have for free, throwing in heat and electricity.

Osgoodby called the system "rotten." Hetrick's opponents said corruption was driving Asbury Park to its knees. "How is it possible," one demanded, just days before the 1933 election, "to spend in one year $3,332,864 for the government of a city of 15,000 people but one square mile in area?" Against the background of the Depression and in the atmosphere of the New Deal, that question had finally grown some teeth.

In addition, Hetrick's West Side coalition was beginning to seem vulnerable. With New Jersey repealing Prohibition in 1933, many of the underground businesses were surfacing, and the status of the ethnic outcasts was changing. Over in New York City, the first Italian-American ever elected to Congress, Fiorello La Guardia, was now waging a successful campaign for mayor. Asbury Park's Civic League was running Louis A. Croce for city council. Croce, born in Italy, had become a prosperous ice cream and candy manufacturer, secure enough socially and economically to step forward and declare, "A dictator runs this city." Another West Sider, Democratic Party leader Joseph Mattice, threw his weight to the reformers, as did the Colored Progressive club. Finally, some of Asbury's middle-class white voters had lost patience with Hetrick's government, which was over three months behind in paying city employees, including its public-school teachers.

You could argue that Asbury Park didn't have much experience with "essential democracy." It had passed almost directly from Bradley's kingdom to Hetrick's dictatorship. Election Day, 1933, was a test, and almost as soon as the voting began, so did the accusations. Poll watchers for the reform candidates accused Hetrick's machine of hiring "floaters": unregistered out-of-towners paid to vote. Word on the street had the going rate at four bits and a shot of rum. Over at Tom Brown's taproom at 1211 Springwood Avenue, a twenty-eight-year-old colored man walked in wearing an anti-Hetrick button, got into an argument, and was shot and killed. But at the end of the day, all five of the reform candidates won. The ecstatic Citizens Association called the victory "a decisive expression on the part of the people that they want that government back in their hands."

Democracy had triumphed. Maybe. Briefly. "Almost from the minute the reform administration took control," the *Asbury Park Evening Press* would later comment, "it was subjected to a bitter campaign of attack." First, the new city manager quit after only six weeks on the job. He cited illness but also "the failure of persons on all sides to give cooperation." Then, two months into the new government's term, a grand jury indicted four of the five reform councilmen for allegedly promising Eugene Capibianco he'd be police magistrate. Capibianco had supposedly delivered them the West Side.

The paper attributed these attacks on the reformers to Clarence Hetrick, specifically to his "genius for organization." The very fact

that the Monmouth County prosecutor was acting on the indictments struck some people as suspicious. The prosecutor was a local
lawyer, Jonas Tumen, and he didn't have a reputation for rooting
out corruption. To the contrary, by that spring of 1934, the only
question Asbury Park had was whether Tumen was in Hetrick's
pocket, or vice versa.

Tumen operated one of the city's most profitable law firms along
with his brother, city judge Louis Tumen. Their offices, Hetrick's
office, and Monmouth's First Judicial Court were all in the Electric
Building. On April Fools' Day, 1930, Jonas Tumen had been
appointed county prosecutor, and according to a special investigating committee of the state General Assembly, things got funny
quick.

Barely three months after Tumen took office, one Thomas
Calandriello was arrested for robbing an American Railway
Express company. Despite Calandriello's long rap sheet—including a case of "atrocious assault"—Tumen never brought him to
trial. In fact, two years after the arrest, the unfortunately named
Monmouth County detective Harry B. Crook was a guest at
Calandriello's wedding. Asked to explain all this, Tumen
couldn't. As the state committee remarked, the prosecutor
"professed a startling lack of knowledge of the affairs of his
own office."

What Tumen did know, apparently, was how to run a shake-
down operation. His Asbury Park bagman was Phillip L. Phillips,
the owner of a men's shop off Cookman Avenue. The committee
heard testimony about how Phillips had visited one speakeasy and
demanded $500 "protection money." When a month passed and
the owner hadn't come up with the cash, Hetrick's chief of police
raided the speakeasy, and the owner was taken before Judge Louis
Tumen and fined $100. The same thing happened the next week.
And the week after. And the week after that, until the place was

finally forced to close. At the same time, other speakeasy owners testified, they'd paid the kickbacks—and stayed in business.

Asbury Park's gambling operation worked much the same way. After the reform government took over, it set out to clean up the city, dismissing Hetrick's police chief and ordering a raid on Walter Hurley, a well-known bookie operating at 724 Cookman in the heart of the commercial district. There, the Asbury police found fifty to sixty people placing bets, as well as racing sheets and other equipment. Under a waiver from the special committee, Hurley testified that he'd been allowed to operate because he was a personal friend of county detective Crook, and that prosecutor Tumen had known all about his operation.

Still other witnesses described a meeting at Harry's Lobster House in Sea Bright, where Phillips had taken control of Monmouth County's slot machine business. If operators didn't come to his men's store and pay ten dollars a week per machine in advance, they were raided. The confiscated slots ended up in Detective Crook's basement, where they were apparently emptied. During Tumen's first year in office, Crook deposited over $10,000 in his various bank accounts, most of it in cash. And in the midst of the Depression, Phillips managed to pay off his mortgage.

Then there was the plot to rob the Berkeley-Carteret Hotel. It seems a vacationing New York City police sergeant, lying in his room at the St. George Hotel, overheard men planning the robbery and went to the Asbury police. He and a local detective tailed three suspects up the boardwalk. First, they stopped to play miniature golf, one of the three keeping score on a package wrapped in brown paper. From there, the suspects walked to the swimming pool on Seventh Avenue. While they swam, the detective got a key to their locker and discovered that the brown-paper package contained a .38 revolver with five cartridges.

The three men, plus a local coconspirator, were arrested. In front of police officers and a local judge, the suspects confessed that they'd been planning a robbery and signed written statements to that effect. A grand jury indicted. Two weeks later, prosecutor Tumen got a letter from a New York City lawyer who was representing the original three suspects. The lawyer wrote that he'd been "conducting negotiations in your State through the office of Joseph F. Mattice." Tumen couldn't tell the committee what those negotiations might be, but attorney Mattice soon appeared before the grand jury to argue that his clients' confessions had been obtained through force. The judge and the police officers who had witnessed the sworn statements were never called to testify. Fifteen days after being indicted, all four suspects walked.

It didn't look good for Asbury's new reform government that one of its prime supporters, Joe Mattice, appeared to be in cahoots with Tumen. And the new officials brought more trouble on themselves by deciding that a reform government meant a dry city. Just before the Fourth of July, 1934, the council declared no liquor could be served on the beachfront. Methodist mayor Sherman Dennis cast the deciding vote. Arthur Steinbach, managing director of the Berkeley-Carteret, savaged the decision as "extremely dangerous business judgement [that would] keep thousands of people from visiting Asbury Park." It was the ancient war revisited, though this particular skirmish was brief. The next day, the council was forced to reverse its decision in a meeting that the *Asbury Evening Press* described as "marked with intense personal antagonism on the parts of officials and factionalism in the crowd."

Investigations had revealed the corruption in Hetrick's government. The question was whether the reformers had any alternative to Asbury's "capitalistic system of government." As the city was trying to figure this out, the new government was tested in an almost miraculous way. On the night of September 8, Thomas Burley, broadcasting from WCAP's rent-free studios in Convention Hall, glanced out toward the dark ocean and shouted, "She's here!" Coming straight toward the studio was an enormous luxury liner, its decks on fire, flames shooting into the night sky. As Burley broadcast, the 528-foot *Morro Castle* beached itself about a hundred yards from where he sat.

The ship had caught fire at sea the night before. By breakfast time, it was close enough to land that a crowd of thousands could follow its smoke north up the Jersey shore through Brielle, Manasquan, and Sea Girt. Vendors sold food and coffee to the rubberneckers in what was described as "an almost carnival atmosphere." As dark fell that Saturday, the still-burning ship broke its towline and steered itself onto the Asbury Park beach. By then, the *Morro Castle* was, as one reporter described her, "a huge mass of twisted steel . . . buckled steel plates, gaunt black funnels, and a maze of charred framework." Of her 549 passengers and crew, 134 had died, either trapped belowdecks as the fire raged or drowned trying to jump to safety.

The next day, Sunday, signs went up on the roads into Asbury: TWO MILES TO THE *MORRO CASTLE* WRECK. An estimated twenty-five thousand people poured into Asbury Park. With the summer season done, in the midst of the Depression, a thousand people paid twenty-five cents a head to walk out on the Convention Center pier to get a closer view of the wreckage. Maybe it wasn't a miracle, but it was certainly a bonanza. A typical reaction was a local restaurant's hastily printed advertising card. It stated the number of dead and then urged the public to "See the Wreck S.S. *Morro Castle* FROM the Old Vienna Garden Café. Good Beer— Good Food." By Monday, members of the city council were announcing their intention to "claim the beached *Morro Castle* and use it as an entertainment attraction." The death ship could be a year-round boardwalk amusement—like the junk Bradley had littered over the beach but more popular. Only the reaction of the national press and of some local citizens forced the council to admit the idea came from "a base, vicious and mercenary desire to exploit." The city manager had to promise that all viewing fees would go to "bereaved families." By November, when the hulk was hauled away, a hundred thousand sightseers had paid to see it— and the reform government had lost the high moral ground.

This reform brand of beachfront capitalism looked a lot like the old Hetrick variety. Meanwhile, revelations about the ex-mayor continued to come out. Three days after the *Morro Castle* went aground off Convention Hall, the state began investigating bribes connected to the construction of that building. Hetrick was called to Trenton to testify, as were both his secretary Grace King and his former beach commissioner J. Whitfield Brooks. Brooks never made it. That morning, sitting in his office in Neptune, the fifty-four-year-old put a bullet through his head.

Brooks had already given the state committee private testimony admitting financial "irregularities" during his term of office. It seems Hetrick's government had paid a firm out of Newark some $2,800 to lay some terrazzo floors. Then, a second check for $2,000 had been made out to the same firm—"with erasures." The papers reported that this additional money had been turned over "to a mysterious messenger identified as Eddie Nelson." Eddie had passed the money to Commissioner Brooks, who then, a witness testified, called the offices of Tumen and Tumen to say he had the cash and would see them in the morning.

It's just coincidence that in Bruce Springsteen's 1975 song about small-time hoods, "Meeting Across the River," the shady, un-named deal going down involves an "Eddie" and that the payoff, as the eager narrator says, is "two grand . . . practically sitting here in my pocket." But it's no coincidence that Eddie's best and only hope—what Springsteen calls "our last chance"—is an illegal scam. By Springsteen's time, it was past clear that for many the only real access to a promised land was through the underworld. There had been hints of that since Asbury Park's founding. What the Hetrick investigation was bringing into the open was that the real money from the beachfront didn't come from tourism—from charging admission to the rides or the city-sponsored dances. That was small change. The real money passed beneath that façade: not from the dancers, in this case, but from the dance floors.

Beach Commissioner Brooks had denied the specifics of the bribe, but he couldn't face having to give public testimony. Meanwhile, ex-mayor Hetrick seemed undisturbed. The morning of the suicide, the most he would admit about the double payment was that "the circumstances were peculiar." He not only walked away from the investigation unindicted, but he seemed more determined than ever to regain control of his city.

In mid-December, a new organization announced itself: the Asbury Park Civic League. It appeared to be another reform group, except it aimed to reform the reformers. Accusing the city's new government of "inefficiency in office," it started circulating petitions for a recall election. A month later, a group of creditors sued the city for defaulting on its bonds, demanding that the next budget include the $1.3 million they were owed. That was impossible, the city solicitor announced: the city was bankrupt. What's more, he was suspicious about the timing. "There is something back of it," he told the press, "something not kosher."

The hits on the reform government started falling faster and faster. The new Civic League quickly gathered enough signatures, and a recall election was announced. In early March, a New Jersey Supreme Court justice signed an order to put Asbury Park's finances in the hands of the state. The *New York Times* described Mayor Dennis and his reform government as being "uncertain . . . as to the consequences of the decision." Councilman Croce wasn't uncertain. He declared that this "vicious measure" was designed to put Hetrick's allies back in power, and that analysis gained a good deal of support when the state named as its special auditor a man who had once been Hetrick's budget consultant. When this auditor called for the city's "ridiculously low" budget to include the $1.3 million owed, Councilman Croce countered by calling for the people "to know as much as Hetrick does about the matter."

Then, three weeks before the recall vote, Mayor Dennis died of a heart attack. His reform party splintered. Suddenly, there were half a dozen factions putting forward more than a dozen candidates. One of Asbury's most successful Negro businessmen, electrical contractor William Knuckles, ran as an independent. "Democracy and true Americanism," Knuckles announced hopefully, "[have] a kindred spirit along our beautiful shore." But two weeks before the vote, the Civic League "cast aside its nonpartisan cloak" by nominating as its candidates ex-mayor Clarence Hetrick and two of his former councilmen. In a city reeling from political infighting, voters now had to choose between a reform government accused of being inefficient, a former government being investigated for corruption, and a confusing array of "independents."

The waters grew even murkier. With the West Side still the key voting bloc, the reform government suddenly did an about-face. A week before the election, it fired the city manager: he who had gotten rid of the corrupt police chief. The reformers seemed to be signaling that housecleaning was over and, like Hetrick, they were willing to leave the city's black market economy alone. Councilman Croce voted against the move, calling it "cutthroat" and declaring himself "strictly against liquor and games of chance."

On the eve of the vote, one citizen paid for an "Open Letter to the People of Asbury Park" in the *Evening Press*. "Last night," he wrote, "I sat down to think seriously about the election next Tuesday. I tried to pierce the fog of charges and counter-charges."

He concluded that the election came down to a fundamental principle. "This principle," he wrote, "is the very foundation of democracy, of good government, of honest government. It is this: can a young man play square in politics and remain in office?"

It was a good question. If Asbury Park's April 1935 election was a referendum on whether the "capitalistic system of government" was inherently corrupt and corrupting, the answer was yes. By a resounding four-to-one margin, the city voted Clarence Hetrick and his cronies back into power. You could argue that Hetrick had manipulated the recall election. You could argue that he'd orchestrated attacks on his opponents. You could argue that he'd once again bought voters. But the only form of democracy there was in Asbury had spoken. Knowing all it now knew about the specifics of corruption under Hetrick's rule, the city had reelected him.

Why? Asbury Park's idea of "essential democracy" started with a strong man at the top, and Hetrick certainly was that. While he had helped get the city into its fiscal mess, he'd also kept it afloat. In the 1920s, the amusement-park industry had peaked with some fifteen hundred parks nationwide. By now, there were only four hundred, and voters may have thought it was thanks to Hetrick that Asbury was one of them. They may also have figured that those "not kosher" demands from the city's debtors would now go away as mysteriously as they'd appeared.

Finally, and maybe most important, there was the continuing threat of a state takeover. Asbury Park wanted to stay independent, and Hetrick would fight for that. He wanted the city (and its profits) under his control. There was obvious irony in Hetrick, Asbury's machine boss, accusing the state of wanting "virtually dictatorial powers"—but the city stood behind him. When New Jersey governor Harold Hoffman called for a state commission to run the beachfront, Asbury Park suspected Hoffman's real concern wasn't reform. The papers made headline news out of the revelation that the governor had admitted in private letters that what he really wanted was to break Hetrick's "political organization." Later, it turned out that even as he tried to take control of the beachfront, the governor was in the midst of stealing some $300,000 of public money. Clarence Hetrick might be a crook, but he was Asbury's own crook. He took the city's case for independence all the way to the U.S. Supreme Court, losing at each step but still refusing to give the state the records it needed to take over the beachfront.

Meanwhile, the reelected mayor quickly rehired his old police chief. By the Fourth of July, 1935, bookie Walter Hurley was back in operation on Main Street, as was Detective Crook's son, James. It was business as usual. Though Asbury, like most shore towns, couldn't afford fireworks displays that year, the Steeplechase building off the boardwalk was still headlining a minstrel show. The Rialto Theater hosted the Hot Harlem All Colored Revue, and July 5 through 7, Paul Whiteman's big band played Convention Hall. Whiteman was the new, white "King of Jazz" in the tradition of Sousa and Pryor. When he failed to draw much of a crowd, he blamed the atmosphere in Convention Hall: a remnant of the old beach censor days. "Young people," Whiteman explained, "they're the ones who dance. And what do they like? . . . Low lights, dim corners, a romantic background."

Mayor Hetrick celebrated that Independence Day by ejecting the owner of the refreshment stand on First and Boardwalk for owing the city back rent. Others in the same position—the operators of the Casino restaurant and of the rolling-chair concession—he treated more lightly: they had supported the Hetrick ticket in the last election. The mayor also replaced the head of bathhouse concessions with his own man, meanwhile reducing the lease from $85,000 to $40,000. According to a contemporary, outside study by the National Municipal League, the fees that the city charged for its rental properties depended on who was leasing. They varied from sixty-five cents a square foot to $11.11: a factor of nearly twenty. "We have no proof of improper influences . . ." the League concluded, "but inequalities so glaring as these are indefensible, even if graft or political favoritism had nothing to do with it." The study called beachfront leases, in particular, the "traditional footballs of politics in Asbury Park."

But by this time, talk of reform had just about faded. FDR's Works Project Administration had created some local jobs, including a $160,000 project on the beachfront, but unemployment just kept growing. In the decade between the mid-twenties and mid-thirties, for example, Asbury's electrical workers union went from a hundred members to eighteen. Down in Trenton, unemployed members of the socialist Workers Alliance, furious at the inaction of their elected representatives, took over the legislative building. Calling themselves the Army of Unoccupation, they began passing mock bills to show up what one leader called "the bunch of miserable buffoons that you usually witness in this building." Their protest legislation included a system of unemployment insurance, a thirty-hour workweek, and heavy corporate taxes. One of their leaders described New Jersey's legislators as "cynically, brutally indifferent representatives of finance capital."

He could have been talking about Asbury Park's reelected mayor. As the city's finances continued to flounder, the Hetrick government, as one opponent put it, "bled its people white." In 1938, the city foreclosed on 313 properties for failure to pay taxes. Many of them were middle-class houses in prime residential neighborhoods, now little more than "empty shells." When the city took possession of these properties and resold them, Mayor Hetrick's friends managed to prosper. For example, clients of Tumen and Tumen bought twenty-four properties, putting down only $14,000. One estimate said the real estate was worth a good

$60,000 more than that. Tumen and Tumen picked up another foreclosed property for $1,500 and quickly sold it for $4,500. Why couldn't the city find buyers willing to pay these prices? Why were the Tumens prospering from the city's decline?

In Asbury, anyway, the New Deal did little to save capitalism and even less to reform it. The Depression continued, and what money there was continued to flow through the underground economy, ending up in familiar hands. When, in 1941, the tide began to turn, it was the prospect of war that changed things. A huge influx of military personnel and dollars poured into the area. The U.S. army, for example, foreclosed on the old KKK headquarters outside Long Branch and added it to Fort Monmouth as a top-secret radar lab.

Asbury Park wanted its share. But as the editors of the *Asbury Evening Press* pointed out, Hetrick's machine was doing next to nothing to attract military dollars. "And the reason for the indifference, of course, is the fact that defense measures cannot easily be adapted to serve the political machine." Asbury's reform parties regrouped. For the city elections of 1941, an updated version of the 1933 alliance, now calling itself the United Citizens League, ran a five-man ticket including a veteran police captain. Joe Mattice, still heading the city's Democratic Party, chaired the League. The owner of a string of movie theaters, Walter Reade, campaigned on an independent liberal ticket. And Hetrick ran as a Republican with his usual slate.

The challengers hammered away at the mayor's machine, citing the "vicious and notorious land grabs" and publicizing the enormous debt that the city had built up under "Boss rule." "This town is broke," Reade declared, "and it's going to stay broke." Most recently, Hetrick had installed parking meters in Asbury, allegedly to lower the high tax rate. The opposition argued that the meters only inconvenienced shoppers—and the income never made it to the city treasury.

The mayor paid his critics little attention. As he had in most elections, Hetrick barely went out in public. When he did address a rally at the Berkeley-Carteret Hotel, he urged voters "not to be bothered by the past," but to consider a future that would include "10-story apartment houses and more federal funds for housing projects." Hetrick cited statistics: with less than 10 percent of Monmouth's population, Asbury accounted for nearly a quarter of the county's retail business. In an unintentionally amusing phrase (given the Hetrick machine's tradition of secret side deals), the mayor guaranteed, "This town will take so many forward steps in the next few years that you won't know it." What steps had it taken so far? Hetrick's special attorney declared that among the mayor's major accomplishments were the 250,000 tulips that the city had planted. "Did you ever try to eat tulip soup?" candidate Reade countered. The *Asbury Evening Press* ran an editorial: "Tulips for the Homeless."

"A vote for Hetrick," the Citizens League warned, "is a vote for Tumen. They are inseparable." The Hetrick campaign countered by reminding voters of 1933's failed reform government: "Don't Change Experience for Another Experiment." The key to the election was still the West Side, but its demographics were shifting. The 1930 census had found that other ethnic groups had moved out, leaving the Springwood Avenue area almost totally Negro. Ninety-nine percent of Asbury's thirty-five hundred Negroes lived in the First Ward, one third of them officially unemployed. Forty percent of West Side housing was deemed "sub-standard," and the city Housing Authority had designated the area "definitely blighted." To woo these voters, the reformers enlisted local Negro leader George Fleming. "I don't blame Hetrick," Fleming told a West Side rally. "I blame the Negro who has kept him in power for 24 years. We have been beaten, kicked, and downtrodden, and . . . never let out a word of protest till now." Hetrick, meanwhile, courted the West Side vote by pushing through the city's first Negro housing project, the long overdue Asbury Park Village, with 126 low-income units.

Joe Mattice warned that the mayor had ways of winning the West Side. Mattice said he'd overheard a "Mr. Nick" boasting he could "deliver the colored vote." And according to George Fleming, Asbury's police officers were forcing Springwood Avenue to support the mayor—bringing in its "women of the street" and telling them they'd better "get together with the old board" or else "they wouldn't be able to work." Hetrick's city magistrate, following directions from the Boss, started "a little cleanup" of various "joints." He called in Minnie Lopez, who ran one of Springwood's biggest nightclubs, and allegedly told her, "You've been doing a lot of ballyhooing for the new ticket, and if you don't shut up, I'll close Cuba's."

On election day, one of the Citizens League's colored workers and two of Walter Reade's supporters were arrested. Hetrick's city magistrate denied the mayor had ordered the arrests, denied they'd been held all night without bail, and denied he'd said to their attorney, "I have no idea what the charges are but we'll find something good."

In one of its pre-election ads, the Citizens League had contended that Asbury would save $220,000 ("over $600 a day") if it could defeat Hetrick and "take the political hacks off the pay roll." Maybe that purely fiscal argument worked. Or maybe Hetrick was just getting old. Though he and one of his colleagues won reelection, the sub-headline on page one of the *Asbury Evening Press* read MACHINE LOSES CONTROL OF CITY.

Which is how three reform candidates wound up waving from the lead car of the rain-delayed July Fourth parade of 1941. By then, they'd already fired nine employees of the city's publicity bureau, abolished the jobs of public safety director and engineering clerk, and gotten rid of the two men hired to maintain parking meters. The new government had also suspended the city magistrate and was investigating the Hetrick machine's last-minute "emergency" spending spree of $28,000.

The Independence Day crowds cheered. But it's understandable if they had their doubts about the triumph of democracy. Or, for that matter, about the reform of capitalism. The flow of military dollars into town was still a trickle. And Clarence Hetrick was still a councilman. Then on October 13, 1941, the lead sentence in the lead article of the *Asbury Evening Press* read "The hand that held an iron grip on Asbury Park's municipal affairs for more than a quarter century was stilled in death today." Hetrick, sixty-eight years old, had died of thrombosis and diabetes. The *Evening Press* went on to say that his "once strong organization" had been "virtually dissipated" in the last election. Then, the paper admitted that no one had ever quite understood the workings of that organization: "Up to the last, Mr. Hetrick had remained a political enigma to friends and foes alike."

The enigma may have been dead; his organization was not. In the special election to fill Hetrick's seat, the reform coalition fell apart. The new mayor endorsed the independent, Reade. And at the last minute, Joe Mattice bolted, throwing his support to the Hetrick man—who ended up winning by 123 votes. In dismay, George Fleming took out an ad on behalf of Asbury Park's Negro population. "The gang which has been smashed must remain smashed," Fleming wrote. "I say to my people we will not betray, we will not sell out, we do not want a return of the old clique." But the *Evening Press* conceded that Mattice had joined "the remains" of Hetrick's machine to sweep the West Side. "The bitter contest," it concluded, was liable to "leave wounds that may be long in healing."

Post-election, with winter coming and the tourists returned to the cities, the citizens of Asbury Park could stroll the empty boardwalk and consider the future. By December, war would break out, Convention Hall would be requisitioned for an officer-training center, and the year-round population—especially among Negroes on the West Side—would dramatically increase as local factories geared up and enlisted men poured into Forts Monmouth, Hancock, and Dix.

But that fall, it was still quiet. And if there was bitterness from all this political infighting—if there was a sense that no matter how you voted, the crooks stayed in office—well, those that walked along the boardwalk had the perfect sound track. "This Love of Mine" was *the* hit song that fall of 1941. It was part of the new, immensely popular sound being forged by the skinny kid from New Jersey, Frank Sinatra. Sinatra's bandleader, Tommy Dorsey, called its understated approach their "Sentamentalist" sound: just a rhythm section, some backup singers, and Frank. It wasn't a big band at all but something smaller, more intimate. Within the year, Sinatra would leave Dorsey's band altogether and go out as a solo act.

That fall of 1941, all up and down the boardwalk, from the jukeboxes and the radios, you could hear Sinatra's drawn-out notes, his yearning cries, what he called his bel canto styling. In Asbury, after decades of being looked on as little better than the colored, Italian-Americans were making their way out of the West Side ghetto and into the halls of power. To them, Sinatra's styling had a brash, familiar confidence. "This love of mine goes on and on."

Yet, even as he proclaims himself, there's something so fragile in his voice—and sad—that it threatens to leave the singer himself speechless. "This Love of Mine" is one of the rare examples of a song where Sinatra wrote his own lyrics, and he doesn't so much describe feeling as allude to it, betting that his listeners will understand. So, after he's explained that he's lonesome during the day, all he has to add is "and, oh, the night." He knows his audience will know what he means: they share a background of despair. When he admits that his heart is bound to break, his voice drops to a hush. "Nothing matters," he sings, and pauses. His voice gets even quieter, a whisper in your ear. "So, let it break."

It was more intimate, more openly revealing, than any popular music Asbury's boardwalk had heard. Sinatra would claim that he'd learned some of this technique from Billie Holiday, the soft way she phrased pain. But Billie Holiday, of course, wasn't likely to be heard on Asbury's boardwalk. If this was the background music to the promised land on the eve of war, it was a long way from Arthur Pryor's martial band. In fact, toward the end of "This Love of Mine," the resignation—the sense that things go wrong, that they corrupt, that they conspire to screw the little man—is so complete, it's hard to believe the song can continue.

But Sinatra asks one last question. He asks it of the sun, the moon, and the stars, and when he sings the word *stars*, his voice rises to an almost frightening intensity. At the end of the day, at the end of 1941, on the almost empty Asbury Park boardwalk that had been subject to decades of greed and deception, you could hear the young Sinatra ask the stars, "What's to become of it, this love of mine?"

And the sound—extraordinarily—is the sound of hope.

FOURTH OF JULY, 1956

ON THE FOURTH of July, 1956, Asbury Park was recovering from an unexpected and seemingly inexplicable fistfight that had broken out on the boardwalk just days before. The papers were calling it the Convention Hall Riot. Hundreds of people had gone on a rampage, starting at the beachfront and continuing on into the business district. The police had arrested dozens, scores had been injured, and with the assistance of out-of-town cops and soldiers, six blocks had been put on lockdown. City officials seemed confused about what the trouble was all about. But they knew what had gotten it started: this new teenage music, this stuff they called rock & roll. It threatened the very values Asbury Park had been built on—threatened the city's central strategy of containment—and it had to be stopped.

Some had escaped the West Side with the cool style of Sinatra. Some had fought their way out through the political system: men like Joe Mattice who made their deals with the old Methodist power structure. Some had taken the merchant's route, establishing little clothing and food stores on Springwood Avenue, leveraging their profits to buy a house on the north side and maybe even a shop on Cookman Avenue. And some had never left.

Through the war years of the 1940s, the "colored" population around Springwood Avenue had skyrocketed. Negroes assigned to Fort Montgomery's signal corps lab, Point Pleasant's Coast Guard station, and the local Naval Ammunition Depot didn't have much choice about where they'd live. One scientist remembers taking a room at a boardinghouse for maids and chauffeurs: the only place in Monmouth County that would rent to him. And you couldn't buy in most areas because banks wouldn't okay mortgages. By 1944, unofficial studies found that Asbury's Negro population had risen to more than a quarter of the city's twenty-six thousand residents. The West Side was brutally overcrowded, and it wasn't just from military families. Wartime labor shortages had forced businesses to hire minorities. In Red Bank, the all-white workforce of the Sigmund Eisner company became thirty-five to forty percent black. The same thing happened at Asbury's Atlantic Sports Wear Company and at Thomas A. Edison, Inc. in West Orange.

With jobs, the wartime economy also brought promise. "During the war years," as one contemporary put it, "the general attitude of the Blacks in Monmouth County was characterized by faith in the American way of life—a faith in things hoped for, but not yet seen." The city decided that the best way to contain the population boom was to have the colored patrol themselves, and West Sider Thomas Smith became one of Asbury Park's first Negro policemen. It was less a concession than an accommodation, but the result for men like Smith was a good salary and the chance for advancement.

By June of 1944, the last remaining councilman from Hetrick's machine had passed away. For the first time in Asbury's history,

Democrats controlled the city council. Yet, instead of picking a Democratic mayor, the council opted for George Smock II: a Republican whose family could be traced back to pre–Revolutionary War Dutch settlers. As a partner in Buchannon & Smock Lumber Co. ("since 1873"), Mayor Smock believed firmly in the Merchants' Vision. Some observers thought the Democrats had appointed him mayor because the party leader, Joe Mattice, had said so. In return, Smock reappointed Mattice judge of the First Judicial Court. "There was no sleight of hand," Mayor Smock had to declare, "and no deals."

If you gauged democracy by how it worked in Asbury Park, you'd have to conclude it was a basically conservative system. Once you got into office, you stayed. Between founder Bradley and Mayor Hetrick there had been a brief interregnum. Now, with Hetrick gone, Smock's ticket won the May 1945 election and would remain in power for more than decade—from the Nazi surrender well into the Cold War. The administration's goal was simple: to maintain the status quo. Smock ran what one councilman lauded as "a conservative economic government," slowly repaying the city debt left over from Hetrick's days and carefully fending off change. In his official capacity, he followed the Asbury Park resort calendar. Each Fourth of July he declared the crowd a record-breaker; in August he presided over the annual baby parade; through the winter he boosted the Merchants' Vision; and each spring he renewed the beachfront leases.

Other traditions continued, as well. For their first three years in office, Smock and his fellow councilmen were under investigation by a Monmouth County grand jury. Indictments charged the Asbury city government with eleven counts of illegal activity, ranging from the purchase of lumber, coal, and steel without getting competitive bids to handing out beachfront leases based on friendships and/or kickbacks. Over at Convention Hall, the owners of the Whirl-O-Ball concession sued the city when they suddenly lost their space on the boardwalk. They claimed the mayor was playing favorites, but Smock defended himself, insisting, "All of our actions were for the best interests of the city of Asbury Park." What's more, the mayor explained, the council's procedure was "similar to that of the preceding governing body for more than twenty-five years." In other words, Smock was just doing what Hetrick had always done—which was pretty much what Bradley had always done—so what was the gripe?

But even as Mayor Smock and Asbury Park stuck to the business of business-as-usual, the world that began outside its borders was transforming itself. Between 1944 and 1954, nine million U.S. citizens moved into new single-family homes, creating vast suburbias. Housing starts jumped from fewer than 115,000 in 1945 to nearly 1.7 million in 1950. Long since developed, Asbury Park proper didn't take part in the construction boom. Bradley's basic zoning plan steadfastly remained: beachfront backed by bungalows backed by shops, then the railroad separating what were now being called the slums. But out in New Jersey, there was an explosion of split-levels, cul-de-sacs, and two-car garages. Not far from Asbury, you could buy a three-bedroom Catalina ranch for under $12,000 ("No down payment for G.I.'s"). Add a new Oldsmobile for a little more than two grand, and you were all set to make one kind of American dream come true. All you needed were the connecting highways.

The New Jersey Turnpike opened in 1952. It linked the Northeast metropolitan corridor from the George Washington Bridge down past Philadelphia. And on Friday, July 1, 1955—just in time for the holiday weekend—the last four miles of the Garden State Parkway officially opened, tying the Jersey shore into the loop. The parkway's 165 miles of road had cost $305 million, but there was every reason to believe it would quickly pay for itself. Those first six months of 1955 were the biggest in the history of the auto industry, with Detroit turning out 4.25 million passenger cars.

The day the Garden State opened, the *Asbury Evening Press* announced, "City dwellers by the thousands, spurred on by the forecasts of hot, humid weather, began pouring into the Shore area." The next day, homeowners within five blocks of the beachfront found their driveways blocked. According to the Asbury police, "every available foot of parking space along Ocean Avenue" had been taken. Photos of the beach showed it packed with white bodies. And the influx was only going to get more intense with the scheduled widening of the feeder roads that led from the Garden State into Asbury.

Visitors found a city whose changes were mostly superficial. Convention Hall still featured old-fashioned attractions like Zoo-A-Rama and a mechanized miniature circus. Sure, you got a glimpse of the nuclear age: a show of radioactive automobiles from the Yucca Flats atomic bomb tests. And a changing morality allowed moviegoers to catch Marilyn Monroe in *The Seven Year Itch* over at Walter Reade's Mayfair. If you wanted something even racier, there was *The Game of Love*, which The Ocean proudly advertised as "Shocking!" But a survey conducted in 1956 concluded, "The last 10 years have by-passed the town." That seemed both accurate and intentional. There hadn't been any major beachfront improvements since the Klan had marched through Long Branch. The city had been granting its merry-go-round lease to the same operators since 1932.

There was something reassuringly nostalgic about Asbury, but by standing still, the city had also gotten seedier. According to some, the place needed fresh blood and new ideas. The local paper began supporting a new civic group that was calling on Smock's city manager to resign. Suddenly, in February 1955, to the surprise of the city, the mayor himself stepped down. The reason given was his health, but his wife was quoted as saying he had "no specific complaint. It's just a lack of energy."

New energy was exactly what Asbury Park wanted. More and more, the boardwalk crowds were made up of modern day-trippers, driving into town for quick thrills before heading home. The city had to decide how to adjust without becoming, as one critic put it, a "Coney Island type venue." You had to go back in history to understand that distinction. As Stephen Crane had put it long ago, Asbury's self-image was one of "singular and elementary sanity" compared to Coney Island's "profanity." Where Coney Island had been wide-open, appealing to the ethnic mix of New York City's tenement communities, Asbury saw itself as morally and racially segregated. The most popular ride in James Bradley's city had probably been the Ferris wheel: a gentle, steam-driven trip up above Lake Avenue to an observation deck. There, a proper middle-class couple could admire the view of the ocean and the line of church spires that stretched down Grand Avenue. In comparison, Coney Island's premier attraction was the Steeplechase. After racing wooden horses down a track, you had to crawl through a low "dog house" into "The Insanitarium." There, on the stage of what was known as the Blowhole Theater, you ended up face-to-face with a dwarf in outlandish costume. Before a man could react, the dwarf would shock him with an electric prod to the ass or the crotch. A woman would have her skirts whipped up over her head by a blast of air. Out of the darkness, there'd come a roar of laughter as those who had just gone through the same humiliation shouted their approval.

From Coney Island's perspective, the national character was clear enough. "We Americans," Steeplechase proprietor George C. Tilyou declared, "want either to be thrilled or amused, and we are willing to pay well for either sensation." The symbol of all this was a caricature of Tilyou called Tillie. Painted on his fun-house walls and reproduced in his advertisements, it was the toothy face of a grinning adolescent with hair neatly parted, a high turn-of-the-century collar, and a slightly crazy stare. Tillie stood for bright lights and loud music and the sticky comingled smell of sweat and candy.

In the past, Asbury had had its own Steeplechase and its own Tillies, but even in its wildest heydays, the city had always tried to project an image of middle-class respectability. Now, in the mid-1950s, with Mayor Smock gone and the Parkway practically leading the masses to its shore, the city took another look at itself. And found there was no danger of turning into Coney Island because that had already happened.

Yes, people still came to Asbury Park to swim and lie out in the sun. But even over the sound of surf, you could hear the dinging of the boardwalk. Like most towns on the Jersey shore, the predominant amusement at Asbury Park had become the not quite legal "games of skill." In wooden booths just off the beach and at arcades inside Convention Hall, you could drop a nickel in a "catchpenny game" and enter a dazzling atmosphere of bells and flashing lights and payoffs. There was Fascination, a kind of tic-tac-toe, where you rolled a rubber ball into a grid of holes and tried to light up five in a row. In Skee Ball, you bowled up an inclined ramp and tried to land in the ring worth the most points. One of the most popular was Skil Bingo, where your nickel bought you a bingo card. The "skill" was tossing dice or marbles to determine what numbers came up. On all of these, if you won, you got a prize, or tickets you could turn in for a prize. Up and down the boardwalk, players aimed for the bull's-eye or tossed big colored rings onto milk bottles or chased goldfish down a colored track with a metal shark.

By 1955, the most popular game on the boardwalk was pinball. And in many ways, pinball proved to be rock & roll's precursor:

the advance army that opened the way to the boardwalk. Pinball had begun during the Depression as just another gravity-fed maze game. By 1933, lights had been added and, a few years later, bumpers. But it was after World War II, with the invention of the flipper, that the game came into its own. Now, you could keep the thing alive, banging on it, lifting it off its legs, flipping the ball back and then rattling the entire pleasure machine. It might last just a minute, or it might go on for a delicious half hour. When you finally lost and looked up, hot and sweaty and strangely exhausted, the world continued to ring.

This wasn't healthy exercise. This had nothing to do with Robinson Crusoe. Almost as soon as it appeared, pinball was denounced as "a perverter of innocent children." The most popular versions—like Bingo Pinball—paid off in cash. According to a *Better Homes and Gardens* of 1957, "Pinball feeds on vast sums siphoned from the worn pockets of those least able to afford the sucker's games of rigged odds." It was a poor people's game, a democratic game, and word on the street was that the pinball empire was Mob operated. A lot of the little mom-and-pop stores didn't much care: the machines brought in customers. That riled their competitors, the big new department stores, and they led the campaign against Bingo Pinball, calling it a direct descendant of the slot machine.

On the surface, Asbury Park tried to distance itself from this lower-class amusement. The city didn't allow the kind of machines that paid off with cash. But it couldn't afford a total ban. The pinball concession for Convention Hall brought in $8,000 a year (through a lease to a corporation that included the president of the school board). Fascination, Whirl-A-Ball, and Skee Ball all made obvious what had been true since the city's beginning but had been kept hidden: Asbury's "guests" were rubes. As visitors lined up on the boardwalk, banging on the flashing games, it was clear that the city had a carny economy. Even now, Asbury tried to save face by maintaining that the games weren't gambling per se. But in 1954 the state of New Jersey ruled they were. The court decided there was no real difference between slot machines and pinball games: both involved "price, chance and prize."

Up and down the shore, concessionaires tried to ignore the law. But the next year, a judge confirmed the ruling, and in June of 1955—just at the start of the high summer season—all the Skillo-Basket games on the Jersey shore were ordered shut down. According to Police Chief Fred Lembke, Asbury Park didn't suffer because its boardwalk didn't allow this variation on the roulette wheel. But Asbury did have Fascination and Bingo, and by 1957, the state would broaden its definition: whether you played for money or a prize, relied on skill or chance, no matter how "innocuous" the game might be, if you put down your cash in the hope of winning something of value, it was gambling—and illegal.

The *Asbury Park Evening Press* took the position that this was a good thing. The operation of these games, it editorialized, "disguised with a phony 'skill' element . . . has been the measure for the deterioration of many resorts." Asbury Park, the paper assured its readers, wasn't dependent on this petty gambling. It was a "successful and thriving community" with an "attractive residential center," hotels, boardinghouses, and a commercial street that was the top retail trade area in Monmouth County. In other words, it still was—or could still be—James Bradley's ideal community. The paper worried about the "long range effect upon the character of Asbury Park," if it focused on "the immediate dollar." The city had to get back to attracting "desirable" tourists who came with their families and stayed awhile. "If Asbury Park's prosperity depends upon spinning wheels in order to separate the visitor from his cash," the editors declared just before the Fourth of

July celebrations of 1956, "or upon chasing goldfish up and down a tank to see which one crosses the line first, then we are indeed in a sorry way." At least one local clergyman agreed, writing that a community dependent on gambling "or any other form of evil" wasn't the sort of place where he and his family wanted to live.

But the dependency already existed. All you had to do was ask the people who actually worked the boardwalk, who made their living there. One Toms River man had spent more than a decade running a game he described as "throwing balls at cats to win a prize." He pointed out that it wasn't just undesirables who played these five-and-dime games, but exactly those all-American families that Asbury claimed it wanted to attract. Another concessionaire took the argument a step further: "A vacation resort such as this gets a shot at an alleged sucker perhaps once a year." So they lost five bucks trying to win the stuffed animals and cheap jewelry that the boardwalk operators called plush. Afterward, they'd go and spend a lot more on "legitimate" amusements like dinner. What was so wrong with the immediate dollar? The Beach Merchants' Association got ten thousand signatures on a petition to reopen the games, while the First Methodist Church was telegramming the governor to uphold the ban.

Next door, Ocean Grove seemed to reproach Asbury with its very presence. There, in the fall of 1955, evangelist Billy Graham delivered a sermon on the revival of religion. It drew twelve thousand people. In the other direction, Long Branch was enjoying the benefits of an amendment to the state constitution that once again allowed betting on horses. Monmouth Park had finally reopened a half century after James Bradley had helped close it. But where did that leave Asbury? "Everyone will sell hot dogs and hamburgers," one concessionaire predicted, "and all the old ladies can go to the race tracks instead of playing skee ball or Skil Bingo." In other words, the city would slowly but surely fade away.

But besides those old ladies, there was another kind of visitor. The owner of the Palace just had to look down Kingsley to see them. Night after night they cruised the strip, modeling their cars, their clothes, their hair. They were the new discovery—or was it invention?—of the 1950s: the teenager. Like the rest of Asbury's beachfront, Palace Amusements hadn't changed much since the 1930s. Its carousel house dated back to 1888, its Ferris wheel to 1895, and its most recent addition—the Crystal Maze hall of mirrors—to 1903. But these kids didn't come roaring off the highway to ride a merry-go-round. By the Fourth of July, 1956, the owner of the Palace had completed renovations specifically designed, as he said, for "teenagers looking for a good time."

First, he'd torn down the old Turner and Ocean Spray hotels (so much for the "desirable" long-term tourist). In the newly opened space, he built two big additions. That made room for rows of new pinball machines under the now-required sign FOR AMUSEMENT ONLY. More importantly, the Palace enlarged its Tunnel of Love by over eighty feet, giving teenagers that much longer to sneak a kiss, a touch. The Palace's other new wing—three stories high—contained what were known in the trade as "dark rides." The Ghost Ride spooked your date into your arms. The Twister carried you, screaming, in and out of whirling lights. The Oriental Express, the Whip, and Rock-O-Plane would eventually be installed. And the bumper cars gave teenagers coming off the Garden State a chance act out head-snapping collisions under mirrored sparks of electricity.

Old Asbury objected, of course. One civic leader declared that the city mustn't allow the boardwalk to "denigrate to the level of a carnival midway." But by 1956, the writing was quite literally on the wall. The new and expanded Palace rose in garish green, its outside covered with murals of giant clowns, kids in bumper cars, and the promise of FUN FOR ALL. Dominating all this were not one but two grinning Tillies. Asbury Park might not have electric prods and upraised skirts, but the caricatures of George Tilyou promised the equivalent: wild times, slightly out-of-control thrills, dangerous fun.

It was a new kind of promised land, and it had a sound track. Long Branch residents called it "excessive noise" and complained that it was booming out of the Ja-Da La Martinique Club at all hours of the day and (mostly) night. "[It] isn't loud," the owners explained. "It's just repetitious." More importantly, the music drew a bigger crowd than the club could hold. The beachfront was dying. And this new music had the potential, the owners declared, of making "the Long Branch–Asbury Park area into another Wildwood instead of a graveyard."

The comparison was to Wildwood, New Jersey: a party town a hundred miles farther down the shore. There, a round-faced country-western singer named Bill Haley had helped invent "excessive noise." Playing a summer gig on the Wildwood boardwalk, Haley had become friends with the act appearing across the way. The Treniers, black twins out of Mobile, Alabama, had started off with Jimmie Lunceford's big band and now played an extroverted, beat-heavy dance music. Early in 1952, they'd released "It Rocks, It Rolls, It Swings," and later that year, Haley produced his own version, a record called "Rock the Joint." The song became a regional hit as clubs up and down the Jersey shore competed for the new teen market. His follow-up, "Crazy Man Crazy," made it onto the national charts in 1953, and by late that summer Bill Haley and the Comets were whipping boardwalk crowds into a frenzy with something called "(We're Gonna) Rock Around the Clock."

"Rock Around the Clock" briefly made the charts in 1954, but it only became a massive hit when it was included in the 1955 movie *Blackboard Jungle*. Like Marlon Brando's *The Wild One* and, later that summer, James Dean's *Rebel Without a Cause*, *Blackboard Jungle* lionized and capitalized on the phenomenon of the teenager. But *Blackboard Jungle* was the first to make an explicit connection between juvenile delinquency and rock & roll. All these movies showed the teenager as antisocial. Anti, that is, the kind of status quo that Asbury had struggled to maintain. By the end of *Blackboard Jungle*, tolerance and understanding win out. There's even racial harmony as the young Sidney Poitier leads the white kids away from gangbanging. But teenagers in the movie audience were less interested in the happy ending than the beginning. That's when "Rock Around the Clock" kicked off with its count-up ("one, two, three o'clock, four o'clock, rock!"), its triple-time drumming, and its crazed guitar. For teenagers, the message was crystal clear. Mayhem. Stand and dance! Which is just what they did, in the aisles of movie theaters across the country. *Blackboard Jungle* propelled "Rock Around the Clock" to number one. And brought Bill Haley to Asbury Park.

The promoters who hired him, the Redicker brothers, weren't rebels; they were jewelers—and insiders in local government. Through their contacts at city hall, they controlled a bunch of beachfront leases. Right after the war, they'd gotten a permit to promote dances on the boardwalk and in 1946 had kicked off with Tommy Dorsey's big band. (By then Sinatra had gone solo.) For the Fourth of July weekend, 1955, they booked Bill Haley and his Comets into the Casino. The city couldn't afford to ignore this new attraction, rock & roll, but it wanted an acceptable, clean-cut performer, and Haley was an obvious choice. Ten years older than Elvis Presley and Little Richard, he presented himself as an odd but basically trustworthy grown-up: moonfaced and spit-curled. "We can show the youngsters," he told the national press, "that fun can be clean." When it came to this new, worrisome, mixed-race music, Haley was the Arthur Pryor of his day, modifying the wild, dirty freedom of rock & roll into something Asbury could live with. And on top of everything else, the Comets were a shore band out of Philadelphia: a local, known commodity.

The 1955 concert went just as planned. Publicity was no problem with *Blackboard Jungle* (advertised as a "Drama of Teen Terror") playing at the Eatontown Drive-in and "Rock Around the Clock" about to top the charts. Hundreds of well-behaved kids showed up at the Casino for the Saturday and Sunday night shows. At $1.50 a head, the Redickers quickly got back the $250 lease on the Casino. At the end of the Independence Day weekend, rock & roll had showed a good profit—and with no trouble, no rebellion. Just like in the movies.

So, as the Fourth of July, 1956, rolled around, the Redickers must have felt that Asbury Park would be able to use rock & roll the way it had ragtime, jazz, and the blues. Like those, the new music mixed cultures that the city kept carefully separate. Bill Haley had learned his rock & roll by crossing the street to hear the Treniers, and by 1956, the new sound was already starting to bring its audiences together. DJ Alan Freed's dances at the Brooklyn Paramount were notably mixed-race. Chuck Berry appealed to white girls; Elvis moved like a black man. Plus, all this was going down within the context of a reenergized civil rights movement. The Supreme Court's *Brown v. Board of Education* decision threatened separate-but-equal schools; Emmett Till's battered body haunted the American judicial system; and Rosa Parks had refused to move to the back of a Montgomery, Alabama, bus.

But official Asbury seemed convinced that it could contain and exploit these changes. In 1956, the city still advocated a brand of benevolent paternalism that dated back to James Bradley. The local paper came out strongly against discrimination. In March, it spearheaded a fund-raising drive to pay the fines of the young preacher leading Montgomery's bus boycott. "This newspaper," the *Asbury Evening Press* editorialized, "feels that the treatment accorded the Rev. Dr. King is a disgrace to the state of Alabama which must, in part, be shared by the whole country." And locals were beginning to admit that the whole country included Asbury Park.

On the boardwalk, Mayor Smock's decade of maintaining the status quo meant run-down facilities and few new attractions. But inland, the same laissez-faire policy led to even deeper poverty. The West Side had never had enough decent places to live, but by the summer of 1956, the waiting list for low-rent housing had grown to seven hundred families. Thousands of Asbury's Negroes qualified for subsidies—which meant they didn't earn as much in a year as a suburbanite spent to buy a new Olds. Back in 1940, Mayor Hetrick had begun construction on the low-income Asbury Park Village. Washington Village was added in 1943, and Smock had overseen a further small expansion there. But all of the West Side's 308 low-rent units were chock-full, and plans to add 63 more would address less than a tenth of those on the waiting list.

In the summer of 1956, the Asbury paper ran a series on what it called Asbury's "official skeleton in the closet." It included a profile of a Negro family of eight living in a two-room Springwood Avenue storefront with no hot water and only a kerosene stove for heat. While half a million federal dollars were available for West Side redevelopment, to get that money the city had to demonstrate its interest. And the city had demonstrated just the opposite. It had no redevelopment plan. Its building ordinances dated back to 1911, its plumbing code to 1906, and its health code was essentially the one that James Bradley had enacted in 1897.

When Asbury had incorporated the West Side a half century before, there had been talk of a "complete house-cleaning." But the area was worth more to its white owners if it was left to decay. Springwood's slumlords could charge four times the rent of federally subsidized housing. And the ancient safety codes meant they didn't have to fix up their buildings. As the *Asbury Park Evening Press* pointed out, "Landlords who have tenants lined up waiting to pay $10 a week for a room in a squalid shack aren't going to make improvements unless they have to." And those landlords were going to support—with contributions and votes—a city government that kept the safety inspectors at bay.

And kept the races separate. On the Fourth of July, 1956, black residents could go to Cuba's nightclub and catch Candy Bishop and her All Stars, fresh from Harlem's famous Small's Paradise. Meanwhile, on the beachfront, the ethnic attractions were aimed at white tourists: Cisco and his Los Americanos played mariachi music at the Monterey Lounge, and the hot spot at the Alan Hotel was Rocky's New Club Zulu. For the nostalgic, the daytime band concert on Eighth Avenue would have a rendition of "The Jolly Farmer Goes to Town" with a tuba solo. And Convention Hall featured acts like the McGuire Sisters, off the Arthur Godfrey TV show. They were racking up number one hits by sanitizing rock & roll: turning out sparkling-clean cover versions of the Moonglows' "Sincerely" and other R&B songs.

The Redickers wanted 1956's rock & roll show to feature an act just as popular and nonthreatening as Haley. Frankie Lymon and the Teenagers must have seemed the perfect choice. Here was a Top Ten group that featured an adorable thirteen-year-old lead singer. Their big hit, "Why Do Fools Fall in Love," was infectious but apparently meaningless feel-good music. Over a catchy doo-wop beat, little Frankie Lymon asked a string of naïve questions: Why do fools fall in love? Why do birds sing so gay? Why does the rain fall? The teenager's high, sweet voice exuded a kind of innocent desire. "I fell in love the minute that record came on," Ronnie Spector recalled. She was twelve, a few years away from becoming lead singer with the Ronettes. "I couldn't tell if he was black, or white, or what. I just knew that I loved the boy who was singing that song."

The fact that you couldn't tell his race was deliberate. The Teenagers were a crossover act. They wanted to appear not just in rock & roll but in mainstream venues—venues like Asbury Park. Onstage, the group often dressed in white cheerleader sweaters with a big red T for "teenager" on the chest. It was a dazzling, clean-cut, collegiate look that presented the Teenagers as ambassadors from the nonthreatening wing of rock & roll. At the end of 1956, they would even cut a single called "I'm Not a Juvenile Delinquent."

It didn't matter that Frankie Lymon had grown up pimping on Harlem street corners ("I learned everything there was to know about women before I was 12 years old"). Or that he'd already developed a heroin habit that would eventually kill him. Or that the Teenagers were hooked up with some of the shadier Mob elements in the shady world of early rock & roll. No, what mattered to the Redickers were the group's clean-cut image and its popularity: "Why Do Fools Fall in Love" went to #1 R&B and #6 pop. The Asbury promoters had to know that the Teenagers were "colored" with both Negro and Puerto Rican members. Maybe the Redickers assumed that only white kids would go to a concert in the white part of town. Maybe they figured if both races did show up, it wouldn't be a problem. After all, kids in Asbury knew their place. For proof of that, you only had to look at the city's version of school integration.

Before 1946, Bangs Avenue Elementary School had, in every sense, been divided in two: physically, socially, educationally. Bangs Avenue North was for white children with an all-white faculty and administration, and Bangs Avenue South was for the colored. The children came in through separate entrances and went to separate classrooms. Use of the only facility they shared, the auditorium, was scheduled so the races never mingled. A West Side citizens group called this "unlawful, against the ideal of brotherhood, a social evil and a breeder of fascism." But up until September 1946, that's how Asbury educated its children. Then, New Jersey passed a statewide civil rights law, and the city had no choice. Asbury Park promptly ended a half century of segregation, and just as promptly, white families moved out of town or sent their children to private schools. "They had three hundred white folks [enrolled in 1946]," one black graduate of Bangs recalls, "and every one of them went over to Ocean Township!"

A decade later, the teenagers who had lived through both sides of this white flight were the potential audience for the Frankie Lymon concert. They went to separate schools, lived in separate neighborhoods, attended separate churches. If the two races interacted, it was pretty rare. They both listened to rock & roll but not in the same room.

At dusk on Saturday, June 30, the crowd began streaming into Convention Hall for the eight-thirty show. The day had cooled from the high nineties, but it was still over eighty degrees when the opening act, Freddie Price and His Orchestra, went on. If the teenagers paid any attention, they heard proper, out-of-date Merchants Music. By the time Price was done, some twenty-seven hundred eager rock & roll fans were ready for the real thing. The Redickers had hired five "reserved policemen" to provide security, and the usual three city police officers were outside patrolling the Saturday-night boardwalk. Chief Lembke looked in on Convention Hall around ten-thirty. Price was still playing at that point, and everything seemed peaceful enough, so he headed back to the station. "Boardwalk crowds," as the chief put it, "always have been very orderly."

Frankie Lymon and the Teenagers finally came on a little before eleven. A cry went up from the crowd. In their sharp outfits and with their tight choreography, they created an immediate sensation. Out front was Lymon: a foot shorter than the other members, with high cheekbones, a round face, dark brows, and a perpetual, mischievous grin. If you squinted a little, you could see him as a darker version of Tillie. Asbury's acting mayor, Roland Hines, watched as the group doo-wopped into its opening number. "When they started singing," he reported later, "I watched some of the kids. They just seemed to lose control of themselves." Apparently, it looked fine to him; wasn't this giddy excitement what the new music was all about? After the first few notes, he, too, headed home.

Then, the fighting began.

According to the Convention Hall custodian (backstage at the time), "The Teenagers had just started their second number, and suddenly fists started swinging." It began over by the soft-drink stand. Scared kids tried to climb onto the stage to get away, and the custodian scrambled forward to protect the sound equipment. The trouble, said producer, Joseph Redicker, "just seemed to break out."

The Asbury police got their first call at 11:06. All available backup was sent—which turned out to be four officers including Thomas Smith, by now the force's only Negro detective sergeant. Smith and another officer took charge of a scene that included four separate fights. They got Convention Hall under control, and soon the dance started back up.

But punches kept being thrown, scattered incidents flaring up here and there all through the crowd. At around midnight, Redicker ordered the doors to the hall closed so nobody else could get in. Still, the fighting continued. After huddling with the cops, Redicker announced that the dance was canceled and told the kids to go home. Which, as anybody from Asbury Park knew, would automatically separate the crowd by race.

But as the fans spilled out onto Ocean Avenue—the music

finished almost before it had begun, the night still young and hot—more fighting broke out. Within moments, a couple hundred kids were going at it. And now they were fighting in public, on Asbury Park's boardwalk, where a convention of the Veterans of Foreign Wars had swelled the pre–Fourth of July crowd to an estimated seventy-five thousand. Angry teenagers, white and black, herded out of a canceled concert and let loose in the midst of thousands of celebrating veterans? Smith and the other officers put in an urgent call for backup.

No one was left in Asbury's police station, so the operator broadcast an alert: "All available help for mass fighting on Ocean Avenue, Asbury Park." Soon, support started streaming in from as far south as Point Pleasant and as far north as Red Bank. In the end, officers from a dozen Monmouth communities responded. Miltary police came down from Fort Monmouth and state police from Shrewsbury.

The combined forces closed down six blocks of Ocean Avenue and transformed the heart of Asbury's beachfront into a no-traffic zone lined with uniformed officers, police cars, and paddy wagons. The papers the next day made no bones about it: this was a riot, the "Convention Hall Riot." As the fighting continued, the cops waded in with nightsticks. It was a foreshadowing of scenes from the modern civil rights movement. At one point, according to the local paper, "Police even considered calling firemen to turn hose lines on the milling Ocean Avenue crowd."

And then the riot spread. City officals weren't particularly disturbed by reports that there were "arguments" in the Springwood Avenue slums. Those were considered common occurrences. But a half hour after the cops closed Ocean Avenue, news came of "roving cars filled with young people" smashing windows on Cookman Avenue. Suddenly, teenagers and their rock & roll-inspired violence threatened the heart of the business district.

According to the local paper, "only the prompt and effective work of local police and the help they received from other police forces prevented far more serious consequences." "Scores" were taken into custody, though few were actually booked. Twenty-five were injured, most of them with minor cuts and bruises, and three people hospitalized. It was one thirty in the morning before the crowd was dispersed and traffic back to normal. The police continued to guard the boardwalk into the morning hours. After all, they weren't clear why the fighting had broken out, so there was no saying when it might erupt again.

In the aftermath, Chief Lembke characterized the disturbance as "a case of hot music and cold beer not mixing. You put beer in the stomachs of kids 15 to 20, and you've got nothing but trouble." It was a reassuring explanation. Drunkenness, after all, was as all-American as Saturday night. And it wasn't Asbury Park's fault since Convention Hall didn't sell beer. What's more, the chief told his city, the troublemakers had come from out of town. "From the information I got, a bunch of colored boys from Newark started a fight with some colored boys from down this way." Unfortunately, the evidence didn't support this. Of the eight kids arrested, five were from Asbury Park and the others from towns right nearby. If the chief was right that outside agitators had caused the fighting, Asbury's police hadn't caught any.

What Chief Lembke insisted on was that the riot was *not* what it looked like. Yes, the rock & roll crowd had been racially mixed, but this was, he reported, "definitely not a race riot. There were colored fighting colored, white fighting white and white fighting colored." It was just an odd thing, inexplicable. In his thirty-five years on the force, dating back to before the Klan marched through Long Branch, Chief Lembke had never seen this kind of "mass fighting . . . on the beachfront."

By the Fourth of July, Asbury's local paper was less interested in the cause than the cure—which struck them as obvious: the city needed more law and order. "Whereas psychologists may help explain it," the *Asbury Park Evening Press* editorialized, "only police vigilance will prevent recurrences." Never mind *Blackboard Jungle*'s happy ending where understanding saves the day. And never mind conditions on the West Side: Asbury's "official skeleton in the closet." The paper mentioned neither, and the city council agreed. Except the council felt it knew the cause of the trouble. It wasn't substandard housing or segregated schools. Acting mayor Hines had been right there in Convention Hall when Frankie Lymon had started singing. He'd seen that strange look come over the teenagers. He knew it was the music that had done it. The government of Asbury Park unanimously agreed there would be no more teen dances that summer. And if and when they were reinstated, officials would make sure to screen out "rock and roll and the rest of this hot music that seems to stir the kids up so much."

The front-page headline in the local paper read CITY TO BAN ROCK 'N' ROLL. Asbury Park had once again rallied around James Bradley's American values. And as with beach segregation and the KKK, the city's position put it at the forefront of a national trend. Just days before, San Jose, California, had been the scene of what was being described as a rock & roll riot. And Jersey City officials had decided to refuse a permit for a teen concert—even though the headliner was Bill Haley and the host Paul Whiteman.

Asbury's voters supported this law-and-order response. In the next city council election, the winning ticket consisted of a veteran of the police department and three lawyers, including Joe Mattice. Asbury also sent a message by defeating Dr. Lorenzo Harris (though he had "the best showing ever by a Negro candidate") and electing instead another West Side doctor, Henry Vaccaro. Some "ethnics" were now allowed in the government; some weren't. The new city council upheld the ban on rock & roll and added that it would remove the batting cage that had turned the boardwalk into a "honky-tonk area."

The problem was that while the city council could try to maintain the status quo, the status quo couldn't maintain the city. The shopping district was in serious trouble. By March 1956, Bamberger's department store anchored a new cluster of shops outside the city. Forty-three acres had been purchased on Route 35 to build the Eatontown Shopping Center. The Monmouth Mall would open in 1959. Malls were easy to get to by car, safe, plus they had the excitement of the new. And thanks to a 1954 revision of the U.S. tax code, developers could write off some of the real estate costs, helping shopping centers undercut prices at local stores.

As for the beachfront, without Bingo and the other games, the boardwalk was, in the words of longtime beach commissioner Kendall Lee, "dead." The publicity around the Convention Hall riot didn't help, but the beachfront hadn't been self-sustaining for years. And far to the west, another blow struck Asbury's economy: a blow from so far away it may not even have been felt, at first. Two weeks after Bill Haley played the Casino, a new promised land opened. "Here," its founder declared, "age relives fond memories of the past . . . and here youth may savor the challenge and promise of the future. Disneyland is dedicated to the ideals, the dreams, and the hard facts that have created America."

If that sounds like James Bradley, the dream that Walt Disney built on 160 acres in Anaheim, California, shared a lot of Asbury Park's original values. It was set off from the outside world. It promised safety and reassuring middle-class fun. It looked backward. In many ways, what Disney created was a replica of small-town America. Or, more accurately, a replica of towns like Asbury that sold nostalgia for those good old days. Brass bands, sounding like John Philip Sousa's, toured Disneyland's spotless streets. Places like Asbury, Disney pointed out, had gotten "honky tonk with a lot of questionable characters running around." Disneyland replaced those characters with its own—Mickey Mouse and Snow White—and that first summer drew four million visitors. The way the malls would drain Cookman Avenue, the new theme parks would help empty Asbury's boardwalk.

By the Fourth of July, 1956, the question was what vision could possibly revitalize the dying city. Or, as the *Asbury Park Evening Press* put it, how to "go forward instead of back." The editors counted themselves among those who still believed in Asbury Park's future. After the Convention Hall Riot, they could "visualize a vital, growing municipality." But the only path to that which they could muster up was a variation on the Merchants' Vision. "Asbury Park is a multimillion dollar business," the editors wrote, "owned by some 18,000 citizen-stockholders." Not a promised land. Not a moral community. Not even a city, really. Asbury was a business, like Disneyland, and it needed a business model. That, the editors wrote, or James Bradley's dream would become "a moribund political sub-division to be looted and then deserted for greener fields."

But that was already happening. The West Side had been looted for decades. And white families had been deserting at least since school desegregation. What rock & roll helped reveal on Asbury's boardwalk were divisions that no business model addressed. The voice that did evoke an alternative vision—that called on the city to "dedicate [itself] to the fight against social stagnation"—came from a guest speaker at Asbury Park High School. Four years after the rock & roll riot, in the spring of 1960, Dr. Martin Luther King Jr. was in Asbury to address the General Baptist Convention of New Jersey. Civil rights sit-ins were sweeping the South. Dr. King argued that the nation's fight against social stagnation had to include "the subtle and hidden segregation in the North." It wasn't enough to be a citizen-stockholder. To succeed, any vision of the future had to combine business concerns with moral ones. "We must learn to live together as brothers," he told the thirteen hundred listeners packed into Asbury High, "or we shall perish as fools."

It's easy to imagine the West Side responding with a simple "Amen." As to the city's businessmen, they might be willing to make some concessions. You could see the city was dying. Cars whizzed by for the bigger, cleaner, safer beaches farther down the shore. Joe Mattice, who was now emerging as Asbury's new boss, had come of age in the era of Hetrick and Tumen. He was willing to work with Detective Sergeant Smith. He might let the Tilt-A-Whirl be open to all—as long as you paid your admission. But that didn't mean living as brothers.

And what about Asbury teenagers? After all, they were the ones who'd fought on the boardwalk. They might be forgiven if they heard in Dr. King's words an echo of Frankie Lymon's. The one declared that a separate society like Asbury's made self-destructive fools out of them all. The other came snapping out onstage, admitting from the start that, yes, of course, they were fools. Then singing what sounded like nonsense, he kept returning to the same unanswerable question. An apparently ridiculous question. And in some ways, the only one worth asking. Why *do* fools fall in love?

FOURTH OF JULY, 1970

ASBURY DIDN'T EXPLODE in 1964. Jersey City and Paterson did, in what a presidential commission called "a series of extraordinary and probably unprecedented racial disorders." The next August, it was Watts: the routine arrest of a drunk driver led to six days of rebellion and thirty-four deaths, almost all of them African-Americans. In 1966, it was Chicago, Cleveland, and San Francisco. Still, Asbury remained quiet. Then, in 1967, it was Newark.

On a Wednesday evening eight days after the Fourth of July, two white cops roughed up a black cabdriver with the generic name of John Smith. "The spirit and the feeling of the moment a rebellion breaks out," Newark native Amiri Baraka would write in *The Autobiography of Leroi Jones*, "is almost indescribable. Everything seems to be in zoooom motion, crashing toward some explosive manifestation. As Lenin said, time is speeded up, what takes years is done in days, in real revolution. In rebellions, life goes to 156 rpm and the song is a police siren accompanying people's breathless shouts and laughter."

By Wednesday, July 12, thousands of Newark's citizens were singing that song. Though most of them couldn't have quoted Lenin, their target was clear. They shattered the plate-glass windows of (especially) white-owned stores, looting and celebrating. New Jersey governor Richard Hughes described Newark as "a city in open rebellion. This amounts to criminal insurrection against society." By the end of the weekend, with twenty-six dead, a thousand injured, another fifteen hundred in jail, and an estimated $5 million in property damage, the governor told the press, "The line between the jungle and the law might as well be drawn here as any place in America."

And then the rebellion spread. Sunday, Newark experienced its first quiet night in five, but Jersey City erupted. At the same time, in Plainfield, eighteen miles south of Newark, a white cop was shot and beaten to death in what the mayor called "planned, open insurrection." New Brunswick and Paterson followed.

Asbury Park was next in line. It had, as the *Asbury Press* wrote, its own share of the "injustice and the frustration that provoke riots." After another decade of being looted and deserted, the city barely had an economy. Typical of the deterioration on the boardwalk, the Casino had burned the year before and still hadn't been fully restored. Across the tracks, thirty-five percent of the city's black population was living below the poverty line, and that number was rising. Plus, the West Side had a close connection to what went on in Newark, fifty miles to the north. Some Asbury residents belonged to Newark's Muslim mosque; others were in contact with its Black Panther Party. "Yea, I paid attention to Newark" is how one teenager explained it.

Five days after the Newark rebellion and the night after Plainfield's, Asbury's city officials called a special meeting to discuss the situation. Mayor Frank Rowland heard a member of the city's housing committee describe the West Side's mood as "explosive." Word was on the street: what had started in Newark was coming to Asbury. It was only a matter of time.

The recently appointed acting police chief, Thomas Smith, rose to deny that. According to a fellow Negro officer, Smith had been owed the chief's job for a while. After going to the black side of Bangs Avenue Elementary School and then to Asbury High, Smith spent two years at Howard University. When he returned from serving in World War II, he rejoined the city's police force, working his way up to captain in the detective bureau. Booker T. Washington was one of his inspirations, modeling how a Negro could achieve by working within the system. When Smith took the police officer's exam, an African-American colleague recalled, he'd come out first, but town officials had balked at making him chief. Instead, they'd asked the middle-class leaders of the Negro community to take Smith aside. "Tell Tommy the town ain't ready for him" is how the whisper supposedly went. "[That he's] a good captain of detectives . . . stay there." But now, as one officer put it, the riots had scared them all: "After Plainfield, shit! They saw the writing on the wall. They got out, and it was, 'Hey, Tommy! You can stop anything.'" So, Smith rose to assure city officials that he could, indeed, stop a rebellion. And some of the other blacks in the room remember exchanging looks as he spoke. If this was what having a black police chief meant . . .

Councilman Vaccaro spoke next. Clearly, the West Side needed more jobs for youth, more recreation, and better housing. The all-white council, including the Democratic boss, Joseph Mattice, listened quietly. The Vaccaro family, with fourteen properties, was the largest single landlord in the ghetto. The day before, in its lead editorial, the *Asbury Park Sunday Press* had lambasted the local government for decades of delay on the West Side's urban renewal. "It has been next to impossible to define accountability," the *Press* complained, "[but] it has been apparent for some time that those with a voice in either project [there was also supposed to be a new middle school] have not shown enough impatience to get action. No one is asking for miracles. At the present rate of accomplishment, less than a third of the urban renewal area has been developed in 10 years and there is no Middle School after almost half that time. It may take a miracle to see these projects completed."

Joe Mattice had controlled Asbury's government at least since his election in 1957, and the newspapers had been going on in this way for as long as he could remember. *Look* magazine would describe Mattice as "standpat," leading a city council "unresponsive to the needs and demands of the growing black population." What he'd learned from more than a quarter century in Asbury politics was the power of silence. Mattice kept quiet now, as Donald Hammary, the representative of the Monmouth Community Action Program (MCAP), stood to speak.

A black activist with a charismatic, fiery personality, Hammary was pure street. And as someone paid by the federal government rather than the city, he could say what others in the room couldn't. He began by making clear that the West Side was past any easy or slow solutions. "The youth today," he declared in his rough, high-pitched voice, "aren't gonna take what their fathers did." A lot of them were smoking reefer just for something to do, and they'd beg, borrow, or steal to get the money for it. "Families," he went on, "have to rent two or three apartments," because there weren't enough decent-sized ones to go around. And what they could rent were run-down and disgraceful. "People on the West Side can't take no vacations to get away from it," he said to the well-dressed councilmen. ". . . [They're] ready to explode . . . And the young people are saying to hell with it."

"We'll handle them" is how Hammary remembers Tommy Smith's law-and-order response. "We have enough police to keep any kind of disorders down."

"Man," Hammary jumped in, "when people get angry enough, a cop ain't nothing but another man!"

The argument went back and forth. Arthur Polite, a Negro businessman, weighed in on Springwood Avenue's moral sins. "That," he said, "will be the crux of any trouble." There were dealers hanging outside Cuba's bar on Friday night, and what Polite called "faggots" showing off their wigs and rings: their numbers "out of proportion" to the size of Asbury Park. "These people on the block," he concluded in disgust, lumping all into one, "have a code of language all their own. Many have been in Freehold jail or prison together." They were what the assistant city attorney, Norm Mesnikoff, called "a different kind of black," not solid Republicans like Polite.

In national reports, sociologists had recently labeled this "the riffraff theory." It held that the majority of Negroes were law-abiding citizens and that these riots weren't political rebellions at all but, as a governor's commission in Louisiana wrote, "formless, quite senseless," and so, "meaningless." As applied to Newark, the riffraff theory blamed "young people with nothing to do and nothing to lose" and "outside agitators." Maybe, one Asbury councilman wondered out loud, if they could just close down certain places, or arrest certain people?

About then, the black police detective in charge of youth, David Parreott, decided to say his piece. Parreott basically agreed with Hammary, but where the MCAP employee let loose with a street hustler's fury, Officer Parreott was a broad, levelheaded man who spoke in measured tones. The people on the West Side, Parreott explained, "want something to do other than to stand around on the corners." This was no new breed. "They are seeking," he went on in his soft but firm voice, "the same things that their fathers sought: security, love, affection, social status, and new experiences."

Parreott looked at Mattice, at Mayor Rowland and the other councilmen, trying for what seemed like the thousandth time to explain what living on the West Side was like. The kids stole cars to prove themselves. They joined gangs for status, security. "They can't take a trip," he said, searching the faces in the room, "so they turn to glue sniffing, drinking, and drugs." Parreott had said it all before, but maybe now, with Newark still smoking, they'd listen. There were three "outstanding fermenting complaints," he concluded, trying to win them over with the urgency in his voice: "housing, recreation, and jobs."

In the end, nothing was resolved, and the meeting broke up near ten P.M. At about that time, across town on Springwood Avenue, a group of twenty teenagers had started throwing rocks at the side of a building. A brick went through the plate glass at Etoll's Grocery on Prospect; a bottle broke inside the open door of the New Asbury Liquor store. But acting chief Smith was right— this time, anyway. Extra police were called into the area, and by midnight, quiet had been restored.

The next weekend, other cities went up across the country. In Detroit, it took seven thousand National Guardsmen to restore order: 43 people were killed and 450 injured. New York City's Spanish Harlem burst into flame; so did Rochester, Birmingham, and Cambridge, Maryland. By the end of 1967, there had been nearly four dozen "riots" and more than a hundred cases of something labeled "civil unrest." Historians would categorize these insurrections as "the greatest wave of urban violence the nation had ever seen." But Asbury Park had stayed quiet. As quiet as the empty lots, long ago leveled for urban renewal, still gaping on the West Side.

The next spring, Dr. King was assassinated in Memphis. There were rebellions in 110 U.S. cities; fifty-five thousand troops were called up. The Sunday after the shooting, with the national death toll at twenty-four, Asbury Park held a silent protest march. Two thousand people (mostly Negroes according to the local paper) walked the length of Asbury's boardwalk, from Casino Hall to Convention Hall, carrying candles and trying, through their silence, to bring this national issue home.

A year later, in May of 1969, Joseph Mattice was elected mayor. His victory over Frank Rowland made the city's long-term shift in power official. By then, Eugene Capibianco had been city judge for decades, and Councilmen Vaccaro and Albarelli were serving with Mattice. The children of Asbury's ditchdiggers and gardeners were now in power. Born and educated in Asbury, with a law firm on Mattison Avenue, Joe Mattice devoted his first public pronouncement to denying one of the central facts of the city. "There is no east or west side as far as I'm concerned," said the new mayor. "I'm going to work for the best interests of Asbury Park."

As Independence Day, 1970, approached, the page-one headline in the *Asbury Park Evening News* confidently predicted A TRADITIONAL 4TH. It was true, the story went on to say, that "human events these days are causing most Americans to pause apprehensively to reassess the state of the union . . . [but the Fourth] still is basically a happy occasion."

The apprehensive pause wasn't only because of a half decade of urban uprisings. By 1970, a series of political assassinations had left many wondering how—if—democracy could function. They saw a law-and-order national government whose power was based on Asbury's kind of racial and economic division. And then there was the war in Vietnam. Over forty thousand U.S. military personnel had died there, with more than a hundred deaths just in the week before the Fourth. There were peace protests all across the country, and death there, too: four students killed at a protest at Kent State in May, two students shot to death at Jackson State ten days later. Over a million men had already been drafted, and coming into the Fourth of July weekend, the Selective Service conducted its second national lottery to determine which eighteen-year-olds would be next.

In New Jersey over the past decade, the population had increased by eighteen percent, much of it in the suburban rings expanding around New York City and Philadelphia. Jersey had become the eighth most populous state and exemplified the trend away from manufacturing jobs to what was starting to be called the service economy. By 1970, this trend helped Jersey "shift towards a more unequal income distribution." Asbury Park, of course, had had a service economy since the days when Stephen Crane said it made nothing. By now, nearly thirty percent of the city's population was on welfare. While the sixties had continued to hollow the town out, Asbury's exterior looked much the same. The antique carousel still spun; there was still the smell of saltwater taffy, the ping of pinball machines, the "dark rides" in the Palace. True, beachfront renewal had never happened. On the other hand, the decay had been long-term, so that tourists used to coming down for their traditional Fourth of July visit found something sweet and familiar in the fading city.

In fact in this, Asbury Park's centennial year, you could argue that the change over the past hundred years had been more stylistic than anything else. Instead of matched teams of carriage horses trotting down Ocean Avenue, shiny convertibles cruised the strip. Instead of women twirling parasols, there were girls in bikini tops and shorts, their fingernails glowing under the streetlights. The tough crowd that had managed to find beer in the nineteenth century had transposed into greasers, arriving in the roar of Harleys. Instead of listening to brass bands, long-haired teens gathered at a club called Mrs. Jay's Heart and Mind Machine. "Tonite," its July 1970 ad proclaimed, "forget about the war . . ."

July 3, fireworks flared and boomed and fell back into the dark ocean, as they had almost every Independence Day weekend since the town was founded. Tourists and local families clapped from the boardwalk. Some old-timers might still remember when these "guests" would have walked home to one of the grand hotels where they'd rented rooms for the season. But those days—and hotels—were long gone. The seven-story, 364-room Monterey Hotel had been demolished in the mid-sixties after a decade and a half of continuous financial problems. Now, most of the crowd got in their cars and drove back to the suburbs. And while there was still Steinbachs, Levin's "King of Values," and the College Shop, "Monmouth and Ocean County's Only Women's Haberdasher," the era of Asbury Park being a premier commercial center was also over. There was downtown parking for a thousand cars, but the spaces were rarely filled.

July 4, 1970, was perfect: sunny and in the eighties. *The Asbury Park Press* went onto Cookman Avenue and conducted a patriotic survey. How many people could quote any part of the Declaration of Independence? No one, as it turned out. As one shopper put it, "We may not know much, but we mean well." By midday, the beaches were thick with sunbathers. Transistor radios formed a chorus of the latest pop hits: the laid-back, summertime feel of "Groovin'" by the Young Rascals; the Association's "Windy." Just offshore, surfers pretended they were in California, waiting for the big wave that never quite came.

As dusk fell, some of these same kids began to line up outside Convention Hall. Asbury had long since lifted its rock & roll ban: the music was too popular to ignore. The Rascals and the Association had played Convention Hall, as had acts ranging from Mitch Ryder and the Detroit Wheels to Motown's Temptations to San Francisco's Jefferson Airplane. For this Fourth, Convention Hall had booked the British group Ten Years After.

The band had a Top Twenty album on the charts but was best known for having played Woodstock a year earlier. Back then, Asbury might have been threatened by the counterculture that Ten Years After represented. But by 1970, *Woodstock* was a movie playing over at the Strand in Lakewood; the antimaterialistic Summer of Love had already been bought and sold; the Beatles were breaking up. Asbury may not have approved of the long-haired kids in bleached jeans and tie-dyed shirts, but they posed no danger. And the blues rock of Ten Years After—the psychedelic pounding, Alvin Lee's ten-minute-long guitar solos—were already mostly a reminder of what had never quite been.

In some ways, rock & roll had become just another boardwalk attraction, bringing in much-needed cash. Tonight, there wasn't likely to be much mixing of races: Ten Years After's appeal didn't extend across the tracks. After the Convention Hall concert, some of the hippest kids—their ears still ringing from the cranked-up guitars—would walk inland a few blocks to the deserted business district. On Cookman Avenue, they'd pass Steinbachs, closed for the night, and find their way to the Thom McAn shoe store, also closed. There, by an unmarked side door, they'd form a line while a woman screened the crowd and took admission.

Once she let you in, you climbed a flight of steep stairs to a coffeehouse called The Green Mermaid. The Mermaid modeled itself on the Greenwich Village folk scene of the early sixties. The waitresses wore T-shirts that read I EAT THE GREEN MERMAID AT UPSTAGE. The coffee came in little cracked cups, and local singers played covers of Joni Mitchell or Bob Dylan. Like The Head Shop on the ground floor of Asbury's Lincoln Hotel, or The White Rabbit espresso house, The Green Mermaid offered a quietly stoned alternative to Asbury's honky-tonk.

But there was more. At the rear of The Green Mermaid was another door and another long set of stairs. They led to the

Upstage: the real attraction for most of the kids who managed to get in. It was a storage room: a windowless, black hole. Its walls were painted with Day-Glo images that seemed to move under the strobe light. "At first glance," one regular recalled, "they looked like mountains and stuff, but then you started noticing peoples' legs and heads, tongues." Built into one whole wall was a mixed-matched bank of beat-up speakers. And in front of that waited a line of amplifiers, microphones, and a drum set.

Margaret and Tom Potter ran the Upstage. Margaret usually started the music around nine by playing with her own group. Then, at midnight, the local players would put together that night's house band. They sorted through musicians the way you'd pick a ball team out on the sandlot. You needed a drummer, a bass player, and a rhythm guitarist, and every night there was a jam leader. Upstage regular Steve Van Zandt remembers, "They paid you five dollars. [But] you had to earn your way into the band."

The shore had lots of clubs where you could hear rock & roll, and many had tryout nights or open mikes. But the Upstage was unique. The standing wall of amps, the chance for anyone to walk in and play, the resulting competition, made it more like a drag race than a business. There were no limitations on what you could play and no big payday if you succeeded. The way Margaret Potter put it, the Upstage was special "because it was a place for the local musicians—young kids—to find themselves."

A little behind the times, tough, working class, this was Asbury Park's counterculture. The Upstage was not only counter to the nine-to-five world (its nine-to-five ran from nine at night till five in the morning), but also counter to the typical shore bar. On the boardwalk, people mostly wanted to hear covers of Top Forty hits. The bands had to be able to do an okay version of "Groovin'" or "American Woman" by the Guess Who. At the Upstage, the audience came to hear what it didn't know. In April 1970, a local reporter described the crowd as members of "what's come to be known as the Woodstock Nation . . . [or] the tribe." They wanted "plenty of floor, plenty of freedom, plenty of good music, and no hassle."

If you were picked to be part of the jam band at the Upstage, you played all night. Typically, the leader would set up some basic three-chord progression with a plain, drum-heavy beat. Sometimes there would be a singer, sometimes not. What the crowd waited for was the lead guitarist, the "glory hog," who would crank up the volume on his amp, step in front of the band, and rocking his head in ecstasy, wail into his solo, playing what sounded like all the notes he knew as fast as he could find them. After he ran out of steam, the next guitarist would take over—and the next—and the next. For eight hours, the kids would vie with one another to see who could cut the most sizzling lead.

By that summer, the acknowledged star of this scene was the twenty-year-old Bruce Springsteen. With a jutting jaw and long, sun-bleached hair down to his shoulders, Springsteen looked the part. "He was," Van Zandt recalls, "the most single-minded of anyone I ever met." And Margaret Potter remembers Springsteen standing out at the Upstage for "his desire and his straight, right down the line approach to music." He'd plug in to the wall of amps, one fellow musician recalls, and "do these blues songs where he'd make up these lyrics off the top of his head. He had this one called 'Heavy Louise.' He was famous for it 'cause it would go on and on and on. He'd make up like nine stanzas of improvised lyrics . . . and he'd intersperse these made-up lyrics with these burning guitar solos."

The music wasn't "revolutionary," Van Zandt admits. "We were anachronistic. Retro." That was partly because Asbury was a kind of backwater. But also, Springsteen and the other kids in his generation of rock & roll had a sense that, as Van Zandt remembers, "everything good had been done." If Asbury Park's heyday was over, so, it seemed to them, was rock & roll's. There had been the founding fathers: Little Richard, Elvis, Chuck Berry, Bill Haley. After that revolution had come the British invasion— the Beatles, the Stones—which had led to groups like the Grateful Dead and Ten Years After (whose very name implied the distance from rock's first burst of energy). But what did that leave? As Van Zandt puts it, by 1970 the Upstage regulars felt as if they "had missed the boat." They kept the dream alive mostly through imitation: "One was [Jeff] Beck—and [Jimmy] Page—and we had a couple of Alvin Lees—and occasionally Santana."

"There was an audience there," Van Zandt states. "You had a couple of hundred people, sometimes. But I swear half of them were musicians. 'Cause after everybody's gig ended at two in the morning, they'd go into the Upstage." While one of the long improvs rolled out, most everyone who wasn't playing danced. Not the tight strut that went with soul music, or the more controlled steps that people were doing to Top Forty songs, but a languid, wheeling hop and skip that paid less attention to the beat than to the texture of the loud, loud music. Boys bent at the waist so their long hair would cover their faces, and girls spread their arms in euphoria, letting their floor-length dresses spin like the old carousel.

It was an overwhelmingly white crowd. Davey Sancious, a black kid from Belmar, laughs at the memory of trying to move to the unsubtle, heavy beat of Steppenwolf's "Born to Be Wild." The jam band at the Upstage didn't play Marvin Gaye's "I Heard It Through the Grapevine," the kind of syncopated groove that dominated West Side parties that summer. "The only black music being played in there," Sancious recalls, "was by white kids who were fans of black music and trying to learn how to play it." And most of them were more into Iron Butterfly's narcotic "In-A-

Gadda-Da-Vida" and Cream's "White Room." It was music that fit the windowless, insulated Upstage; music that aspired to create its own, quasi-mystical scene; music designed to set you apart from the troubles going down in the outside world.

Margaret Potter's club promised to be a safe zone from, among other things, Asbury's simmering racial scene. Still, the first few times Sancious ventured into the Upstage, he was careful to go with friends: one white and one black. Cookman Avenue, after all, was across the tracks. "I was nervous about it," he remembers. "It wasn't a place where black people went."

Sancious knew the geography of segregation, having grown up on the West Side. His father—an electronics engineer—taught radar and helped maintain the missile system at Fort Monmouth. His mother was a schoolteacher in Neptune. One day, when Davey was five, the family moved. "I put all my toys in this cardboard box and got in the car and drove eight miles to Belmar. And pulled up in this new neighborhood . . . We went from lower class—we weren't poor, but it was a real struggle . . . we went from that to, suddenly, it was like Ozzie and Harriet . . . Instead of going to school and worrying about fighting, you could actually go to school and learn something." After that, when Sancious returned to Asbury, the kids called him a "Belmar boy."

Springwood Avenue remained the center of black culture on the northern shore: the place to get a haircut, to hear the news, to listen to or play music. Davey's father would take him to the Orchid Lounge, a Springwood Avenue club an eighth of a mile and a world away from the Upstage. The Orchid Lounge was a grown-up place that drew top-name jazz acts: Jimmy Smith, Jack McDuff, Lonnie Liston Smith. The crowd dressed for a night on the town: men in dark suits with ties knotted just so, women with perfume so dazzling it took a while to notice their smart hats, the tight string of pearls. "It was like black folks being turned out,"

Davey recalls, "happy about having someplace to go. I don't remember seeing a white person in the Orchid Lounge." The owner would sometimes let the ten-year-old Sancious jam there. One of the musical thrills of his young life was having Lonnie Liston Smith lean over and show him a certain jazz chord that he'd been trying to figure out for weeks.

As he got older, Sancious began playing keyboard in a constantly changing lineup of R&B bands. "Back then, it was five sets a night, forty minutes on, twenty off . . . You'd go out in the car and smoke a thing, have a drink, whatever you're doing. 'Ah, man! Fourth set!'" This crowd wanted covers, too, but unlike the boardwalk clubs, here you had to know how to play James Brown, the Temptations, the Delfonics. You'd stretch out a three-minute radio hit for as long as people kept dancing. It was an almost totally segregated scene. "[White] kids," Sancious recalls, "didn't really stray. You couldn't just walk up Springwood and see what was going on . . . [That was] the kind of thing that would get people pissed off."

Which is why Sancious was cautious about crossing over the other way—to the Upstage. Even recognized local R&B bands, such as Tony Blair and his Soul Flames, didn't work Asbury's beachfront. Blair had sung with Lloyd Price and with the Drifters, had cut four records, and had played all over the country, including at white clubs in other shore towns. But he couldn't get a gig a few blocks east of where he lived on Munroe Avenue. "The owners of the clubs won't hire me . . .," he had told the paper in the late 1960s, "because my group is all Negro . . . They're afraid some of our Negro followers might come into their places."

What finally drew Sancious into the Upstage was the music. You could hear soul, jazz, and R&B in black Asbury; in fact, it cut across generational lines. Sancious remembers when he and his father first heard Aretha Franklin's "Chain of Fools" on the car radio: his father pulling over till the song finished, then driving straight to the local record store to buy the single. But Sancious got fascinated by a different kind of music. One afternoon his brother brought home the first Jimi Hendrix album, and the two of them sat in their Belmar bedroom and played it straight through. "Nobody," Sancious says, "had made sounds like that! Forget about the sonic thing—the textures he was making—his guitar playing was just breathtaking . . . I sat there on the edge of the bed," he recalls, "staring at the cover, trying to read it and understand."

Hendrix had learned his chops as a journeyman R&B player and was as much a part of the black tradition as Lonnie Liston Smith. But in order to pursue the sound he was after, he'd ended up moving to England. And when he crashed into the American consciousness, it was as a weird variation on the British guitar hero. His sly, stoned voice, his feverish solos, and the rage of his controlled feedback might as well have been the sound of inner cities going up in flame. At the same time, Hendrix seemed to offer an alternative both to the ghetto and the middle class: a psyche-delic cool that was neither Belmar nor Springwood but incorpo-rated both. "That was it," Sancious recalls. "I got very serious about guitar. Right on the bed there."

Hendrix grabbed him and led him to the Upstage. In 1970, a sixteen-year-old high school dropout, Sancious had decided to dedicate himself to music full-time. The whirling, stoned-out freakiness of the room above Thom McAn's was as close as he could get to being inside a Hendrix album. It replaced the question of what color you were with Jimi's untranslatable gauge of hipness, "Are You Experienced?" Years later, Sancious would try to de-scribe the racial dynamics at the Upstage. "There was a sense of," he says, groping for words, "a little sense of community, actually. Like, you're not going to get *that* trip put on you here . . . We just thought: we're all here, we're all together, let's have a damn good time! And all the stuff you put up with out in the world—if you just went out in the street . . . being called a name or being disrespected in a store or being suspected of something or whatever—that stuff went on all the time, every day. But amongst that scene of people, especially the musicians . . . there was no funky racial vibe at all. Not at all."

So, on the Fourth of July, 1970, the tribe could walk from the Ten Years After concert at Convention Hall through the empty business district to the Upstage and there, dream its own promised land. Meanwhile, on the West Side, there were two black teen dances this Saturday night: one at the Community Center and another a few blocks away at the Catholic church. Which left Springwood unusually quiet. Donald Hammary closed up his father's billiard hall early because business was so slow. He passed the time out in front of Cuba's, hanging with that crowd that worried Mr. Polite. A few kids, Hammary recalls, were "running and chasing each other, throwing bottles and these things." Routine on the West Side. A traditional Fourth.

At some point, a car with a white guy driving stopped at the light. "Boom! Bottle hit the car. By accident," says Hammary. "He looked and—voom—took off! And everybody laughed. 'Ha, ha, ha,' you know?" Another car came down Springwood, a convertible, and some of the kids decided this was a good joke. They raised a garbage can and dumped it in. Still no big deal, Hammary insists. A guy known as Easy Living stepped out of Cuba's, saw what was happening, and told the kids to cut it out. Which they did for a while but were soon back at it. "They were hitting black cars and white cars. Any kind of car. And laughing! . . . We sit there watching, paying no mind. Then, next thing you know, one of the kids is up on the roof [with] bottles full of water. Waiting for a convertible to come. Ditta-da-ditta-da-ditta!"

Someone called the cops. By the Fourth of July, 1970, Asbury's force of fifty policemen included twelve blacks. These were typically assigned to Springwood and the West Side, just as Tommy Smith had been back in the day. When the two black officers pulled up and asked the people to move along, there wasn't much response. So one of the patrolmen went to a pay phone and put in a request: "I need some back-up here. Ackers and Springwood." The crowd waited; the cops waited. According to Officer David Parreott, white policemen often wouldn't respond to calls from Springwood; they considered it the black cops' turf. When the crowd realized that no one was coming, they pressed forward. One of the officers pulled his gun, told everyone to get back, and began waving his piece in the air. His partner got on the phone, again. Still no response, and the crowd kept growing.

At a little past midnight, both teen dances let out at the same time. West Side dances drew kids from up and down the shore: African-Americans from Red Bank, Long Branch, Toms River. Now, Hammary recalls, "You could see how they were coming together. They all met on Springwood." From down the avenue, they reminded him of ants: how they milled and joined and turned into a single body. That body headed for the crowd already too big for the patrolmen to handle.

"Now is when the hoodlums took over," says Hammary. "[They shouted,] 'Get rid of them black pigs! Get them out of here!' . . . One of [the cops got] hit on the head, and one on the shoulder. And I saw tears in [the cops'] eyes. And they're homeboys! They ran past Second Baptist Church." As soon as the cops retreated, the whole thing escalated. "They kicked in the liquor store: boom! They ran up into the liquor store. Someone hollered, 'The drugs! The drugstore!' Boom!"

Police Chief Thomas Smith was out at a club that Saturday night. The dispatch clerk reached him there, and he put his entire force on duty. As it had three years earlier, the strategy appeared to work. By early Sunday, Springwood was quiet. The "out-of-town agitators" drawn by the teen dances had been sent on their way. And the situation stayed calm as morning broke. Soon, the usual well-dressed West Siders were parading to and from church. Across town, on the beach, tourists were putting on suntan lotion.

But at dusk, crowds began to re-form on Springwood. "It started," Chief Smith would say, "with large groups of teenagers about 14 and 15 years old . . . My men would move in, disperse a large group of about 200 people. They would separate, move a couple of blocks, and form up again." Said a witness who identified himself as a member of Asbury's small Black Panther Party, "I seen more people than I ever seen in my life. There wasn't no cause for it. Ain't nobody go out like Paul Revere and tell them, 'To arms, to arms—come on out on the street and let's go burn down the town!' It was spontaneous, unrehearsed and unprovoked."

One crowd broke into a liquor store. Still, right up until midnight, it seemed to the police that the difficult Independence Day weekend would end up a manageable one. Then, at twenty past twelve, a group of about seventy-five teenagers converged on the Neptune Diner at the inland end of Springwood Avenue and Route 35. "It all happened so fast," said the owner, "that no one knew what was going on until it was over." Eight of the teenagers ran into the place and ripped off $600.

Word spread instantaneously. The city government's response was almost instinctual. As Mayor Mattice and his city manager supervised, the police barricaded off Springwood at Main Street, isolating the East Side from the West. Behind "islands of police cars," officers stood and watched the looting in relative quiet. One cop muttered that it was "just like a party." Then, the paper wrote, he "reached under the protective glass of his riot helmet and drew hard and long on a cigarette."

Across the line, down Springwood, people were grabbing rocks, smashing in windows, and climbing in over the glittering glass to help themselves. "I've been here twenty years," the owner of a Springwood shoe store told the paper later. "My father owned this place twenty years before that. We never had any trouble." But generations of business-as-usual had ended. The way the Springwood economy had always worked, one West Sider recalled, was you took your weekly or monthly check to the local market and left it there. "George would tell [you] to come anytime and get what you want . . . They'd bring George the telephone bill, the electric bill, and George would pay it. If there was anything left over, George kept it." Now years of this plantation economy were coming home to roost. The uprising targeted Peluso's Grocery up on Asbury Avenue, M&B Meats, and Hutters bakery. West Siders threw bottles at the New Jersey National Bank and Trust. Neptune police found a firebomb propped on the window ledge at Wellers Fuel Co. Along the main stretch of Springwood Avenue, three quarters of the buildings ended up damaged. By the end of that night, at least eight would be completely destroyed.

At three A.M. on what was now July 6, the mayor declared a state of emergency. A hundred out-of-town cops came from Neptune, Ocean, Wall, Middletown, Long Branch, Allenhurst, and Ocean Grove. The state police stood by, waiting for orders. At four A.M., the rioting was declared under control. At five A.M., the out-of-town cops were sent home. Twenty people had been arrested, and six city cops had sustained minor injuries. At six-thirty Monday morning, the city's public works department started cleaning up. Mayor Mattice announced a curfew starting that night at ten. A local Baptist minister and the president of the local NAACP agreed the rebellion had been a long time coming, the direct result of joblessness and substandard housing, then cautioned the West Side to "cool it" and "seek proper redress."

But by noon, passing cars were being hit again, fights had broken out, and the *Asbury Press* reported crowds harassing "police and white civilians in the area." Enough rocks and bottles hit passing trains for Penn Central to order its engineers to skip the Asbury stop. At two in the afternoon, the Asbury police again called for backup. At three, a fire broke out in the rear of the Capitol Bar and from there spread to the fifteen-thousand-square-foot Fisch's department store: one of the keystones of Springwood Avenue. "Anybody who was anybody came and shopped at Fisch's," Officer Parreott recalls. Despite fire departments from ten neighboring companies pouring into the area, it burnt to the ground. Mayor Mattice called New Jersey governor William Cahill, and by five P.M. two hundred heavily armed state, county, and local police patrolled the West Side.

Through the early hours of the night, they tried to maintain law and order. Then at nine, they were called back beyond the barricades. "We feared," said a deputy police chief, "that in the dark it would lead to mass slaughter on both sides." Police would come into the West Side only in response to emergency calls. Otherwise, the "jungle" was left to fend for itself.

Trying to head off more trouble, the NAACP called a meeting just at the border of the zoned-off area. Police Chief Smith came to the West Side Community Center and listened to a group of fifteen- and twenty-year-olds insist that "this has been brewing a long time" and listing the same reasons Parreott had given three years before: no jobs, recreation, or decent housing. "When you talk with them," Smith later told the paper, "they can almost bring you around to their way of thinking." But Smith was a policeman first: "My loyalty was to the city of Asbury Park and law and order." After about twenty minutes, the meeting was abandoned.

And the ransacking of Springwood was soon back in full swing. One West Sider watched "women . . . walking around with their arms full of loot, as if they were shopping," and even "respected members of the community" stepping through smashed-in windows, "just like a hungry army foraging for food." Officer Parreott recalls, "Guys were bumping into me with refrigerators and washing machines and sofas." Kids took hammers to the parking-meters or bent hoses so the fires couldn't be put out. The first night, as Donald Hammary puts it, had been "all home people, mostly." Now, the troubles had been "advertised," and out-of-towners had joined in. "Their main target," said one witness of the rampaging crowd, "is to get the police now. They aren't thinking about what led to it all."

City officials claimed to be just as ignorant of causes as they'd been with the rock & roll riot. "There seemed to be no organization to the disorders," said Deputy Police Chief Flannigan, "and no leaders. I don't know of any main issue that would have sparked them." Mayor Mattice would go on record as saying he was convinced "outside forces" were involved.

By two A.M. Tuesday morning the seventh, Springwood was once again quiet, the buildings smoldering, glass all over the streets. Three hours later, the mayor and the city council entered the office of the Monmouth Community Action Program (MCAP) to meet with leaders from the West Side. Willie Hamm, an assistant administrator at Rutgers University, read a list of twenty demands. They included firing both Judge Capibianco and the housing authority chairman; appointing Negroes to the school board, the housing authority, and the planning board; establishing a police review board and a recreation commission; the implementation of rent control; the completion of the urban renewal project; the construction of a recreation center; and the immediate hiring of a hundred "Negro youth" for summer employment jobs. To which Mayor Mattice replied, "I'd like to do something, but I can't." He would study the matter, but he couldn't just fire a judge. And there were no vacancies on the school board. "This doesn't take any more time or any more decision making," was Willie Hamm's response. "It takes an answer. You have the blame for all this on your shoulders."

Mattice and the other city officials retreated to city hall. At noon Tuesday, they returned to the MCAP headquarters. There, in front of an angry crowd of more than a hundred, they agreed to appoint Hamm to the school board. The other issues would just have to wait. The director of MCAP left shaking his head and denouncing the meager concession. "There's going to be more trouble," he declared. "And this time they're going east. It may not be tonight, or next week, but it will happen."

It happened within an hour.

The MCAP office was on the corner of Springwood and Main, right where the barricades were set up. When the meeting broke up, around two in the afternoon, a crowd had already gathered nearby. "As the hot afternoon wore on," wrote the *Asbury Press*, "the youths began edging restlessly toward Main Street." Suddenly, a few started running. "Hey, they're going east!" a young girl yelled. "They're going east! I hope they burn it down!"

The way the *New York Times* reported it, "several hundred blacks came screaming across the Penn Central tracks." After breaking through the barricades and crossing Main, the West Siders stopped at the foot of the shopping district. There was a line of about a hundred state troopers and city policemen on Cookman Avenue. As the two sides eyed each other, a young black man paraded slowly up and down the middle of the street waving a Black Liberation flag. Others joined him, fists raised in the air.

Then, around three-thirty, the impasse broke as the crowd slowly and deliberately started smashing shop windows along Cookman. A rock went through the drugstore's plate glass. A clothing store was looted, one of its mannequins left on the sidewalk "like a corpse." The windows of the Thom McAn store collapsed inward from the pressure of the crowd, and suddenly the air was full of wooden legs from the shoe display. Two flights above, the Upstage sat in silence, its Day-Glo paintings unlit, its wall of amplifiers waiting for someone to plug back in.

Then, "the police suddenly seemed to change character." That's how a television reporter from New York City's ABC affiliate saw it. "Almost as though an order had been given," he went on. "They started firing. I didn't actually see anybody hit, but I did see that the police were shooting *level*—I mean, not into the air. *Shooting level.*" Years later, asked about his force's reaction, Chief Smith spoke softly: "In any organization like the police, you gotta figure you have some people there who just fire at random. At will. A patrolman on the line, his rifle—his shotgun—was so hot I had to take him off the line and put him in headquarters." The local hospitals would report treating forty-six people injured by gunfire.

By four thirty, the crowd had been pushed beyond Main Street back into the West Side. This time, the state troopers and patrolmen followed, apparently with more than peacekeeping on their minds. The cops cut back and forth across Springwood, ordering people inside. West Siders would later testify that many weren't wearing their badges or any other identification. One resident was standing in his front yard talking to a neighbor when twenty-five troopers, guns drawn, marched up. He didn't mind being told to go indoors, he later testified—"This, I know, is supposed to be their job"—but he couldn't get over their attitude as they stomped through his gate, into his yard, onto his property. "If I hadn't been a man who believes in God," he told the paper, "I don't know what I might have done." His wife described the state troopers as "pressing their authority." Said her husband, "This is the way the white man acts down south."

In neighboring Neptune and Red Bank, disturbances rocked the night. In Asbury, men reported state troopers beating them at random. Women reported sexual attacks. Years later, Willie Hamm still remembered his "total surprise." "Prior to that," he said, "I had held police in high regard, especially the state police . . . But they broke windows out [and] some appeared to be intoxicated." The next day, the mayor met again with Hamm and other West Side leaders. Now their most pressing demand was the removal of the state troopers. That night, a twenty-eight-member, self-appointed black peace patrol walked Springwood, trying to maintain law and order without bloodshed.

On Thursday, after touring the scene, Governor Cahill asked President Nixon to declare the city a major disaster area. Not until Friday afternoon, July 10, did the city announce state troopers would be withdrawn from the West Side. They remained in other sections of the city. That afternoon, Mayor Mattice met with Willie Hamm. It was a quick, twenty-minute meeting. Convinced he'd regained the upper hand, the mayor refused to answer the list of West Side demands, including urban renewal. Hamm emerged from the meeting stone-faced and announced there would be no further communication between the mayor and Negro leaders. And the volunteer peace patrol would be pulled off the streets. Within an hour, the mayor had called an emergency meeting of the city council. By eleven that night, he'd backed down enough to promise that the city would at least answer "either yes or no" on all demands.

Saturday, July 11, a week after the first signs of trouble, Asbury Park remained tense. Over on Cookman, the damage was mostly broken windows. But the West Side, especially Springwood Avenue, had been torched, gutted, and left for dead. Overall, 180 persons had been injured, 167 arrested, and property damage had reached $4 million. The editors of the *New York Times* saw "a particular irony" in this "aging holiday resort of the white middle class" going up in flames. They called the city "a pleasure dome" and added, "Violence grows out of the catastrophic, smiling neglect of . . . social decay." Was that Tillie's expression, then: smiling neglect? The "cruelest part of this tragic explosion," the *Times* concluded, was that the protest might work: city officials might finally offer the West Side basic amenities. And this would prove that violence pays.

The editors needn't have worried. Years after the Fourth of July uprising, the substandard housing, the lack of jobs and recreation, would all still be in place. Blocks of Springwood Avenue would remain abandoned: fields of weeds. Steinbachs would move out not long after the troubles, and other stores would follow until Cookman Avenue ended up nearly as empty as Springwood. A rash of For Sale signs would spread down James Bradley's broad avenues. The way one city official put it, Asbury Park had become another example of the nationwide "urban pathology." For those on the boardwalk side of town, the riots had done it. That's what happened when things were allowed to get out of control.

But that wasn't how the West Side saw it. For many there, the Fourth of July uprising hadn't done Asbury Park in; it had just confirmed what they'd known all along. "The riots was just the end of it" is how one black employee of Fisch's recalls it, "burning a town that was already dead." And David Parreott insists, "The end of Asbury Park was politicians . . . Those old phony politicians we had. We should have gotten them out of office and put someone in there who would stand up . . . We needed to go out and kick sooner."

In the ruins of the city, politicians talked about starting all over again: rebuilding the beachfront, returning Asbury to its former glory by retracing its steps. Even the fortune-tellers on the board-walk couldn't have predicted what would eventually put Asbury

Park back on the map: its collapse. Or, more specifically, its collapse as amplified through rock & roll. Or, even more specifically, through the rock & roll of that long-haired guitar player and his buddies from the Upstage.

FOURTH OF JULY, 1978

DAVEY SANCIOUS DIDN'T take part in the Fourth of July rebellion. He was hacking around with some friends that night in Belmar and cut his hand badly enough to need stitches. He had no idea what was going down on Springwood Avenue, but as he sat in the local emergency room, people began coming in "covered in blood. And in different states of trauma." Then the cops arrived and started asking everyone questions, and Sancious realized that there was this "other thing going on . . . The whole night changed. It got very serious." Days later, when he figured it was safe, the teenager went by Springwood and saw the smoking ruins. He remembers his first reaction as sadness: for the West Side and the Orchid Lounge and "what it used to be like. In the days. It was like it had been a war."

Davey's buddy from the Upstage, Garry Tallent, agreed. "Just sad," Tallent says. "It was just sad more than anything else." Tallent was one of the few white musicians who was familiar with the West Side. He'd moved to Neptune as a teenager, and his hunger for music had led him onto Springwood. That's where he found a record store with the fifties R&B he loved. That's where he found the Orchid Lounge and became the lone white teenager who hung around outside: "When the door opened, you'd get to listen a little bit. Then they'd close it, and it would be muffled again." Finally, that's where he found—and plugged in to—the soul scene. Two, three times a week, a big black Cadillac would pull up to his mother's house, and it would be a guitar player/ singer named Melvin looking for "that funky little white boy." ("He kind of liked me," Tallent recalls, "but he never really knew my name.") They'd drive out to Piner's Lounge, an all-black club somewhere out near Fort Monmouth. There, Tallent appeared onstage as the bass player for Little Melvin and the Invaders. Melvin would call out, "Funky thing in G," and they'd wing it, playing nameless, floor-shaking, twenty-minute dance grooves. Occasionally, they'd get help from a stand-in saxophonist named Clarence Clemons. "A great, great learning experience," as Tallent remembers it. When he heard about the trouble on Springwood, Tallent drove right down and watched as his favorite record store burned: "All that vinyl melting!" As he gawked, one of the protesters threw a brick at his car, "and we got the hell out of there."

At the time of the riots, Springsteen was living in a surfboard factory out on the edge of town. When he heard about the riots, he climbed a nearby water tower. As Springsteen remembers it, he wasn't surprised that the West Side was burning; after all, this kind of thing had been happening all over the country. Not surprised, but stunned by the sheer magnitude of the event. From the top of the tower, looking out across Route 35 toward the ocean, Springsteen felt as if he were watching his whole city go up in flames.

A lot of the kids at the Upstage weren't even curious enough to see what had happened. "The best parts of those days was playing," says drummer Vini Lopez: playing till dawn and then a bunch of the musicians would "just sleep on the beach." There wasn't room for anything much except music. "We were so obsessed with getting at the mystery of it—learning how to do it—that really took up almost all your time," Sancious says. "Learning how to play guitar, learning how to play the keyboards, writing music, making some money so you could buy the guitar—so you could buy the guitar strings!"

Steve Van Zandt barely recalls the 1970 uprising. He knew the West Side burned, but what mattered at the Upstage, he says, wasn't politics or social issues but "some kind of sacred, mystical, shaman thing": the heart of rock & roll. The core group of musicians were on a quest, sure that the heart still beat somewhere down under the current pop hits, back among the songs of their adolescence. They searched not only the Beatles catalog, but less well-known sounds like the passionate R&B of Gary "U.S." Bonds and the sweet inner-city edge that connected Frankie Lymon to Phil Spector's Wall of Sound. They returned to Elvis, whose comeback TV special aired two years before Asbury burned and reminded the tie-dye crowd of their black-leather history. There was Roy Orbison, Sinatra from their parents' day, and beyond that, a dim pantheon—Muddy Waters, Robert Johnson—whom they knew mostly because someone had covered a cover of a distant, down-home masterpiece. "I was doing research" is how Van Zandt puts it. "I was going back, studying the blues guys, rediscovering the R&B guys, a lot of the fifties guys." If the crew at the Upstage didn't pay much attention to Asbury's racial uprising, there's an ironic reason: they were too caught up in traveling back through America's racial history—from rock & roll to the beat of slavery.

No one was more obsessed than the long-haired guitar hero,

Bruce Springsteen. A working-class kid out of Freehold, he lived, breathed, and dreamed the music. As a teenager, he'd played the underage Hullabaloo clubs in a band called The Castilles. Then, he'd founded Child, which according to its bass player "was going to do original songs in a style that was close to what Cream and Jimi Hendrix were doing." That had evolved into Steel Mill, a heavy-metal unit, guitar-driven.

"We used to play from Jersey down to Carolina," Springsteen remembers. "For a lot of colleges . . . I don't know how many." The spring of the killings at Kent State, as antiwar protests closed campuses across the country, Steel Mill was touring Ocean County College, Monmouth College, down to Richmond, Virginia, back to the Ice Palace in Bricktown and the Clearwater Swim Club in Atlantic Highlands. In a way, the venues were an extension of the Upstage: an alternative circuit that was neither the white Top Forty beach bars nor the black inland R&B clubs. "We were popular in a small area" is how Springsteen puts it. "It was a band that rocked. It got you on your feet, set you in motion, and kept you there."

Not quite two weeks after the 1970 uprising, with the West Side still smoldering and disturbances about to break out once again, Steel Mill played Asbury's boardwalk. The venue was a recently remodeled rent-a-car garage now called the Sunshine In. Its manager saw Steel Mill as a perfect booking because the band's "following reaches into the thousands." Even in troubled times— or maybe especially in troubled times—rock & roll was one of the few things that could draw an audience into the ravaged city. When Steel Mill played the Sunshine In, one patron recalls, the place was "jam-packed. Jam-packed! People spilling out into the streets."

Steel Mill's local popularity was spreading. The previous winter, the band had driven across country to California, where it had earned a rave review for an appearance at the Matrix Club in Berkeley, auditioned for rock impresario Bill Graham at the Fillmore West, and even been offered a recording contract. But for Springsteen, something about the music still wasn't right. He found himself searching for a sound that, as he put it, "rocks a little differently—more in the rhythm and blues vein than rock & roll." It needed to include a blistering lead guitar like Ten Years After, plus the hokum and party atmosphere of the boardwalk. But Springsteen also wanted the feel of the soul music that he and Van Zandt loved. Or, more specifically, the feel that the Irish rocker Van Morrison had gotten on that summer's *His Band and the Street Choir*—a fusing of R&B sounds with Woodstock perceptions.

In Asbury, the implications of that blend went beyond the musical. Steel Mill's sound was powerful enough to bring the hippie crowd into the ruined city. But it was primarily a white party. To add R&B flavor was to remind the audience not just of rock & roll's multiracial past but also of the complicated world right outside. Springsteen didn't hang on Springwood the way Tallent did; his love for soul music came mostly off records. But for Springsteen to achieve the mix he heard in his head, his dream band would have to integrate in a way Asbury Park never had.

One night in late 1970, Davey Sancious came into the Upstage and found Tallent and Springsteen "standing next to each other at the top of the stairs and talking about this jam session they're trying to organize for the one o'clock start up." Garry introduced the sixteen-year-old Sancious to the twenty-one-year-old Bruce: "This is my friend, Dave. I met him a couple of weeks ago, and we did something. A really good keyboard player." (Garry and Davey were in a short-lived band called Glory Road.) Then Tallent added, "You want to sit in with us?" Sancious's one word answer was yes.

That first night, Sancious recalls, "We ended up playing for hours. We did this one jam that lasted for hours and hours." If Sancious was, in his own words, "blown away" by Springsteen's chops, the feeling was mutual. "When we first played together," Springsteen says, ". . . he was a real wild man. He had that rock & roll thing in him—it always seemed like he might be the next Jimi Hendrix. He had the potential to be that." As Sancious remembers, after they'd finished playing, "closed this place up, then we just hung out and talked. [Bruce] had a band called Steel Mill, which was very popular. He said, 'I'm thinking about breaking the band up, and I'm going to start something new. And, uh, I want to know if you'd, um, be interested in being in it?' And I was, like, 'Yea! Absolutely!'"

Even as Springsteen was trying to form a funkier, integrated band, Asbury's racial situation was getting worse. Sancious remembers the West Side after the rebellion: "Just razed. Buildings burnt out. And after they put out all the fires and stopped it, they bulldozed it. They leveled so much of it . . . like a ghost town." In response to the uprising, the Ku Klux Klan had reappeared. The Klan had stayed active in central Jersey, Springsteen recalls, but it hadn't been "needed" in Asbury Park for fifty years—not since its values had triumphed in local elections. Now, crosses burned across New Jersey: in Hightstown, Princeton, Long Branch, and Neptune. On March 13, 1971, three Klansmen were formally accused of the Hightstown and Princeton incidents. That night, a six-by-four-foot cross blazed in downtown Asbury. It was strung up right on Cookman Avenue in John F. Kennedy Park—eight feet in the air and pointing south so Ocean Grove could see the flames across the polluted waters of Wesley Lake. Police Chief Thomas Smith called it "an isolated incident" and "a prank."

Other members of Asbury's police force made some attempts at healing the divided town. During the rebellion, police sergeant Joseph Monteparo had appeared on the David Susskind television show and gotten into a shouting match with Donald Hammary. The police accused Hammary of having helped incite the riots. Now, community seminars were set up so that black leaders and white police could talk through their grievances. Hammary and Officer Monteparo had even uncovered some begrudging admiration for each other. Then, on a Saturday night in late April, Sergeant Monteparo was stabbed to death on Springwood Avenue. His killer was a former mental patient and a black man. Chief Smith immediately assured the public that it wasn't a racial incident, and Officer David Parreott would eulogize Monteparo as his "liaison not only with the white community, but also with the hard-nosed white police officers." But at three A.M. on the morning of Monteparo's massive funeral, a kerosene-soaked cross was set on fire at Hammary's place of employment, MCAP.

In the midst of all this—or maybe it's more accurate to say on its outskirts—Asbury musicians were developing what would come to be called the Shore Sound. The week of the MCAP cross burning, a new band debuted at a dingy little Asbury club, The Student Prince. Led by Van Zandt, including Tallent and Lopez as well as John Lyon (already better known as Southside Johnny), the all-white Sundance Blues Band aimed to play "a lot of roots, and the rock and roll that evolved from blues roots." That in itself was something of a departure: a back-to-basics sound that shed the ornate decoration of seventies rock. In addition, Van Zandt declared that this band wouldn't play the hippie alternative college circuit but the shore bars. Usually, Van Zandt acknowledged, that meant having to "sell out" by playing Top Forty. But he thought it might be possible to get the drinking crowd to listen to "something a little more fulfilling and challenging." The Sundance Blues Band was a crossover move for the long-haired Upstage musicians: out of the windowless psychedelic room and back toward their working-class roots. Within a couple of months, the band was performing with Springsteen, and though it all proved to be a temporary alignment, the idea—an ambitious bar band—pointed the way to the future.

By this time, the spring of 1971, there was no denying that rock & roll had become big business. Bill Graham, announcing the closing of his Fillmore East and West, said the music was "joining America. It's General Motors." Asbury Park reaped some of the benefits—events at Convention Hall and places like the Sunshine In drew much needed tourists—but the scene still made the city fathers nervous. That summer, the popular James Gang played the Sunshine, and some twelve hundred teenagers showed up. "We had to fight our way to get through the doors," acting city manager Sicilino testified. Inside, they found "open drinking and smoking of 'home-made cigarettes.'" Mayor Mattice wanted the year-old club closed down, and the police made the owners cancel Ike and Tina Turner's R&B concert for fear "it might cause racial tensions."

Springsteen had finally managed to put together a band that would "rock a little differently." Featuring a horn section that turned out early-sixties soul lines, the ten-piece unit incorporated the soul sound of Springwood Avenue as brought over by Tallent and Sancious. "Basically," Tallent remembers, "we would have been happy to have been Van Morrison and his band." To back up his vocals, Springsteen had put an ad in the local paper: GIRL SOUL GOSEPL [sic] SINGERS (2). When Delores Holmes and Barbara Dinkins showed up to audition, Holmes was frankly scared. It was late at night, they'd left the black part of town, and the surfboard factory looked deserted. "Maybe," Holmes told Dinkins, "they're bringing us up here to rape us!" Years later, Springsteen can only imagine what it must have been like for the singers to cross Asbury's racial lines.

The resulting Bruce Springsteen Band played mostly local gigs that summer and fall, including regular weekends at The Student Prince over at 911 Kingsley. Springsteen has called it "the darkest, dingiest, dampest place you ever seen." They played for the door, and as he and Van Zandt would joke later, "We split $13.75 between us." While the sound was funkier than Steel Mill's had been, Sancious admits that at the clubs they played "the only black people would be us in the band." Asbury's boardwalk was still segregated—enough so that just having Sancious and the girl singers was making a statement. The band didn't dwell on it. "It wasn't like we had this thing of, like, okay . . . we're the only integrated band," Sancious recalls. "We never said, let's present some picture to society: look at us, we're cool, why can't you do it? Nothing like that. Ever. Just five or six guys playing this music and just having a ball." Delores Holmes recalls being in the Bruce Springsteen Band as "the safest that I ever felt in my life."

But the tensions of the outside world inevitably filtered in. Holmes remembers that after she brought the band by to meet her father, he took her aside. "Don't you bring those people in my house again!" They were long-haired, they dressed funny, and they were white. Springsteen's small but devoted following had its own problems with the mix. Holmes describes trying to get through the crowd to the stage at a concert in Richmond, Virginia, as "the first time I really encountered prejudice. Nobody called me the N-word, but they might as well have."

By winter, the band had broken up—not from these outside pressures but because there wasn't enough money to pay everyone. The core musicians continued to play together: Springsteen, Van Zandt, Tallent, Lopez, Sancious, and keyboardist Danny Federici. They'd also met Clarence Clemons, the black saxophonist from Tallent's time with Little Melvin and the Invaders. Clemons would eventually personify Springsteen's integrated E Street Band and, mythically, lead them to success. But at the time, success looked a long way off. Everyone except Springsteen had day jobs, and soon even this smaller band had to break up. During the winter of 1971, Springsteen went back out to California (where his parents had moved), played some solo shows, then came back East, where he moved into Tom Potter's old apartment, two doors down from the Upstage. Tom had moved to Florida, Marge was working as a hairdresser on Main Street, and the Upstage had closed: another victim of Asbury's hard times. Springsteen's apartment on Cookman was over an abandoned beauty salon. "Amidst the old hairdryers and washing sinks," Springsteen remembers, "I wrote the songs that comprised *Greetings*."

The full name of Springsteen's first record was *Greetings from Asbury Park, N.J.* The cover was a classic tourist postcard of the city, complete with glimpses of the boardwalk and a packed beach. It was an up-front acknowledgment of where he was from—and where he was from had almost no rock & roll glamour. Not only was it Jersey, that industrial mix of suburbs and swamp, but it was some crumbling shore town way past its prime. Columbia Records signed Springsteen as a solo act in the singer/songwriter mode of Dylan or James Taylor, and he made what he calls "primarily an acoustic record with a rhythm section." The rhythm section consisted of his old Asbury band, and they added another layer of sound to songs that already gloried in excess. The lyrics Springsteen wrote in that empty beauty salon looked at the world through a smeared, poetic lens that owed a lot to the Upstage. "Your cloud line urges me," Springsteen shouts in his rough voice, "and my electric surges free." There isn't time to figure out if this makes any sense: the music boils and bubbles, and characters emerge out of the stream of words only to slip right back under. "We get into those great funky riffs" is how Springsteen put it at the time, "that Gary U.S. Bonds stuff that is lost forever in the annals of time. You can get into that groove, get it *there*, and sing weird words to it, too!"

The band went on the road to support *Greetings* after its release in January 1973. President Nixon was starting his second term, promising "peace with honor" in Vietnam. In Asbury Park, another cross had been burned, this one on Willie Hamm's front yard. The city had finally made the last payment on its debt of nearly $11.5 million that dated back to Mayor Hetrick's reign. There had been almost no beachfront improvements since then. The Casino had burnt in the mid-1960s and still wasn't fully repaired. The city had poured more than a million dollars into Convention Hall, but the ocean still ate away at its foundation. Over by Deal Lake, what had been billed as "the world's largest swimming pool" caught fire and had to be closed. And the city couldn't lease its paddleboat concession because Wesley Lake was too full of garbage. That May, reformers finally defeated the seventy-one-year old Joe Mattice. He'd been in the job sixteen years and was facing an eighty-seven-count indictment for "conspiring to retain political control in the Democratic Party." He eventually pleaded guilty to falsifying names on petitions: helping the dead to vote.

That summer Asbury tried to revive its baby parade, last held in 1949. Though there were three hundred entries and what the paper called "one of the biggest crowds in years," few residents were fooled. If the sun was out and the day hot, Asbury's beach could still draw tourists. A fifth of the city's income—about a million dollars annually—came from rent on ninety boardwalk concessions, but it wasn't nearly enough to meet expenses. In 1974, city employees would be forced to take a ten percent wage cut. As a member of the Beachfront Association of boardwalk concessionaires put it, "We have no money, and the city has no money."

Given this depressing picture and the poor sales of a record he'd called *Greetings from Asbury Park*, it would have been understandable if Springsteen had shied away from small-town subject matter.

But his second record, *The Wild, the Innocent, & the E Street Shuffle*, does just the opposite. Its "cast of characters," Springsteen would later say, "came vaguely from Asbury Park at the turn of the decade." You can hear it in the opening cut, "The E Street Shuffle," which refers obliquely to the West Side uprising: "The heat's been bad," Springsteen sings, "since Power Thirteen gave a trooper all he had in a summer scuffle." The teenagers hang in a club called Easy Joe's, "where all the riot squad goes." The record came out of a time, Springsteen has written, when he "watched the town suffer some pretty serious race rioting, and slowly begin to close down."

What Springsteen watched wasn't just beginning. It had started decades before. And it wasn't simply that the city was closing down. For Springsteen and his friends, Asbury was opening up. Because of its failing economy, rents were low enough for the band members to afford, if barely. Because the city was desperate for business, the Upstage and the shore bars had been allowed to operate, late and noisy and disreputable as they were. What was closing down was the old Merchants' Vision. And that left room among the ruins for something new.

Springsteen's "E Street Shuffle" is based on "Monkey Time," an R&B summer hit from ten years earlier. Its recycled funk is all about how kids manage to survive by dancing on the wreckage of the past. But it's on the album's second cut that Springsteen makes Asbury his own. The song is a piece of romantic journalism, its title a kind of dateline: "4th of July, Asbury Park [Sandy]." Like Stephen Crane's early reporting, Springsteen is covering a dream landscape we all recognize; he calls it "Little Eden." As fireworks rain down on the city, his throaty voice describes the scene. "Switchblade lovers" drive the circuit, "wizards" play pinball in the arcades, the boys from the Casino dance with their shirts open, and greasers sleep on the beach. The girls either flirt in the shadows under the boardwalk or dance in "them cheap little seaside bars." The details are realistic, but you know this scene even if you've never spent a summer on the shore. You know it from the movies, from a century of postcards and parlor music, from the calliope sounds in the background. Springsteen calls it the carnival life. It's the older, failing, fading America.

The song's alternative title could have been "Farewell from Asbury Park." Because this boardwalk is the opposite of a tourist attraction; it's a place to leave. Why exactly, Springsteen doesn't and maybe can't say. "I just got tired," he sings, "of hangin' in them dusty arcades, bangin' them pleasure machines." By the end of the song, he's made up his mind. "For me," he declares, "this boardwalk life is through." And almost as an aside, he adds softly, "You ought to quit this scene, too."

Davey Sancious, who's playing the cascading keyboards, remembers that the whole band felt that way. "We all wanted to get out. Absolutely! . . . It was just: let's go. Let's go!" Springsteen has written that this Asbury Park is "a metaphor for the end of a summer romance." It could just as well stand for adolescence itself. Or, for the larger idea behind those pleasure machines: what the founding fathers called the pursuit of happiness. However large you want to make the metaphor of Asbury Park, the song says it's over. With Federici's oompah accordion behind him, you can hear Springsteen simultaneously kissing the past good-bye and holding it close. His nostalgia for the old American shore town—for summer romance, for the promised land that once was—makes this a declaration of independence, but not of freedom.

Springsteen's second album turns, at the end, to New York City, which he calls "my getaway from small-town New Jersey." The rave-up, "Rosalita," announces that rock & roll is his ticket out, and his destination is the big time. But this record didn't get him there. Released in the summer of 1973, it earned good reviews and, again, few sales. "It was," recalls drummer Vini Lopez, "like they shelved it." This despite a fall and winter tour that extended the band's reputation for exhilarating, exhausting live shows. When they got back to Asbury, they were still playing The Sunshine In and The Student Prince.

Asbury had entered what Sancious delicately describes as its "post-prime era." On the beachfront, the massive old hotels were getting razed. On the West Side, city fathers had decided to change Springwood Avenue's image by calling it Lake Avenue. The change didn't go much deeper than that despite the election of the city's first black councilman, Dr. Lorenzo Harris. Whether you called it Springwood or Lake, it remained what the *New York Times* described as "a vista of gray, lifeless buildings." The city's last public housing project had been completed in 1958. Almost sixty percent of the West Side's housing stock dated back to before 1940.

With two not very successful records behind him, Springsteen was twenty-five. He was making he recalls, maybe $200 a week and living in a ratty shotgun apartment in West Long Branch. He spent his time listening to sixties pop artists like Roy Orbison and the Ronettes, changing the personnel of his band, and trying to discover *that* sound. He knew it was some mix of the old reliable chords and the contemporary reality of gas shortages and a president about to resign in the disgrace of Watergate. All around him, the music scene was fat with nostalgia. An Asbury club called The Magic Touch on Second and Ocean featured the Coasters, the Chiffons, and the Drifters, while Convention Hall would headline the pseudo-doo-wop band Sha Na Na and Frank Sinatra Jr.

Springsteen's third record wouldn't come out for another year and a half. But he had the title track, "Born to Run," well enough in hand to premier it in the spring of 1974. Springsteen describes the song as a "turning point," and the album that would grow up around it as "where I left behind my adolescent definitions of love and freedom." Years later, Springsteen would perform acoustic versions of "Born to Run" that highlighted the doom built into it, but the song as first recorded is a raving, saxophone-driven roar of hope. By day, he's out on the streets of what he calls "a runaway American dream." Without naming it, he announces, "This town rips the bones from your back / It's a death trap, it's a suicide rap / We gotta get out while we're young." And then he rams into the one-line chorus: " 'Cause tramps like us, baby, we were born to run."

Not till the break do we get to see where we are. Then, Springsteen focuses in on the boulevard by the Palace, the amusement park, the kids "huddled on the beach in the mist." As the song finishes—on a highway "jammed with broken heroes"—we expect this heartbreak of a town to disappear into the distance. Thanks to rock & roll, the lovers have broken free, right? They're about to find out, once and for all, "if love is real." But that moment doesn't come. Someday, maybe, they'll reach a better place. Till then—for now—forever?—they're born to run.

Springsteen's tramps don't make it any farther out of Asbury than Stephen Crane's did in their horse and buggy. Instead, "Born to Run" sets up the parameters. These kids start with broken promises, with the future as a lie. Asbury Park personifies that collapse. It's a death trap. The only way out is down a road that, gauging by the revved-up nostalgia of this song, leads back through Ronnie Spector to the whisper of Frank Sinatra and beyond: back to the sacred heart of rock & roll. "Born to Run" set the standard. Then, as Springsteen says, he spent the next year trying to make the best rock & roll record ever.

As Springsteen was creating music from the ruins of Asbury Park, its city fathers were looking for ways to rebuild. But they were caught in a kind of undertow. What economists called "the longest and deepest economic recession since the end of World

War II" began late in 1973. While nineteen million new jobs would be created during the 1970s, ninety percent of them would be in the service industry. The irony was that the country as a whole seemed to be headed for the kind of make-nothing economy that Asbury was trying desperately to leave behind.

Back in 1970, after the "urban unrest," the New Jersey state Assembly had proposed a new growth industry: legalized gambling. That bill died, but in 1974 the Assembly once again called for a public vote on establishing state-run casinos. Supporters included the mayor of Atlantic City and Mattice's successor in Asbury Park, Mayor Ray Kramer. Both old resort towns were on their last legs: their boardwalks collapsing, their pleasure domes out-of-date, their ghettos expanding. The only economy they'd ever known was the tourist trade. The only future they could imagine involved revitalizing their beachfronts. If gambling would do that, bring on the casinos.

New Jersey governor Brendan Byrne led the movement. Legalized gambling, the argument went, would fight unemployment, which was at six percent nationally, nearly eleven percent for blacks. Plus, it would do so without raising taxes. And state overseers would make sure organized crime didn't get its foot in the golden door. That fall, a group calling itself the Tourism Development Council of New Jersey launched a half-million-dollar publicity campaign supporting the bill. Two weeks before the November vote, a poll showed almost sixty percent in favor. It looked as if New Jersey was about to become Las Vegas.

But the pro-gambling forces hadn't factored in the strength of the moral opposition, which dated back to Prohibition and beyond. Religious and civic groups united in what they called the No Dice coalition. The church led the way. In Red Bank, a Baptist pastor worried that gambling would "create a carnival atmosphere . . . just like in Nevada." Honky-tonk towns like

Atlantic City and Asbury might want that, but as a Methodist minister pointed out, nothing in the bill "contained" gambling to just the shore. "If it first came to Atlantic City, and then to Asbury Park," the papers quoted a Catholic spokesperson, "it would eventually spread throughout the state like a cancer." A leader of the Christian Scientists added, "We don't need the temptations of getting something for nothing."

It sounded like Asbury's old battle against sin, and the Methodist Church weighed in heavily. On the Sunday before the vote, a letter from the bishop of the United Methodist Church was read from pulpits throughout the state. The bishop called on Methodists to telephone "out-of-town friends, relatives, and Christmas card lists and urge a no vote." By then, twenty of New Jersey's twenty-four newspapers had decided to oppose the bill. Though the *Asbury Press* could see the obvious economic advantages, the editors worried that the open-ended language meant the state was "handing the casinos to private interests, including mobsters." In the days just before the vote, that fear took over, fueled by the testimony of the U.S. attorney in charge of investigating Jersey's organized crime: "The very same interests which have allowed Atlantic City to deteriorate will be the sole financial beneficiaries of casino gambling."

In a last-minute moral stampede, New Jersey voters defeated the referendum by an overwhelming three-to-one margin. Asbury's Mayor Kramer was "frankly disappointed." So was the mayor of Atlantic City, who called on the state "to come to the aid of [its] resort towns." If gambling wasn't going to lead the revival, something had to.

Asbury Park turned, as it always had, to its beachfront. City leaders came up with a proposal to extend the boardwalk inland to Cookman Avenue. The idea was to turn sunbathers into shoppers, even if there weren't many sunbathers anymore—or shops. Forty percent of the city's seventeen thousand residents were African-Americans; citywide unemployment was running at eighteen percent; thousands waited for low-income housing. Meanwhile, kids still roamed through the charred remains of Springwood Avenue without the recreation or jobs that had been promised decades before. And Asbury wanted to extend its boardwalk. At the hearing on the proposal, a resident described only as an "elderly black man" rose to speak: "All my life here, I've always heard 'boardwalk, boardwalk, boardwalk,' and never has there been any similar concern for the West Side." No response was reported.

Springsteen built his third album, *Born to Run*, around the title track. It came out in the fall of 1975 to a wave of critical enthusiasm and publicity, including the singer appearing simultaneously on the covers of both *Newsweek* and *Time*. The *Asbury Press* ran a small item, but there's no indication the city felt that this tramp music had anything to do with Asbury's real-life problems, or its future. After all, this was only rock & roll: teenage talk about cars and guitars and girls.

In some ways, that's right. As soon as you drop the needle on *Born to Run*, the narrator's asking his girl to come down off her porch, get in his car, and leave town. This is their "one last chance to make it real." And as the song "Thunder Road" rises and booms like the surf itself, Springsteen announces their destination: together, they'll drive into the night to "case the promised land." Where that is—where Thunder Road leads—he doesn't say. Except that it's elsewhere. "Mary climb in. / It's a town full of losers, and I'm pulling out of here to win."

A triumphant sax solo follows, but the song ends before Mary ever actually leaves the porch. Soon, the next cut promises, they're going to "bust this city in half," and Springsteen knows just how it'll happen. Asbury's avenues run north to Eighth, followed by

Deal Lake Drive, which means you could count the lake itself as the city's Tenth Avenue: the barrier to the outside world. Rock & roll is how you break what Springsteen calls the "Tenth Avenue Freeze-Out." And the key to Springsteen's brand of rock & roll, the song declares, was found when Clemons—the "Big Man"— joined the band. "Tenth Avenue Freeze-Out" doesn't mention race; it doesn't have to. The cover of *Born to Run* shows Bruce leaning on Clarence's broad shoulder. With Sancious and interim drummer Ernest Carter departed to play jazz, Clemons is now the only black member of the E Street Band and carries the full weight of symbolism. During their live shows, Springsteen would famously slide the width of the stage on his knees to kiss the saxophonist full on the lips. The band was still playing to almost all-white crowds. But here was the world as it might be: rock & roll equality, the integrated boardwalk.

At the same time, Springsteen's breakthrough album is also, as he says, full of dread. "Desperate lovers" park by the beach. "Sometimes," he sings, "it seemed you could hear the whole damn city crying." And at the end of "Backstreets," Springsteen's lovers realize they might not be able to walk free. "After all this time / to find we're just like all the rest / Stranded in the park / and forced to confess." When Robinson Crusoe was stranded, he'd turned to the Christian life; James Bradley had founded Asbury on that ideal. But in this twentieth-century version, the stranded want out. And because there weren't many legitimate ways to escape, people found illegitimate ones. "Meeting Across the River" is the black-market version of the one last chance: a hustler's dream of scoring a quick two grand and making everything all right. All a listener needs to hear is the slow, minor-key melody to know that this deal's not likely to go down. But it's the guy's only shot, and all through this collection of songs, Springsteen keeps putting hope next to disappointment like bars in a cage. He celebrates the ones

who "reach for their moment / and try to make an honest stand"—
then describes how they wind up "wounded / not even dead." This
is Jungleland. "You're not necessarily on the Jersey Shore anymore," Springsteen says of his record. "You could be anywhere in
America." The other way to put that is that anywhere in America
has become Asbury Park.

Born to Run rose to number three on the charts and carried
Springsteen beyond Tenth Avenue once and for all. The heroic
themes, high-octane music, and the small-town imagery struck a
nerve. Springsteen might still be a cult figure—without a hit single
or Top Forty radio play—but the cult was now huge and growing.
A live show broadcast from New York City's Bottom Line helped
spread the word. And with Springsteen's fame came Asbury
Park's. A new club, The Stone Pony, opened on the boardwalk
where the old Mrs. Jay's had once stood. The Pony quickly became
the focus of the Shore Sound, which included Springsteen, Southside Johnny and the Asbury Jukes, and a handful of less well-
known bands. "When the Upstage closed," as one musician put it,
". . . The Pony became that place." Fans started coming to Asbury
to hear the music but also to find the promise in the songs. To see
exactly where "the hungry and the hunted explode into rock &
roll bands." They found a city that, officially anyway, seemed to
ignore their local hero. The Asbury Press had a small item about
Springsteen's old music teacher and how remarkable it was that
this shy boy had ended up famous. But beyond that, even if it had
wanted to, the resort town was too drained to capitalize on its
growing fame.

By the summer of 1976, Born to Run had sold a million copies.
On the Asbury beachfront, most of the old hotels had closed and
stood facing the ocean with plywood nailed over their windows.
The big brick Berkeley-Carteret had shut down, and there was talk
of making it a residential center for seniors. In the two years since

the defeat of the gambling bill, New Jersey's unemployment rate had jumped to nine percent, one of the highest in the nation. As the state joined the rest of the country in celebrating the nation's bicentennial, there didn't seem to be any new ideas on how to restart the economy. So, the state Assembly turned once again to gambling. In this new proposal, the casinos would still be state-regulated, but there were two major changes. A percentage of the gaming revenues would now go to help "the elderly and disabled." And this bill proposed casinos in Atlantic City only.

That didn't please Asbury Park. Mayor Kramer opposed the referendum. But the pro-gambling forces had soon amassed a war chest of $1.4 million. They took out ads arguing that gambling was not only a "painless" way of increasing revenues but "a unique tool of urban redevelopment." Atlantic City had a ghetto a lot like Asbury's. Casinos would provide hundreds of entry-level jobs. Working on the assumption that the majority of these would go to Atlantic City's underemployed blacks, forty branches of the state's NAACP came out in favor of the bill. For those worried about organized crime, proponents argued that legal casinos meant "undercutting" the Mob and reducing the "temptations" that corrupted state politicians. The governor repeatedly assured voters the state would oversee the whole operation. Finally, the state's Gambling Study Commission took the position that this bill was about freedom and democracy. To forbid gambling, the commission argued, was "puritanical, hypocritical, repressive and archaic."

In what the *Asbury Press* called "a money-tight, job-tight state employment picture," the bill passed by 250,000 votes—a result that many felt was even more surprising than Jimmy Carter's successful presidential bid. Atlantic City was jubilant. Resorts International, which had largely bankrolled the publicity campaign, raced to be the first legal casino on the East Coast. By the

Fourth of July, 1978, this most recent variation on the American dream was open for business. Atlantic City's old Chalfonte-Haddon Hotel had been totally remodeled, and seventy-five thousand people a day were rolling dice, playing poker, and pulling the slots. The local gambling industry was well on its way to creating over fifty thousand jobs and attracting billions of dollars in investment.

But folks were already beginning to see the flip side. Nearly all of the investments were centered on gambling. In the new gold rush, ninety percent of local businesses failed. By 1985, casinos would own a quarter of Atlantic City's real estate. Plus, the gambling jobs didn't go to the city's poor. Cooks and croupiers were brought in from outside the community and, far from revitalizing the ghetto, tended to settle out in the suburbs. Atlantic City's unemployment rate stayed higher than both state and national rates, sometimes nearly twice as high.

Part of the problem was that the casinos followed James Bradley's vision. Or was it Disneyland's? Visitors not only bet their money in the shiny new pleasure domes, they ate, drank, slept, shopped, exercised, and were entertained there. As one expert put it, "The laws that established casinos made them islands unto themselves." Prosperity on the beachfront didn't spread inland. As a study by the Twentieth Century Fund put it, "You don't see any spillover. The casinos are walled-off universes . . . In terms of revitalizing the city, it [legalized gambling] is a disaster."

The money went to the people who owned the casinos, and despite all the state's assurances, organized crime had gotten in at the very start. The owner of the first casino, Resorts International, had grown out of the Florida gambling operation of the famous mobster Meyer Lansky. Inspectors investigated other ties, including the influence of the Gambino family, led by Carlo Gambino, the model for *The Godfather.* On the Fourth of July, 1978, Resorts International was extending its hospitality to Carlo's nephew Joey and his wife, Rosario. They were put up in the casino's luxury suite with all expenses paid. Less than two years later, Mr. and Mrs Gambino were both indicted on charges of importing $60 million in heroin.

Atlantic City proved what Asbury Park had been proving. That the trickle-down theory didn't work. That the money tended to stay in a few hands. That this top-down vision of the promised land had corruption built right in.

As the Gambinos slept in the only legalized casino on the Jersey shore, Asbury had officially been designated the twelfth most distressed urban area in the United States. In fact, with its falling tax base, crumbling housing stock, and ongoing redlining, some experts were calling the city a "model of deterioration." It was a prime example, according to its director of community affairs, "of a Northeastern city that could not make the transition from railroad to an automobile-oriented society." The president of Asbury's Chamber of Commerce had another explanation. The city's "precipitous decline" was a product of the 1970 riots. "You can find whole rows of downtown stores that have closed up and resurfaced in Monmouth Mall, four miles outside of town. We simply have not gotten out from under the shadow of the civil disorders."

If it could rehabilitate itself, the *New York Times* wrote, Asbury Park could once again become a national symbol: this time "a small-scale model" for post-Vietnam urban renewal. The city's new Development Corporation set out to address the problem with what the *Times* called "the current 'pragmatic' social consciousness." That consciousness anticipated the era of Ronald Reagan, which was about to begin. The 1960s War on Poverty had proved, this argument went, that there was nothing to be gained by governmental programs aimed at improving the ghetto. The key was making sure private enterprise thrived. So, the board of Asbury's new Development Corporation didn't bother to include representatives from civic groups and/or the West Side. As the head of the board put it, "It's not so much a question of black and white as a question of green."

If some Asbury Park residents thought all this sounded mighty familiar, their suspicions were confirmed when the Development Corporation revealed the "most striking feature" of its $200,000 plan: extend the boardwalk into town. Boardwalk, boardwalk, boardwalk! This constant return to the same idea—and the constant insistence that it was, in fact, a new idea—was almost funny. Except that the situation had gotten that much more desperate.

By the Fourth of July, 1978, the desolation had spread to once-prime residential areas. On Fourth Avenue, where Stephen Crane's mother had bought her cottage, the collapse of the tourist industry had forced hotels like Lang's Guest House to look for other ways to fill their rooms. Already zoned for high-density use and desperate for dollars, many had turned to the state of New Jersey, which needed places to house its "deinstitutionalized." A year before the West Side "riot," Lang's had converted to a boardinghouse and, by 1978, was home to some twenty ex-patients of the Marlboro Psychiatric Hospital. Enough old hotels had followed this model for the city manager to declare Asbury Park "a dumping ground for ex–mental patients."

According to the pragmatic social consciousness of the Development Corporation, this made the area between the beachfront and Main Street a "dead space." This Fourth of July would prove that the designation had more than one meaning. Many of the old hotels were out of code. Over the decades, as the population had shifted, safety inspections had gotten less frequent and less strict.

The city treated this "dumping ground" as it had always treated the West Side. In fact, to what remained of Asbury's white middle class, it may have seemed as if the West Side had spread east: their worst nightmare. On this Independence Day, a torrential rain flooded the roads and forced Asbury to cancel its fireworks. In the midst of the downpour, Lang's Guest House caught fire. The exact cause wasn't known: faulty wiring, the fire chief thought, or maybe someone smoking in bed. Three people died.

"You can't have community pride unless there's something to have pride in." That was retiring Police Chief Thomas Smith's description of his old neighborhood around Springwood Avenue, and it was becoming true of more and more of the city. The record Springsteen had out that Independence Day seemed to reflect that. Its characters, he's said, live "in the middle of a community under siege." You could be excused for thinking that the title of the record, *Darkness on the Edge of Town*, referred to the West Side or to Asbury's racial problems in general.

But the songs don't bear that out. If anything, *Darkness* is whiter-sounding than *Born to Run*: the music tilted away from dance beats toward urgent, punkish guitar—and its characters drag racers and factory workers. The multiethnic funk of "The E Street Shuffle" is gone. Instead, Springsteen focuses in on the white working class and on the darkness that is left to them once the work is gone.

Two years had passed since *Born to Run*. In that time, rock & roll had bankrolled Springsteen's escape from Asbury Park. Financially, he was doing fine, but the new record grappled with what the twenty-eight-year-old called his "sense of accountability" to those he'd left behind. While there's hope on *Darkness*—and the shouted demand that "these badlands start treating us good"—the characters are older, the odds of getting free even slimmer. As Springsteen says, he deliberately kept out "any hint of escapism."

From the first lines, "Lights out tonight / Trouble in the

heartland," the theme is set. For the first couple of songs, we could be any place that's racked with fear and in any family where a son inherits his father's sins. But on the album's third song, "Something in the Night," when Springsteen wants to call up a landscape where all chance of escape has been cut off, he takes us back into Asbury. On a slow, harrowing melody, we're suddenly "riding down Kingsley . . . looking for a moment when the world seems right." It's almost dawn in the shore town, and the only people in sight are "wasted" kids. The narrator tries to get away, but he's stopped at the state line. Behind him, on the inside, are all "the things we loved . . . crushed and dying in the dirt."

The rest of *Darkness* either refers to other parts of the United States—the Utah desert, little towns in Louisiana—or, more often, leaves the landscape generic. Springsteen's "streets of fire" run anywhere people are tricked and lied to; his "mansions of pain" exist wherever the factory whistle blows. And though he borrows the title of "The Promised Land" from Chuck Berry, Springsteen's song isn't nearly as specific—or as cheerful. Berry played on the idea that the payoff to the American Dream lay west, in California. Two rock & roll generations later, Springsteen defines his promised land in the negative: where you *aren't* "lost and brokenhearted," where your dreams *don't* "tear you apart," where your blood *doesn't* "run cold."

Springsteen's dream isn't James Bradley's moral community: upright, separated from the world, segregated. In fact, what Springsteen wants can only be found in the ruins of that kind of place. Not on Main Street, down Kingsley, or up in suburban "Fairview," but "in the darkness on the edge of town." There, you can see what's gone wrong and who's been left out. There you "pay the cost." Which is why, in that darkness, there may finally be a chance of taking an honest stand. It is, in its own way, as religious a vision as Bradley ever had.

Darkness marks the end of Springsteen using Asbury Park as a metaphor. It'll be twenty-five years before he writes another song about the city. He moves on, not so much changing his subject matter—it's always that question of whether love is real—but extending it out across the horizon. This Fourth of July, as Lang's Guest House burns in the rain—as the Gambinos sleep in their luxury suite—Springsteen's career has taken him far from the Jersey shore. On tour in Los Angeles, he watches the fireworks from the Santa Monica pier. Eight years before, he'd climbed a water tower and watched Springwood Avenue burn. Now, he climbs to the top of an office building where a huge billboard advertises *Darkness*. It stretches his face across half a block, and Springsteen jokes that it's "the ugliest thing I've ever seen in my life." So he and Clemons and Tallent and some of the others celebrate the Fourth by spray-painting the billboard with graffiti.

By then, *Darkness* has gone gold, shipping more than half a million units, and Springsteen is a star, whether he likes the image or not. Asbury Park is behind him. He's started performing a new song about leaving that past behind. He calls it "Independence Day": a sort of bookend to "4th of July, Asbury Park [Sandy]." No fireworks boom, here. Instead, a son says good-bye to his father and their town. It may be Asbury Park, if you go by the calliope sound at the beginning. It may be Freehold. It could be anywhere. It opens with the son telling his father, "There's a darkness in this town that's got us, too." It's time to leave. "They ain't gonna do to me," the son says, "what I watched them do to you."

Then the landscape broadens. It's not just the son who's going to quit this scene. All the rooms are empty down at Frankie's joint; the highway's deserted. Everyone's leaving, and Springsteen tries to explain what's happened. "There's just different people coming down here now," he sings. "Soon, everything we've known will just be swept away." The song moves to a familiar funereal beat, like the one Springsteen used in "Factory": that slow, inevitable march Stephen Crane heard in the workingmen's parade.

The song's chorus keeps calling out, "Say good-bye. It's Independence Day." But nobody says it. As if nobody can leave. Finally, there's a last confession. It's about how generations pass, about the other side of progress, about the way each vision of a better world destroys the one that came before. And it's about how we are bound to each other. The son knows all the things his father wanted. And looking out over this empty promised land, he swears, "I never meant to take those things away."

EPILOGUE:
FOURTH OF JULY, 2001

YOU CAN READ the future at Frank's Deli. Up at the counter, the locals sit: a black woman with braided hair, a Hispanic woman whose English is slow, an Italian-American guy with a loud voice and dark glasses. Someone's left a copy of today's *Asbury Park Press*—July 4, 2001—and that's how you read the future. It says there's going to be a parade in Ocean Grove and something called an Oceanfest over in Long Branch. Asbury Park will be hosting a sand-castle competition, and at one P.M. a bunch of local bands will play Convention Hall in "A Call for Freedom" concert. To end child slavery in Sudan.

A waitress talks with a gray-haired woman: "They're gonna have a whole beachfront fair today."

The gray-haired woman nods. "Used to be so many people that my kids would get lost."

"Oh, I remember."

In the back of Frank's, they've hung framed pictures from the

1940s and '50s: Convention Hall, the boardwalk, the train station. It's eight-thirty in the morning, and the oldies radio starts playing "On Broadway" by The Drifters. The song's so familiar that the lyrics tend to blend with the room's general chatter: how when you walk down Broadway without enough to eat, "the glitter rubs right off, and you're nowhere."

Out on Main Street, some stores have closed for the holiday, and some are closed for good. Driving north toward Deal Lake and the end of town, you can hear the local radio station playing the air force anthem and then, in honor of the holiday, John Philip Sousa.

Across Deal Lake, the houses sit quiet and prosperous in the morning light. But here, on the Asbury side, it mostly feels abandoned. Down the length of Asbury's coastline, the beach-front looks like a war zone: Ocean and Kingsley avenues reduced to rubble and ruined buildings. Nearby, the James A. Bradley Motor Inn has been shuttered and painted a uniform military brown; its only speck of color comes from an orange-and-black sign: No Trespassing. In the distance, Convention Hall and the Berkeley-Carteret occupy emptiness. At Fourth Avenue, the gaping skeleton of an unfinished high-rise dominates the skyline.

The beachfront might look like a war zone, but it isn't. There's been no fighting here. For the past quarter century—longer—the city's leaders have made agreements, exchanged handshakes, and signed contracts. That's what produced this landscape: not war, business.

As you start down the boardwalk, it's all but deserted. Its planks—laid in a chevron pattern—are rotting out at the ends. The old concession stands have been nailed shut: white paint peeling off, leftover signs reading THE CUCKOO'S NEST and JOE'S #1. Out on the rock jetty, three men are throwing lines into the mist. A few words of Spanish drift back to shore. Beyond them, the hum of fishing boats is pitched a little lower than the onshore air conditioners. Lifeguards set warning flags and tip their tall white chairs upright.

In 1978, when Springsteen's *Darkness* came out, Asbury's city council was calling for a new, comprehensive waterfront-redevelopment plan. Two years later, the government officially declared the boardwalk a blighted area, making it eligible for state funds. That was the year Samuel J. Addeo became city manager, a position he'd hold into the nineties.

Addeo, along with Mayor Frank Fiorentino and a council that included the ex–police chief Thomas Smith, managed a city on the skids. Of Asbury's seventeen thousand residents, a quarter lived below the poverty line. The median annual household income in 1980 was about $17,000; on the West Side, it was half that. Unemployment in Monmouth County was around seven percent; in Asbury, it was over twelve percent. And of the city's eight thousand housing units, almost eighty percent were rentals. By 1980, white flight had helped make Asbury's "minority" population the majority, but the people who stayed in the city didn't own it. Out-of-town landlords did. Services were few and, with President Ronald Reagan starting his first term, getting fewer. As the black owner of a West Side market put it, "Reagan is reality. People have got to understand Uncle Sam is not your uncle . . . It's now sink or swim."

Asbury didn't swim. It took four years for the city to adopt (unanimously) a Waterfront Area Redevelopment Plan. In 1984, as Reagan swept into his second term, the city declared that it was changing direction. The beachfront would no longer be a honky-tonk tourist attraction. Instead, Ocean Avenue would become a pedestrian block surrounded by condominiums and apartment buildings. The city's central article of faith was unshaken: the economy had to begin with the beachfront. But now it would draw people to live, not just visit. The way the local paper reported it, Asbury Park would be "exchanging its character as an amusement-oriented seaside resort for that of a residential community." And when its ship came in—not the burnt hulk of the *Morro Castle*, but a string of condominium towers and town houses—the real estate boom would trickle down from the shore to the rest of the city. That was the theory.

The 1984 redevelopment plan covered the 240 acres along the beach and inland to Grand Avenue. Changing this area to the city fathers' definition of "residential" would mean displacing the current residents, many of whom were the "elderly, deinstitutionalized, and handicapped." After accidents like the fire at Lang's Guest House, the state had tried to improve safety by issuing loans to boardinghouse operators. Taking advantage of this, landlords had enlarged the dead space. Soon, Asbury Park had seven hundred state-licensed beds for ex-patients and an uncounted number of unlicensed ones. Asked what would become of these people under Asbury's new development plan, City Manager Addeo said it was the state's problem. Asbury had done more than its fair share, had been so welcoming to "the socially disadvantaged," Addeo said, that "the Statue of Liberty should have been restored and set on our beaches."

Up on Fifth, between Ocean and Kingsley, the redbrick wings of the Berkeley-Carteret Hotel still stand. During the early eighties, the old hotel became the model for Asbury's future. Two local brothers, Henry and Sebastian Vaccaro, bought the fifty-year-old landmark for $325,000. Their immigrant grandfather had worked there as a gardener. (Meanwhile, buying up property across the tracks until, by 1980, his widow was the largest single landlord on the West Side.) Though local banks refused to finance this rags-to-riches story, the Vaccaros managed to raise some $16 million, including over $3 million in an Urban Development Action Grant and a reported $8 million of their own funds.

A lot of it was rock & roll money. Henry Vaccaro was one of the founders of the Kramer Guitar Company, known for electric guitars with patented aluminium necks. Kramers were hip enough to be endorsed by the new generation of guitar heroes, Eddie Van Halen included, and produced big profits. By the time he was investing in the Berkeley-Carteret, Henry Vaccaro had been elected chairman of the board, and Kramer Guitar was heading for over $15 million in annual sales. Vaccaro parlayed his music connections to convince rock & roll pioneer and country-western star Johnny Cash not only to invest in the hotel and maintain a suite there but to promote the reopening with a concert appearance in the fall of 1985.

The Vaccaros claimed that the renovated Berkeley-Carteret was soon operating at seventy percent capacity and was "booked for every weekend until 1990." Asbury's city fathers could almost taste the influx of new money. A federal spokeswoman cited the project as a prime example of Reaganomics: "the private sector working to benefit the public." But by the beginning of 1986, the beachfront still looked much the same, and the total value of Asbury's square mile of real estate had declined to $164 million. Citywide unemployment was at twenty percent. That spring, Mayor Fiorentino and Manager Addeo signed a $500 million contract with the Vaccaro brothers. It called for the construction of twenty-four hundred residential units between Grand Avenue and the beach. "The start of a new Asbury Park," said Addeo.

While it looked like a case of local boys make good (Henry's daughter, a councilwoman, recused herself from the deal), the Vaccaros were actually only responsible for a third of the project. The bulk of both the financing and the construction went to Carabetta Enterprises of Meriden, Connecticut. The Carabetta family, which had built and managed thousands of federally subsidized apartments across New England, now controlled a sixty-four percent interest in Asbury's rebirth. In essence, the city had sold its shoreline to a private developer.

The idea was to proceed in stages. To start, sixteen town houses (each going for around $150,000) would be built in the south part of town on Wesley Lake. As construction began, Manager Addeo announced, "Things are looking up." Then, in September 1987, the nearly completed town houses burned down. Two local subcontractors were arrested for setting the fire; they claimed the Vaccaros' paychecks had been bouncing. "It just means we take a larger step forward," Sebastian Vaccaro announced, promising to start work on fifty new and improved town houses. Meanwhile, Carabetta began tearing down the old Jefferson Motel at the beach end of Fourth Avenue. The two condominium towers scheduled to rise there were going to hold a total of 224 luxury residential units, with prices ranging from $115,000 to half a million.

And that was just the beginning. The plan called for the other two thousand apartments to be ready for occupancy by 2003. With that many high-income residents, Asbury would indeed change character. The problem of the "socially disadvantaged," of the poor and the colored, would be solved: they'd be pushed out. The "new Asbury" would once again be middle and upper class. City property values began to rise just on the prospect, the net worth nearly tripling between 1985 and 1991. In November of 1988, the council unanimously granted Carabetta's Ocean Mile Development Group a twenty-year tax abatement.

Three months later, the Vaccaros had to pull out of the deal. Despite claims to the contrary, their model of redevelopment, the Berkeley-Carteret, hadn't turned a profit in three years. The brothers gave a number of reasons: construction on the beachfront had made it inaccessible, sewage and garbage spills had ruined Asbury's beaches. In April of 1989, they stopped making payments on their bank loans, and that fall, Joseph and Salvatore Carabetta agreed to buy them out. The Toms River bank that had taken a flier on the Vaccaros now loaned the Carabettas $12 million.

Meanwhile, Asbury Park had elected its first African-American mayor: former police chief Thomas Smith. Far from changing the city's emphasis on "boardwalk, boardwalk, boardwalk," Smith had helped approve and continued to support the redevelopment plan. But even as Asbury piled all its chips in one place, the speculative real estate boom of the 1980s was coming to an end. Soon, Carabetta Enterprises began to implode.

Joseph Carabetta blamed "the five or six year depression in the Northeast." The *Asbury Park Press* refused to hold anyone responsible: "The right things just didn't happen to the Carabetta organization." Nor did the Carabettas do the right thing. Starting in 1990, their management company had been diverting rent money from its federally subsidized projects to prop up its corporate finances. The way a source at the U.S. Department of Housing and Urban Development described it, Carabetta had "raped" its project accounts. In May 1991, their local source of capital, the high-flying Toms River bank, went under altogether: the largest bank failure in New Jersey history. In Asbury, construction stopped. Owing the city almost $450,000 in taxes, defaulting on $13.6 million in loans, Carabetta filed for Chapter 11 bankruptcy on June 8, 1992. At the same time, the developer refused to give up its exclusive rights to build on the waterfront. Which left the decaying skeletons of the unfinished condos: a daily reminder that Asbury's shore was being held hostage.

If you walk down past their jagged shadows, you come to Convention Hall. On this Fourth of July, the high church of the Merchants' Vision smells of damp and piss. Back in 1986, when the Vaccaros were flush, they announced their plan to refurbish the hall, bringing in "name acts" and building a recording studio in its theater area. The idea was to capitalize on the "music image of the city," as Henry Vaccaro told the *New York Times*, adding, "Rock music has kept Asbury Park on the map."

He mostly meant Springsteen. In 1984, *Born in the U.S.A.* had created an international sensation, selling 18 million albums worldwide. With its American flag cover and its title song (based on Ron Kovic's Vietnam memoir, *Born on the Fourth of July*), the record made Springsteen not only a major star, but also a patriotic figure. Depending on how you heard the record, he was either extolling traditional American virtues (see Ronald Reagan's attempt to claim the rocker as his own), or extending his Asbury Park vision of a broken promised land. As Springsteen led the longest-running and highest-grossing concert tour in rock history, the city's fame grew. The year Vaccaro announced he wanted to build on Asbury's music image, Springsteen released a best-selling compilation of his live shows, and another kid from the area, Jon Bon Jovi, went platinum with his album *Slippery When Wet*.

Asbury Park once again had a national profile, but not as a model of deterioration nor of post-Vietnam urban renewal. The depressed little resort town had become a rock & roll landmark. Fans who had never been within a thousand miles of the city knew to turn left off Kingsley to find the Casino. Asbury was an icon, a miniature. Shake it, and the real-life landscape disappeared in a swirl of music.

The Vaccaros could never take advantage of "the music image." They went under without accomplishing much more than getting a new roof put on Convention Hall. Joseph Carabetta then signed a deal to build an "entertainment center" on the beach and, through his connections, tried to get Michael Jackson's family involved. As the Carabettas and the Vaccaros sued and countersued, what commercial value there was to the Shore Sound tended to go elsewhere. On this Fourth of July, there's a free concert by Southside Johnny and the Asbury Jukes, but it's up at Monmouth Park. Convention Hall stands empty. The posters stuck to its walls advertise ROAD WARRIORS WRESTLING NIGHT: GRANDMASTER TOO COOL AND VAMPIRO.

Across from Convention Hall is Atlantic Square Park, with a larger-than-life statue of a man, bronze hat in hand. It's James Bradley, the last private developer to own Asbury's waterfront. This morning, over Bradley's shoulder, Sunshine Amusements is setting up kiddie rides. FUN POWER it reads on one trailer and, in pastel pinks and blues, THE TUNA CAN. Along the length of the boardwalk, where the Ferris wheel used to compete with the Steeplechase, these are now the only operating rides. And they're just here for the weekend. Two black kids in do-rags sit at the foot of Bradley's statue. A carny man hands them free passes, and they move along.

Past Convention Hall, the boardwalk's been ripped up for repair. You can look down and see the crisscrossed beams of the bulkheads, designed to break the impact of the waves and retain the upland. Despite these—and the stone jetties and groins—the latest estimates say over three hundred thousand cubic yards of sand get transported north off the Asbury Park beaches each year. The coastline would be losing two feet annually, except the Army Corps of Engineers keeps pumping sand back onto the shore. Between 1998 and 2000, they dumped 3.1 million cubic yards.

South of Convention Hall is the Howard Johnson's. Dusty boxes of saltwater taffy sit next to dusty postcards of girls in bikinis. Overhead, on the restaurant's roof, is the Arthur Pryor Memorial Bandshell. Down a ways, one of the concession stands has been converted to the HOUSE OF GOOD INTENTIONS HEALTH MINISTRY. Not far from it is Madame Marie's: a closed-up concrete booth.

The sign for READINGS—TAROT CARD—CRYSTAL BALL remains, probably because Springsteen mentioned it in "4th of July, Asbury Park (Sandy)." In the song, Marie gets busted for telling fortunes better than the cops.

Down the boardwalk is the former Ocean Mile Sales Center. Through its dirty plate-glass window, you can see an old model of Carabetta's proposed waterfront development. Tiny condo towers rise around tiny parking lots. Blue awnings the size of matchbooks shade little balconies. Some have fallen off and lie on the ground. Some of the model people have fallen over, too.

On a table by the beach, volunteers have arranged red, white, and blue trophies for the sand-castle competition. The miniature-golf course is covered in sand; PLAY GOLF now reads I AY GOLF. Kitty-corner down the street, The Stone Pony stands against a background of eyeless boarded-up motels. It's one of the few functioning reminders of the city's rock & roll past, and Springsteen has dropped by from time to time to make surprise appearances. The marquee promises Hot Tuna on July 18, Marshall Tucker on July 20, Nils Lofgren (a member of the E Street Band) on August 18.

The sun's trying to break through. Up the beach comes a black man with the build of an ex–football player. He's shirtless, with shorts, sandals, and a big straw hat. As he strides along, slamming into the sand with each step, he waves his arms and swears.

An official-looking white guy shouts at him from up on the boardwalk: "You cursing?"

The black man turns to face him. "I'm talking to myself."

"Well, you can't be throwing F's around in public."

There aren't more than eight people on the whole stretch of beach and boardwalk.

"I'm talking to myself." The black man looks the white guy over, then goes on. "I'm fishing with my kids. They say I need a goddamn beach badge. Ain't nobody in the water! Since when do you need a goddamn beach badge to fish?"

"That's the rule."

"Whose rule?"

The two men stay a certain distance apart, shouting at each other from boardwalk to beach.

"In most towns," the white man says, "you can't even fish where people are swimming."

It's still early in the day, but his voice has an edge as if he's been yelling at people for hours. For years. The black man sounds the same way, as if he reached his limit long ago.

"It's a damn *public* beach!"

"And I'm the president of the Asbury Park Fishing Association." Announcing his title seems to calm the white guy. He stands with his hands on his hips. "I'm not gonna bust your stones. Buy one badge: four dollars. I'll let it cover your whole family."

"Fuck that. It's a goddamn public beach!"

The black guy goes striding away, waving his straw hat, throwing his arms out, cursing. When he gets back to where his family sits, he looks back at the official to make sure he's being watched. Then he slams down into his chair, picks up his rod, and keeps fishing.

Out in the low surf, the lifeguards are practicing rescues. Two men row a dory along the tops of the swells, their oars flashing like some nineteenth-century etching. Down at the south end of the beach is the Casino, its entrance framed by stone pillars and topped by green sea creatures. Most of its windows are broken.

Behind the Casino, there's a sign: ASBURY PARK'S SUNBEACH. This is the Mud Hole: the one part of the beachfront where the "colored" used to be allowed. It sits in the lee of the city's sewage treatment plant. On that boarded-up tower is an official warning about asbestos. Near by, someone's scribbled, "This was our place."

Take a few steps out of Asbury into Ocean Grove, and the boardwalk's suddenly clean, the hotels open. People are eating in a little family restaurant so quaint it feels Amish. On the walls hang hand-tinted pictures from the past century and a clipping about Springsteen returning to The Stone Pony. All the customers are white.

If you look back from the Grove, across Wesley Lake to Asbury Park, you see the tall, aqua-green wall of the Palace. Six-foot lettering advertises the Skooter Ride, and ten-foot cartoon images show white couples laughing in red and orange bumper cars. On the east side of the building, a plastic sign says FUN FOR ALL, with a huge hand-painted mural of a roller coaster detailed in spent neon. Walk around front toward Asbury Avenue, and you see the two Tillies: big loony faces. The signage reads PA A E FUN HOUSE. Cracks split the wall. A part of the roof has collapsed.

For the three summers that the Vaccaros ran the Palace, it became the home of the Asbury Park Rock & Roll Museum, featuring memorabilia from Springsteen, Bon Jovi, the Asbury Jukes, and others. But in January of 1989, desperate for cash, the brothers closed the Palace and began selling off its contents. They contracted to have the hundred-year-old carousel dismantled and put up for auction. Some of the carved horses drew estimated prices of $40,000; the whole set of seventy was said to be worth a million dollars. Meanwhile, a group called Friends of the Palace Carousel tried to raise the money to keep the merry-go-round in Asbury "in the interest of preservation."

What they were trying to preserve, one organizer said, was "a memory of a time when life was a little slower." One witness to that time, Stephen Crane, had used the merry-go-round as a symbol not of slowness, but of nineteenth-century repression: old America holding its younger generation back, denying the possibility of change, keeping its young lovers spinning in useless circles. But what the preservationists wanted to save was the *memory* of that time. For decades now, Asbury had been marketing itself as a throwback to simpler times, to old American values. As preservationists rallied around the antique carousel, across the street welfare families watched from peeling cinder-block motels.

The auction eventually took place, with the merry-go-round machinery going to a Mississippi water park called Wonderland. The Vaccaros went on to sell the Ferris wheel, the dark rides, and the shooting galleries. A decade later, the *Asbury Park Press* announced that the Palace building itself was in danger of collapsing, and a "Save Tillie" campaign started up. By now, the preservationists were mostly Springsteen fans. They, too, were trying to save the memory of a time: the memory of a rock & roll landscape. Tourists would be drawn, the argument went, to what remained of the place Bruce had been born to run from, the "death trap."

Heading inland past the Palace, you walk by former hotels: the Belmont, the Atlantic. Folded-up wheelchairs lean against entranceways; the front yards are gated and dusty. Out on their broad porches, sitting in the still spotty morning sun, are the old and the infirm and the poor. Across the way, where Heck Street intersects, the once-white 150-room Metropolitan Hotel rots quietly.

Most of the big private houses through here have been converted into multifamilies: a half dozen mailboxes hang by each front door. This is part of the dead space, which only grew after Carabetta declared bankruptcy. During the Clinton years, the net value of Asbury Park real estate dropped by almost thirty percent. When the market hit bottom, a property-management company started running a shell game in this area. It would buy the old houses cheap and then sell them to out-of-town straw buyers who often didn't know, or care, what they'd bought—only that they were guaranteed a profit. In return for kickbacks, realtors would give unrealistically high appraisals of the properties, and then a wholesaler in Freehold would issue mortgages. The straw buyers would then turn around and convey sixty percent of the title back to the property-management company. Before the FBI closed in, the company had bought over $3 million of Asbury's dead space, which they'd parlayed into more than $9.25 million in mortgage money. Meanwhile, the buildings stayed firetraps; the roofs leaked; renters lived without heat or electricity.

In the distance, from the direction of the shore, come the drum rolls of the Ocean Grove Fourth of July parade. They echo down church row: Grand Avenue. The 1949 synagogue is now the First French Speaking Baptist Haitian Church. Past the Iglesia Presbiteriana, Cookman Avenue intersects. This end of the city's former shopping district is mostly boarded up and shut down. There are bail bondsmen and a medical-supply company and one functioning haberdasher called "Mr. Fashion: For the Man Who Cares." Carl Williams runs Mr. Fashion. He sits with a large-print Bible in his lap and, behind him, a glass cabinet displaying black felt hats and ruffled, sky-blue shirts. He's a former mayor of Asbury Park.

In the newspapers, Williams has described Asbury Park politics as "a let's-make-a-deal kind of thing." In 1993, Williams—a black man—announced his campaign for city council on a reform ticket. He was offered a $30,000 campaign donation and was told it came from "the same place everybody else gets it." Turning the cash down, he won anyway. The victory marked the end of City Manager Addeo's thirteen-year reign. (Thomas Smith, by then, had moved on to become a state assemblyman.) But Asbury's latest version of reform didn't last long. A few months after the election, new mayor, Dennis Buckley, was arrested for buying cocaine in a local bar. A string of leaders followed, including Williams, but redevelopment remained paralyzed. Describing city government in the late nineties, the *Asbury Park Press* wrote, "Something like chaos has taken hold." If you ask Williams, he'll tell you Asbury's downslide began long before that. Bible in hand, he explains that the city's fall from grace started when James Bradley sold the beachfront, and "men started taking women into the parks, and there was band music on the beach."

Across the street from Mr. Fashion, the yellow-brick Steinbachs building stands on its own peninsula. It's been boarded up for twenty-two years. In front of the temp labor center, a few people sit on benches, waiting. Next door is the walk-in medical clinic, then the old bus station. The shoe store on the corner is called Extreme. Above it, on the second story, behind the windowless brick wall, is where the Upstage used to be.

Before Cookman ends at Main, there are some signs of revitalization. In an August 2000 article headlined MOVE OVER, FIRE ISLAND, HERE COMES ASBURY PARK, the *New York Times* announced that "urban gays" were leading a local revival. The old Victorian cottages up by Deal Lake were being bought and restored. Here on Cookman, you can peer into gutted storefronts and see the massive old support beams that used to span this rubble. The buildings are being converted into art galleries and restaurants and retro shops where you can buy 1950s-era turquoise vinyl couches.

This activity ends at Main Street. As you cross the tracks, Lake Avenue starts being called Springwood. And soon you see block after abandoned block, the weeds waist-high.

This *is* an old battlefield.

Here, protesters massed, heading for police barricades and the east side of town. This is where grocery stores were looted and burned. Unlike the boardwalk, this area owes its emptiness to a pitched battle: people fighting over what the past meant, how to divide up the present, and what the future might hold. Nobody died here, not directly from the fighting. Lots of people died here.

The one modern building on this end of Springwood is St. Stephen's AME Zion Church. After it became clear that the city's redevelopment was going to focus on the beachfront, St. Stephen's came forward with its own plan for the West Side. The African-American church proposed ninety-eight garden apartments and town houses, a seven-story senior-citizen building, and a revitalized business district along Springwood Avenue. It formed a not-for-profit that secured $5.5 million in federal and state funding. But for the project to have a chance, the city council had to agree to the kind of tax abatements it would offer Carabetta. Instead, in 1976, the council vetoed the local, black-run project, declaring that it would be better to wait for private builders. The head of St. Stephen's development corporation said the decision smacked of Asbury's "hidden agendas."

By 1981, neglect of the West Side was so severe that a study found it necessary to state, "The area is still part of the city. It will not vanish nor will its problems." Asbury was still hoping for "private money to move things along." That's how one councilman put it, inadvertently summing up the paralysis in one revealing sentence: "The city can't do anything, but we're willing to do what we can."

Another decade passed. Finally, the city sold seventy-two West Side lots to a developer called Philip Konvitz. He put down ten percent of the $750,000 purchase price and agreed to build affordable housing along Springwood. In the next ten years, he completed only fifteen houses and sold only seven. You can see them just past St. Stephen's: a handful of two-story suburban town houses surrounded by abandoned lots. Konvitz claimed the problem was state money that never came through. In the meantime, the weeds grew taller, and none of the city managers, starting with Addeo, or the redevelopment lawyers, or the various city councils were willing to confront the developer.

Konvitz had become the most recent in the string of Asbury Park power brokers. Born on the Fourth of July, 1912, in Zefat (now Israel), he became a bail bondsman in Newark—thanks, he says, to the Mob. "In my business," he explains, "I knew everybody. I knew the good guys, I knew the bad guys." His International Fidelity grew into a $100 million operation licensed in fifty states and Puerto Rico. He invested in Jersey shore real estate that was eventually worth more than $20 million. For years, Konvitz held court in a trailer parked outside a Neptune shopping center. There, dressed in a 1940s-style summer suit with suspenders and an old-fashioned straw boater, he received a daily line of people looking for his legendary no-interest loans. According to his close friend ex–police chief, ex-mayor, state assemblyman Thomas Smith, the loans didn't create political influence. They went to "non-descript people."

When Henry Vaccaro went bankrupt in Asbury's waterfront development deal, it was Konvitz who loaned him $100,000 to save his house from a sheriff's sale—and then invested $200,000 in Vaccaro's guitar business. And council members got loans, too. One was given $35,000—unsecured and with no interest—to open a bar on Asbury's waterfront. Four months later, this councilman introduced a resolution that let Konvitz sell eighteen of the untouched and unpaid-for Springwood lots to another developer. The resolution passed 4-0. "[Council members] respect my opinion," Konvitz said. "I don't try to influence anybody."

In July 2000, when Asbury's council proposed that a state authority come in and monitor beachfront redevelopment, the resolution called for the chairman of the authority to be a local citizen: someone known for his "business acumen, political savvy, and . . . negotiating ability." The name that came up was that of eighty-eight-year-old Philip Konvitz. At a subsequent closed-door meeting about the appointment, a Superior Court judge declared,

"There is one person who controls Asbury Park." The local paper reported that the judge "clearly was referring to Konvitz." The names changed—Konvitz assumed the role of Clarence Hetrick or, before that, of James Bradley—but the perception remained the same: that Asbury was run and could only be run from the top down. The same way the economy had to flow from the beach-front inland.

This Fourth of July, the only sign that Springwood Avenue has anything to do with a beachfront is a lone seagull wheeling above the empty lots. Off in the distance, sirens sound like ghosts of the riot police. It's the Ocean Grove parade drawing to a close. On Atkins, five blocks west of the tracks, there's a one-story building with MUSIC BAR ENTERTAINMENT written over its closed, black door. This is what's left of Springwood's music scene. On this corner, Bill Basie must have played stride piano; Davey Sancious must have searched for that lost jazz chord. This is where Donald Hammary heard the ditta-da-ditta-da of glass bottles thrown from rooftops.

North, on Borden Avenue, tired wooden houses teeter on old foundations. Here's a new, half-finished place, construction ma-terials rusting and melting in the weather. Next to it is the Shiloh Unified Holy Church. Near that, a couple of shotgun houses: two rooms wide by two deep with a narrow hall running down the center. They look at the same time decrepit and ancestral: the architecture of the Deep South brought here by hotel porters and chambermaids. The yards are cluttered with broken plastic toys. Old men sit out front in folding chairs. Families gather around Fourth of July barbecues, joke with each other while the coals heat up.

At Mattison Avenue, some kids are playing in a quiet play-ground; the chains creak on the swings. East is the Asbury Middle School, and on Bangs Avenue, the Faith Baptist Tabernacle, built in 1923, back when the Klan was marching. Past Prospect, the street is as tree-lined as a country road. Old maples three stories high shade frame houses. For every abandoned lot or front yard spilling with black garbage bags, there's a property that's been carefully planted, its walkway swept, its iron fencing tipped and painted. In front of one house, a gray-haired black lady clips the hedge. She looks to be in her eighties, wearing a blue-and-white summer dress, her home whitewashed till it sparkles, blue hydrangea blooming beside her.

You can see the future from here.

Back across the tracks, past the dead space, by the shore, kids will soon be building sand castles. A half hour from now, over on Ocean Avenue, the black man who went cursing down the beach will be packing up his car. "They wanted us to buy a four-dollar badge," he'll tell a friend. "But I said I'd leave first. We got done what we needed to get done."

Two months from now—after the attack on the World Trade Towers—Springsteen will appear on a nationally televised "September 11 Telethon," singing a new song about Asbury Park, his first in years. "My City of Ruins" talks about "Young men on the corner like scattered leaves / The boarded up windows, the empty streets." It ends with a call to "rise up," as Springsteen once again uses Asbury to reflect the state of the nation.

Even before it's in office, a new city council will start working out a deal where a new developer agrees to buy Carabetta's rights and commit to the old formula of high-end condos on the beach. Included will be what one planning consultant describes as a "rock'n'roll entertainment Mecca." In twenty-first-century language, the plan is to make Asbury "a destination location" reborn through "the economic momentum [of] gentrification." Facing a $4 million budget deficit and a state takeover of city finances, with its property value still dropping, the city will resell its beachfront.

Of the three thousand proposed new units, five percent will be labeled affordable ($100,000 and up). The developer will commit to donating funds toward improving the West Side. But hope for most of the current citizens will depend on a familiar theory: money from what one council member calls "the new Asbury Park" is supposed to float the rest. How will this wave of gentrification affect the thirty percent of Asbury's population living in poverty? When a local minister asks, the city manager who structured the redevelopment deal answers: the law requires housing be found for the dispossessed, "but not necessarily in the same area."

Moments after the final planning session for the new Asbury, that city manager will be forced to resign, accused of taking bribes on another matter in another town. The man offering the bribes will be identified as Philip Konvitz. But the waterfront plan will continue to move forward, the new city manager saying—with no apparent irony—that "the people of Asbury Park have been dying for this."

In June of 2004, preservationists will saw Tillie's face out of the wall of the Palace and place it in storage. Then the old amusement park will be demolished. And that Fourth of July, with the city still waiting for reconstruction to begin, Asbury's first Independence Day parade in years will march down Main Street. Bands will play; fireworks will go off that night. "It shows we're back," one resident will say. Another will call it "emblematic."

But all this is in the future. Here on Bangs Avenue, on a shady block, hope makes a different sound. An old woman in a blue-and-white summer dress is working in her garden. As she works, she hums a tune almost too soft to hear.

ACKNOWLEDGMENTS

Many people have made this book possible, some of whom I will forget to thank. All errors and opinions are mine.

First, thanks for all their help to the staff of the Asbury Park Library, including Dorothy Booker, Charlene Jordan, Joan Lager, Patricia LaSala, Lauren Loudermilk, Malakia Oglesby, Robert Stewart, and Wanda Wyckoff.

And then there is the inexhaustible source of Asbury information, Ellis Gilliam.

Among the many people kind enough to share their memories and insights, I want to thank Donald Hammary, Gregory Holland, Delores Holmes, Kate Mellina, Norman Mesnikoff, Paul Onto, the Rev. David J. Parreott Jr., David Sancious, Thomas Smith, Garry Tallent, Steven Van Zandt, and Carl Williams.

For his continuing role as teacher and friend, Dave Marsh.

For his enormous generosity, Bruce Springsteen.

For their enthusiasm and support over too many years, Sandy Choron, Jonathan Demme, Jim and Kath Desmond, Rusty Pedersen, Janey Tannenbaum, Bobby Vergara, Frank Wilkinson, and Wendy Wolf.

For their help on the final leg, Bloomsbury's Karen Rinaldi, Panio Gianopoulos, Amanda Katz, and Greg Villepique.

Finally, thanks to my families: Ma, Pa, and the sisters, the great Marta Renzi and her equally great sons, Amos and Lorenzo.

NOTES

FOURTH OF JULY, 1870

5 For Bradley's version of the founding See his "History of Asbury Park,"
The Shore Press, May 21, 1885. Hereafter, "Bradley history."

6 Jersey wagon Harold F. Wilson, *The Story of the Jersey Shore* (Princeton, NJ:
D. Van Nostrand Co., Inc., 1964) 20. Hereafter, "Wilson 1."

"Born on Valentine's Day" For a history of Bradley's childhood and early
business career, see the front-page obituary, *Asbury Park Press*, June 7, 1921
(hereafter, "Bradley obit"); also *James A. Bradley and Asbury Park: A Biography
and History*, pamphlet at Asbury Park Library, published under the auspices
of the Bradley Memorial Committee, 1921. Hereafter, "Bradley bio."

7 probably from drink Harold F. Wilson, *The Jersey Shore: A Social and
Economic History of the Counties of Atlantic, Cape May, Monmouth, and
Ocean* (New York: Lewis Historical Publishing Co., Inc., 1953), 510.
Hereafter, "Wilson 2."

for 1837 panic and description of the Bowery Edwin G. Burrows and
Mike Wallace, *Gotham: A History of New York City to 1898* (New York:
Oxford University Press, 1999), 612–59.

8 minstrel show Ibid., 643.

hard, hot work See "How Brushes Are Made," *Manufacturer and Builder*
23, no. 12 (December 1891).

9 "distinctively middle-class creed" Burrows and Wallace, *Gotham*, 976.

Helen Packard See Helen M. Bradley obituary, *Asbury Park Evening Press*,
February 15, 1915, 1.

a visitor   *Daily Journal*, July 16, 1885.

1857 panic   Burrows and Wallace, *Gotham*, 844–50.

10 Civil War   Ibid., 874–77.

11 Henry Ward Beecher   Ibid., 976.

12 Josh Billings   See www.boondocksnet.com/twaintexts/pattee02_g.html.

"strangely warmed"   William Warren Sweet, *Methodism in American History* (New York: Abingdon Press, 1933; 1954), 35.

"One condition"   Ibid., 42.

13 "Wither am I going?"   Ibid., 64.

Methodist membership   Ibid., 120.

Love feasts   Ibid., 40.

"bathed in tears"   Ibid., 76.

"the surf blends"   Wilson 1, 46.

14 population   Wilson 2, 466.

"the favorite watering place"   *New York Times*, July 13, 1870.

Bradley's wild woods   See Bradley history.

15 "religious application"   Daniel Defoe, *Robinson Crusoe* (New York: Dell, 1982).

"The great world"   Dr. E. H. Stokes, *The Story of Ocean Grove: An Historical Sketch* (1919), www.oceangrove.org/history2.htm.

16 Spanish silver dollar   Gustav Kobbé, *The New Jersey Coast and Pines: An Illustrated Guide-Book (With Road Maps)* (New York: Walking News Inc., 1982), 48. First published 1889.

preamble   See "Ocean Grove: Growth of A Great Religious Summer Resort," *New York Daily Tribune*, August 2, 1890.

early guidebook   Kobbé, *New Jersey Coast*.

17 "Bless de Lord!"   *Asbury Park Journal*, December 10, 1887.

"worldly delights"   Richard M. Cameron, *Methodisim and Society in Historical Perspective* (New York: Abingdon Press, 1961), 218.

"tendency to worldliness"   Ibid., 219.

dancing   Ibid., 222.

"the practice of the sexes"   Kobbé, *New Jersey Coast*, 51.

"autocratic"   Wilson 2, 80.

1871   Matthew Simpson, *A Hundred Years of Methodism* (New York: Phillips and Hunt, 1876), 195.

18 "He holds the honest people"   Matthew Josephson, *The Robber Barons: The Great American Capitalists, 1861–1901* (New York: Harcourt, Brace and Company, 1934), 19.

Drew Theological   Sweet, *Methodism*, 318.

publishing concern   Ibid., 323.

19 Bishop Asbury   Frank Bateman Stanger, ed., *The Methodist Trail in New Jersey: One Hundred and Twenty-Five Years of Methodism in the New Jersey Annual Conference, 1863–1961* (Camden, NJ: Annual Conference of the Methodist Church, 1961).

early days   See Wilson 1, 25–30.

"grace at each meal"   Ibid., 30.

entertainment   Ibid., 75.

"profoundly pro-Southern"   Graham Russell Hodges, *Slavery and Freedom in the Rural North: African Americans in Monmouth County, New Jersey, 1665–1865* (Madison, WI: Madison House Publishers, 1997), 188–9.

20 "The depot is crowded" *New York Times*, July 13, 1870.

opening day See *New York Times*, July 13, 1870.

"The truth is" Ibid., July 13, 1870.

"I cannot think" Wilson 1, 80.

21 "having our clothes torn" Bradley history.

"I think we have enough" Ibid.

22 "money making was secondary" Bradley bio.

23 "landscape as theology" Glenn Uminowicz, "Sport in a Middle-Class Utopia: Asbury Park, New Jersey, 1871–1895," *Journal of Sport History* 11, no. 1 (Spring 1984): 61.

an incident took place See Bradley history.

24 We know that later *Asbury Park Journal*, December 10, 1887.

FOURTH OF JULY, 1885

26 "The growth of towns" *Shore Press*, April 23, 1885.

grown into a resort See Kobbé, *New Jersey Coast*, and Helen-Chantal Pike, *Images of America: Asbury Park* (Portsmouth, NH: Arcadia Publishing, 1997).

27 "drainage" Bradley History.

1883 season Wilson 2, 487–512.

boardwalk Ibid., 546.

Steinbachs Pike, *Images*, 23, 38–39.

28 "package railway" *Shore Press*, June 20, 1885.

"The tonic saltwater" Wilson 2, 535.

nine-piece John T. Cunningham, *The New Jersey Shore* (New Brunswick, NJ: Rutgers University Press, 1958), 140.

short story "The Reluctant Voyagers" by Stephen Crane (from *Harper's* magazine, circa 1893) Thomas A. Gullason, ed., *The Complete Short Stories and Sketches of Stephen Crane* (New York: Doubleday, 1963), 121–39.

"The surf lubricates" Wilson 2, 533–34.

"cut so low" *New York Times*, July 12, 1886, 5.

29 Modesty Ibid., June 7, 1921, 17.

"Jesus" Ibid., June 12, 1886, 5.

junk See Bradley bio.

"skyscraping" See Bradley obit.

30 "Not a person to be easily understood" See Bradley bio.

enormous contradictions *Asbury Park Press*, December 24, 1887, and *Daily Journal*, July 13, 1889.

immigrants Burrows and Wallace, *Gotham*, 970.

"I give it as my opinion" *Shore Press*, April 23, 1885.

Golden Road T. J. McMahon, *The Golden Age of the Monmouth Shore: 1864–1914* (Fairhaven, NJ: T. J. McMahon Publishing, 1964), 21.

iron pier Ibid., 23.

31 "Satan" *Daily Journal*, August 8, 1889.
"hypocritical cloak" *New York Times*, July 12, 1886.
"In spite of" *Daily Journal*, August 31, 1889.
a contemporary account *New York Times*, July 12, 1886.
The Artesian and local judge Ibid., December 12, 1886, 10.
illegal saloons Ibid., July 12, 1886.
32 "excursion houses" Cunningham, *New Jersey Shore*, 144.
diversions See *Daily Journal*, "Pleasure Guide," 1885.
rink *Shore Press*, June 11, 1885.
Epicycloidal Wheel Wilson 1, 65.
33 unpaved streets See "West Side Story: Profile of a Black Community,"
special report, *Asbury Park Press*, May 21, 1982. Hereafter, "West Side
Story."
Burnham Henry C. Pitney Jr., supervising ed., *A History of Morris
County, New Jersey, embracing upwards of two centuries, 1710–1913* (New
York/Chicago: Lewis Historical Publishing Co, 1914).
Independence Day *Shore Press*, July 9, 1885.
34 "impudent" *Daily Journal*, July 7, 1885.
"Too Many Colored People" Ibid., July 17, 1885.
35 "a big colored picnic" *New York Times*, July 19, 1885.
36 drawn from his religion James S. Thomas, *Methodism's Racial Dilemma:
The Story of Central Jurisdiction* (New York: Abingdon Press, 1992), 13.
African-American congregants Ibid., 28–29.
general conference of 1844 Ibid., 36.
37 The result was Sweet, *Methodism*, 277.
targets Ibid., 313–14.
Cape May Ibid., 329.
Post Reprinted in *Daily Journal*, July 21, 1885.
38 Galveston Ibid., August 17, 1885.
"Bradley always goes off" *New York Times*, July 12, 1886.
"two distinct factions" *Shore Press*, October 22, 1885.
39 welcome-home dinner Ibid.
lynching *New York Times*, March 8, 1886, 1.
editorial Ibid., March 16, 1886, 8.
"Why should I" Ibid., March 8, 1886, 1.
40 "uphill work" *New York Times*, March 31, 1886, 2.
signed simply "Citizen" *Daily Journal*, July 30, 1886.
letter from a writer Ibid., August 5, 1886.
41 "A Colored Man's View" Ibid., August 12, 1886.
unnamed hotel man Ibid., August 14, 1886.
letter from Wiesbaden Ibid., August 17, 1886.
42 "dens of iniquity" *New York Times*, July 12, 1886.
first issue *Daily Journal*, June 20, 1887.
43 open letter *Asbury Shore Press*, July 1, 1887.
250 people Ibid.
44 had it wrong *Shore Press*, July 1, 1887.
reprinted an editorial Ibid.
"agitators" *Daily Journal*, June 29, 1887.

45 St. Mark's *New York Times*, July 6, 1887.
46 "all nuisances" *Daily Journal*, July 7, 1887.
   Bradley statement *Shore Press*, July 8, 1887.
   "commission hours" *Asbury Park Journal*, July 20, 1889.

AMERICAN DAY, 1892

48 Thin, with almond-shaped Stanley Wertheim and Paul Sorrentino, *The Crane Log: A Documentary Life of Stephen Crane, 1871–1900* (New York: G. K. Hall and Co., 1994), 72. Hereafter, "*Crane Log*."
   born in Newark See R. W. Stallman, *Stephen Crane: A Biography* (New York: George Braziller, 1968). Hereafter, "Crane bio."
49 "as soon as he could walk" Ibid., 4.
   a series of tracts Ibid., 5.
   "guilty, condemned" *Crane Log*, 8–9.
   Love Feast Christopher Benfey, *The Double Life of Stephen Crane* (New York: Alfred A. Knopf, 1992), 29.
   At forty-five Crane bio, 1.
50 the white of an egg *Crane Log*, 14.
   moved three times Benfey, *Double Life*, 30.
   "I am much more concerned" Crane bio, 7.
   inherited money Ibid., 9.
   industrial school *Crane Log*, 19.
   "Much encouragement" Crane bio, 6.
51 hotels See Pike, *Images of America*.
   the melodeon *Asbury Park Press*, June 7, 1921.
   Ocean Grove Record *Crane Log*, 32.
   kill time Crane bio, 33.
52 "in and for religion" Ibid., 5.
   fortunes fail *Crane Log*, 32.
   "Strikes" Benfey, *Double life*, 37.
   oyster-like *Crane Log*, 24.
   "extremely ill" Ibid., 34.
   "physical derelict" Ibid., 44.
53 beer Ibid., 15–16.
   Roosevelt Gullason, *Complete Short Stories*, 25
   first newspaper piece *Crane Log*, 37–38.
54 distillery Ibid., 42.
   "Don't the people" *New York Daily Tribune*, July 13, 1890.
   Baby Parade Ibid., July 27, 1890.
   laudatory profile Ibid., August 2, 1890.
55 1891 column *Crane Log*, 63.
   average summer visitor Uminowicz, "Sport in a Middle-Class Utopia," 56.
   "a great lot of trouble" *New York Daily Tribune*, July 24, 1892.
56 "shriveling" Benfey, *Double Life*, 67.

nonfiction version   Stephen Crane, *Maggie: A Girl of the Streets*, ed. Thomas
A. Gullason (New York: W. W. Norton Critical Edition, 1979), 75–76.

57 "no way out"   Ibid.
"The thousands"   *New York Daily Tribune*, July 24, 1892.
"abjectly poor"   *Crane Log*, 74.
Carousel House   "New Jersey Register of Historic Places Nomination" for
Palace Amusements, prepared by Asbury Park Historical Society, April 26,
2000. New Jersey Historic Preservation Offices, Trenton.

58 "watching the surf"   *Crane Log*, 74.
"There is probably"   *New York Daily Tribune*, August 14, 1892.

59 "creates nothing"   *Crane Log*, 77.

60 "made Stevie Crane famous"   Crane bio, 53.
"uncalled-for"   *Crane Log*, 78.
vice president   Ibid.
"I seemed to have forgotten"   Crane bio, 56.

61 July 1890   *New York Tribune*, July 27, 1890.
"noisy dwarf"   *New York Times*, July 24, 1885.
Port Jervis lynching   See Crane bio, 11, 565.

62 "The Monster"   Gullason, *Complete Short Stories*, 430–75.

63 "Coney Island is"   *New York Journal*, Summer Resort Supplement,
August 16, 1896.

64 "a Jerseyman"   Crane bio, 1.

65 "There is a mighty pathos"   "Coney Island's Failing Days," in Gullason,
Complete Short Stories, 181–86.
1893 story   Ibid., 113–121.

FOURTH OF JULY, 1903

68 "greatest patriotic"   *Asbury Park Evening News*, July 6, 1903.
"outdo Atlantic City"   Ibid.
"In reality"   Ibid., June 22, 1903.

68 "wideawake merchants"   *Asbury Park Journal*, November 26, 1902.
"dingy by day"   Ibid.

69 "his next walk"   Ibid., November 28, 1902.
Prohibitionist Party   *Asbury Park Evening News*, June 22, 1903.

70 the deciding vote   See Bradley bio.
"riparian rights   *Asbury Park Evening News*, June 23, 1903.
slot machines   *Asbury Park Journal*, July 25, 1902, 1.
McKay   Leonora Walker Mckay, *Mama and Papa: Volume II, The Blacks
of Monmouth County* (self-published, 1984), 63.

71 African-American   Ibid.
mob   *Asbury Park Evening News*, July 6, 1903, 1.
"Mulatoe"   See McKay, *Mama and Papa.*
"genus tramp"   Uminowicz, "Sport in a Middle-Class Utopia," 64.

72 "patrino"   *Asbury Park Journal*, November 14, 1902.

"the warm impulsive heart" *Shore Press*, April 23, 1903.

Joplin See Edward A. Baker, *King of Ragtime: Scott Joplin and His Era* (New York: Oxford University Press, 1994).

73 infection See Ted Gioia, *The History of Jazz* (New York: Oxford University Press, 1997).

74 Sousa John Philip Sousa, *Marching Along* (Westerville, OH: Integrity Press, 1994. Originally published 1928.)

Chicago World Exposition Rudi Blesh and Harriet Janie, *They All Played Ragtime* (New York: Oak Publications, 1971), 73.

75 Pryor biography See Richard Benjamin, "Arthur Pryor: Ragtime Pioneer," Paragon Ragtime Orchestra (1998-9), www.paragonragtime.com/pryor.html.

"ponderous echoes" Blesh and Janie, *They All Played Ragtime*, 74-76.

hits See Benjamin, "Arthur Pryor."

76 "ethnics" Uminowicz, "Sport in a Middle-Class Utopia," 62.

77 First National Bank "The Asbury Park Bank-Fraud Case: *Twining v. New Jersey*," www.soc.umniedu/~samaha/cases/twining%20facts.html.

"If the beach" *Asbury Park Journal*, September 9, 1902.

"I must say" Ibid.

his pitch Ibid., November 19, 1902.

"people's" Ibid., November 7, 1902.

attorney Ibid.

Hotel Keepers Ibid., September 19, 1902.

78 "Silence Is Golden" Ibid., October 10, 1902.

CITY PROCEEDS Ibid., November 7, 1902.

Appleby *Asbury Park Evening Press*, December 15, 1924.

"remain silent" *Asbury Park Journal*, November 14, 1902.

"farce" Ibid.

79 For the Educational Hall meeting, including quotes See *Asbury Park Journal*, November 28, 1902, 1.

81 old-fashioned oompah music Ibid., November 21, 1902.

resignation and elections Ibid., December 25, 1902.

"injudicious" *Shore Press*, January 8, 1903.

4 to 3 Ibid.

82 "looked sadly" Ibid., April 23, 1903.

$20,000 Ibid., May 7, 1903.

The Crystal Maze See "New Jersey Register of Historic Places Nomination."

middle-class organizations *Asbury Park Evening Press*, June 27, 1903.

Olmsted Ibid.

83 Conterno's band Ibid.

Majestic Theater See Benjamin, "Arthur Pryor."

phonograph record Ibid.

269 concerts See Daniel F. Frizane and Frederick P. Williams, "Historical Notes" to *Arthur Pryor, Trombone Soloist of the Sousa Band*, Crystal Records, CD451.

84 Casino and improvement See Pike, *Images of America*.

"stand aside" *Asbury Park Journal*, February 20, 1906.

85 "most certainly oppose"   Ibid., May 12, 1906.
Reverend Ballard   Ibid., February 24, 1906.
editorial   Ibid., March 15, 1906.
"festering cancer"   Ibid., March 20, 1906.
Bradley   See *Asbury Park Journal*, May 12, 1906.
86 "the longest purse"   Ibid., March 20, 1906.
Appleby   *New York Times*, December 15, 1924.
Booker T. Washington   *Asbury Park Journal*, March 16, 1906.
87 the resolution passed   Ibid., May 17, 1906.
"I want to look down"   Bradley obit.

FOURTH OF JULY, 1924

88 lavender bunting   *Asbury Park Evening Press*, March 25, 1924.
89 "plan the home budget"   Ibid., March 22, 1924.
A hundred city businesses   Ibid., March 24, 1924.
sixty-thousand people   Ibid., March 29, 1924.
"living reproduction"   Ibid., March 24, 1924.
"twice the size"   Ibid., March 30, 1924.
passing a resolution   Ibid., March 26, 1924.
90 Tindall's affidavit   See *Asbury Park Evening Press*, April 7, 1924, and *New York Times*, same date.
"the temperance movement"   Halford E. Luccock and Paul Hutchinson, *The Story of Methodism* (New York, Cincinnati: The Methodist Book Concern, 1926), 465.
"The Rum Coast"   *Asbury Park Sunday Press*, October 7, 1923.
91 "the like of which"   *Asbury Park Evening Press*, April 7, 1924.
"Sinners walk"   Ibid.
front-page headline   *New York Times*, April 7, 1924.
92 "There was no lewdness"   *Asbury Park Evening Press*, April 8, 1924.
founding member   "The Golden Medinah," in Dr. Alan S. Pine, Jean C. Hershenov, and Dr. Aaron H. Lefkowitz, *Peddler to Suburbanite: The History of the Jews of Monmouth County, New Jersey* (Deal Park, NJ: Monmouth Jewish Community Council, 1981).
"a rotten party"   *Asbury Park Evening Press*, April 8, 1924.
laced with corruption   January 6, 1915.
Income on the Casino   Ibid., January 11, 1915.
93 fifty-seven candidates   Ibid., January 1 and 6, 1915.
squeak-in   Ibid., January 8, 1915.
on election day   Ibid., January 12, 1915.
SOUND THE ALARM   Ibid., January 9, 1915.
Hetrick was born   "Shore Pioneers," *Asbury Park Press*, April 9, 1967.
"financial acumen"   *Asbury Park Evening Press*, January 9, 1915.
On November 9   Ibid., November 10, 1910.
94 suspects   Ibid., November 11, 1910.

"Black Diamond" Ibid., November 13, 1910.

"Swear that you" Ibid., November 14, 1910.

"Everything points" Ibid., November 20, 1910.

SWIFT JUSTICE Ibid., November 13, 1910.

"Criminal assault" Ibid., November 20, 1910.

95 mob Ibid., November 15 and 27, 1910.

three citizens Ibid., November 28, 1910.

Burns Detective Agency See *American Legion* magazine, January 19, 1970.

two thousand dollars' bail *Asbury Park Evening Press*, November 28, 1910.

fingerprints *American Legion*, January 19, 1970.

SUPREME EFFORT *Asbury Park Evening Press*, December 4, 1910.

96 "open breach" Ibid., November 28, 1910.

confessed Ibid., April 19, 1911.

shunned its endorsement Ibid., January 7, 1915.

eighteen-page pamphlet Ibid., October 13, 1941. Hereafter, "Hetrick obit."

refused to indict Ibid., April 11, 1924.

"weak-minded" Ibid., April 8, 1924.

"knew before" Ibid., April 7, 1924.

The next day Ibid., April 8, 1924.

a Republican in good standing See Hetrick obit.

97 1919 resolution *Asbury Park Evening Press*, September 27, 1924.

"determined to continue its fight" *New York Times*, April 8, 1924.

"do everything within our power" Ibid.

"the most powerful" Kenneth T. Jackson, *The Ku Klux Klan in the City: 1915–1930* (New York: Oxford University Press, 1967), 251.

four and a half million Howard Zinn, *A People's History of the United States* (New York: HarperPerennial Library, 1980), 373.

"felt most at home" David M. Chalmers, *Hooded Americanism: The History of the Ku Klux Klan* (Durham, NC: Duke University Press, 1987), 3.

98 Woodrow Wilson Wyn Craig Wade, *The Fiery Cross: The Ku Klux Klan in America* (New York: Simon and Schuster, 1987), 115.

private screenings Ibid., 119–32.

Simmons Ibid., 140.

99 Southern Publicity Association Ibid., 157.

"If you are a Native Born" Ibid.

Within fifteen months Ibid.

exposé Jackson, *Ku Klux Klan*, 13.

"Congress" Wade, *Fiery Cross*, 166.

"the larger and more pretentious" *New York Times*, April 13, 1924.

one-tenth of one percent Zinn, *People's History*, 373.

bounced a seven-dollar check *Asbury Park Evening Press*, April 7, 1924.

100 "considerably disturbed" Ibid., April 9, 1924.

whispered a phone number Ibid., April 7, 1924, and *New York Times*, April 9, 1924.

riding in Bell's touring car *Asbury Park Evening Press*, April 9, 1924.

100 "more or less"   Ibid., April 8, 1924.
exonerated   Ibid., May 1, 1924.
red C   Ibid., November 2, 1933.
the week of the orgy   Ibid., April 9, 1924.
101 "The Klan is"   *Inspirational Addresses*, Second Imperial Klonvokation, September 23–26, 1924, author's collection.
forty thousand fundamentalist   Wade, *Fiery Cross*, 171.
"exceptionally large audience"   *Asbury Park Evening Press*, June 27, 1924.
"primitive rhythms"   Sousa, *Marching Along*, 357–58.
102 "unwept"   Ibid.
"the parasite"   See Frizane and Williams, "Historical Notes."
"the abominable jazz"   Paula S. Fass, *The Damned and The Beautiful: American Youth in the 1920's* (New York: Oxford University Press, 1977), 22.
William Basie   See William Basie, as told to Albert Murray, *Good Morning Blues: The Autobiography of Count Basie* (New York: Random House, 1985).
piano contest   Ibid., 35.
Ellington   See John Edward Hasse, *The Life and Genius of Duke Ellington* (New York: Simon and Schuster, 1993).
"the main stem"   Basie, *Good Morning Blues*, 39.
"a very big house"   Ibid., 44.
103 a cutting contest   Ibid.
Fats Waller   See liner notes to *Duke Ellington Masterpieces, 1926–1949*, Proper Records, SV6033.
"the greatest living Negro leader"   McKay, *Mama and Papa*, 52.
"hopeless economic"   "Convention of Universal Negro Improvement Association," August 1924, New York, www.marcusgarvey.com/c23.htm.
"eighty-seven thousand cases"   Chalmers, *Hooded Americanism*, 245.
"The Negro is not a menace"   *Inspirational Addresses*.
104 "Foreign people"   *Asbury Park Evening Press*, March 3, 1924.
butcher shop   Pine, Hershenov, and Lefkowitz, "The Golden Medinah."
Bradley was donating   See Pike, *Images of America*.
"the most dangerous"   Jackson, *Ku Klux Klan*, 22.
forty-four thousand Italians   See Allesandra Di Beneditto, *Italian Immigration to the United States*, Institutus Survey Paper 1/2000, A FAST-US-2(PP2D) U.S.
one out of five   Chalmers, *Hooded Americanism*, 244.
YMCA   *Asbury Park Evening Press*, March 31, 1924.
105 "extending their power"   Chalmers, *Hooded Americanism*, 245.
"borrowed time"   Zinn, *People's History*, 374.
"the first time"   *Asbury Park Evening Press*, March 10, 1924.
"monster crowd"   Ibid., July 5, 1924.
"old maids"   Ibid., March 10, 1924.
106 jazz clubs   McKay, *Mama and Papa*, 78.
ASCAP ban   Ortiz Walton, *Music: Black, White and Blue* (New York: William Morrow, 1972), 64–65.
"Jailhouse Blues"   Gunther Schuller, *Early Jazz: Its Roots and Musical Development* (New York: Oxford University Press, 1968), 143, 230.
Original Dixieland Jazz Band   Ibid., 181–82.

four thousand men, women, and children   *Asbury Park Evening Press*, July 5, 1924.
"We want" Ibid.
Imperial Palace   Ibid., June 26, 1924.
107 baseball game, etc.   Ibid., July 5, 1924.
souvenir program   "TriState Klonklave," July 4, 1924, souvenir program, author's collection.
"Amid the bluffs"   Chalmers, *Hooded Americanism*, 243.
"cosmopolitans"   *Inspirational Addresses*.
"no one but"   *Asbury Park Evening Press*, July 5, 1924.
"the cloud of"   Ibid., June 28, 1924.
"the most un-American"   Jackson, *Ku Klux Klan*, 175.
"first allegiance"   *Inspirational Addresses*.
108 throw hardballs   *Asbury Park Evening Press*, July 5, 1924.
"the multitudes"   Ibid.
four thousand a year   Zinn, *People's History*, 373.
"protect the public"   *Asbury Park Evening Press*, March 3, 1924.
Vanderpool   *New York Times*, August 1, 1924.
"one of the most earnest"   Ibid., December 15, 1924.
109 platform   Ibid., September 19, 1924.
"absolutely false"   Ibid., September 22, 1924.
"The Klan is not"   Ibid., September 20, 1924.
SHALL THE KLAN   *Asbury Park Evening Press*, September 22, 1924.
110 Tindall   Ibid.
The next day   Ibid., September 24, 1924.
KU KLUX BEAT WASHBURN   *New York Times*, September 25, 1924.
"It is clear"   *Asbury Park Evening Press*, September 24, 1924.
"a crushing blow"   *New York Times*, September 25, 1924.
Monmouth County Equal Rights Association   *Asbury Park Evening Press*, November 1, 1924.
111 elected Appleby   Ibid., November 5, 1924.
VICTORIES   *New York Times*, November 6, 1924.
"in closer touch"   *Asbury Park Evening Press*, June 23, 1925.
112 disastrous fire   *Asbury Park Sunday Press*, October 9, 1923.
113 "I pressed my nose"   McKay, *Mama and Papa*, 81.

FOURTH OF JULY, 1941

114 "gigantic patriotic"   *Asbury Park Evening Press*, July 2, 1941.
"palmy days" Ibid.
Germans capturing   Ibid., July 3, 1941.
115 Robert Taylor, etc.   Ibid., July 2, 1941.
residents complained   Ibid., July 5, 1941.
"members of Holy Name"   Ibid., July 7, 1941.
116 lead car   Ibid.

116 $8 million   Ibid., May 12, 1941.

beach erosion   Victor Gellineau, director and chief engineer, *Report by Board of Commerce and Navigation, New Jersey, on the erosion and protection of New Jersey beaches*, MacCrellish & Quigley, Trenton, NJ (see reports for 1922, 1924, and 1930).

indebtedness   *Asbury Park Evening Press*, November 6, 1933.

city's promotional brochure   *The Story of Asbury Park: The Record of Progress and Achievement, 1916-31*, reprinted by the Asbury Park Historical Society (2003).

reacted slowly   *Asbury Park Evening Press*, July 9, 1941.

117 "an enigma"   Ibid., April 9, 1967.

rarely seen on the streets   Hetrick obit.

"ostensibly"   *Asbury Park Evening Press*, April 9, 1967.

Hetrick's employer   *New York Times*, October 9, 1935.

Utilities like UP&L   See a "brief history" of the electricity industry by Senator Jeff Bingaman (D-NM), chairman of the Committee on Energy and Natural Resources, http://energy.senate.gov/news/dem_release.cfm?id=177741.

for UP&L data   See the annual reports of the Utilities Power & Light Corporation, 1927-34.

118 "radical nature"   Ibid., 1934, 3.

"the savior"   *Asbury Park Evening Press*, May 6, 1933.

Asbury's New Deal   Ibid., November 8, 1933.

119 losing even more money   Ibid., November 3, 1933.

"close connections"   Ibid., June 15, 1933.

Waxey Gordon   Ibid., May 12, 1933.

"south of Asbury"   Hetrick obit.

120 "city-wide upheaval"   *Asbury Park Evening Press*, October 11, 1933.

outside fiscal experts   Ibid., October 11, 1933.

Osgoodby   Ibid., November 2, 1933.

121 Burley   Ibid.

"rotten"   Ibid.

"How is it possible"   Ibid. November 3, 1933.

Croce   Ibid., November 2, 1933.

122 "dictator"   Ibid.

three months behind   Ibid.

"floaters"   Ibid., October 11, 1933.

Tom Brown's taproom   Ibid., November 9, 1933.

"A decisive expression"   Ibid., November 3, 1933.

"Almost from the minute"   Hetrick obit.

"the failure"   *New York Times*, January 16, 1934.

Capibianco   *Asbury Park Evening Press*, April 1, 1934, and July 27, 1934.

"genius for organization"   Hetrick obit

123 April Fools'   *Final Report of the Special Committee*, December 17, 1934, Chairman W. Stanley Naughright.

Calandriello   Ibid., 4.

Crook   Ibid.

"a startling lack"   Ibid., 2.

Phillips   Ibid., 12.

"protection money" Ibid.
fined $100 Ibid., 31–32.
124 Hurley Ibid., 53.
slot machines Ibid., 57.
$10,000 Ibid., 73–75.
Berkeley-Carteret Ibid., 12.
125 Mattice Ibid., 13.
never called Ibid.
no liquor *Asbury Park Evening Press*, July 2, 1934.
"marked with intense" Ibid., July 3, 1934.
126 *Morro Castle* story See Gordon Thomas and Max Morgan Witts, *Shipwreck: The Strange Fate of the Morro Castle* (New York: Dell, 1973).
Old Vienna Garden Café Author's collection.
"as an entertainment attraction" *New York Times*, September 12, 1934.
127 "base, vicious" *Asbury Park Press*, October 26, 1975.
"bereaved families" *New York Times*, September 13, 1934.
J. Whitfield Brooks Ibid., September 12, 1934.
terrazzo floors Ibid.
128 "circumstances were peculiar" Ibid.
"inefficiency in office" *New York Times*, December 19, 1934.
creditors Ibid., December 1, 1934.
"something not kosher" *Asbury Park Evening Press*, January 8, 1935.
New Jersey Supreme Court Ibid., March 7, 1935.
"uncertain" *New York Times*, March 8, 1935.
"vicious measure" *Asbury Park Evening Press*, March 9, 1935.
129 "ridiculously low" Ibid., March 15, 1935.
"to know as much as Hetrick" Ibid., March 11, 1935.
Mayor Dennis died Ibid., March 18, 1935.
Knuckles Ibid., April 5, 1935.
"cast aside" Ibid., March 22, 1935.
fired the city manager Ibid., April 2, 1935.
"cutthroat" Ibid., March 28, 1935, and April 2, 1935.
"*Open Letter*" Ibid., April 3, 1935.
130 four-to-one Ibid., April 11, 1935.
"virtually dictatorial" Ibid., July 6, 1935.
131 private letters *New York Times*, July 14, 1936.
Supreme Court See *Faitoute Iron and Steel v. Asbury Park*, 316 U.S. (1942).
Hurley *Asbury Park Evening Press*, July 9, 1935.
minstrel show Ibid., July 3, 1935.
"Young people" Ibid., July 6, 1935.
ejecting the owner Ibid., July 3, 1935.
"traditional footballs" *New York Times*, October 26, 1935.
132 $160,000 *Asbury Park Evening Press*, July 1, 1941.
electrical workers union Nick Mahalic, *History of Local 400*, http://www.ibew400.org/history.html.
Army of Unoccupation Jon Blackwell, "1936: An 'Army' Seizes the Capital," *Trentonian*, http://capitalcentury.com/1936.html.
"bled its people white" *Asbury Park Evening Press*, May 7, 1941.

313 properties Ibid.

Tumen and Tumen Ibid.

133 prospect of war Ibid., July 9, 1941.

old KKK headquarters *Asbury Park Press*, December 12, 1949.

"indifference" *Asbury Park Evening Press*, May 2, 1941.

Mattice Ibid.

"vicious" Ibid., May 2, 1941, and May 7, 1941.

"Boss rule" Ibid., May 4, 1941.

"broke" Ibid., May 6, 1941.

meters Ibid., May 2, 1941.

134 Hetrick's rally Ibid., May 6, 1941.

tulips Ibid., May 8, 1941, and May 7, 1941.

"A vote for Hetrick" Ibid., May 12, 1941.

1930 census See "West Side Story: Profile of a Black Community" *Asbury Park Press* special report, May 2, 1982.

thirty-five hundred Negroes Ibid.

"definitely blighted" Ibid.

Fleming *Asbury Park Evening Press*, April 19, 1941.

135 first Negro housing project "West Side Story."

"Mr. Nick" *Asbury Park Evening Press*, May 3, 1941.

"women of the street" Ibid., May 8, 1941.

Minnie Lopez Ibid., May 12, 1941.

denied the mayor Ibid., July 12, 1941.

"over $600 a day" Ibid., May 12, 1941.

MACHINE LOSES Ibid., May 14, 1941.

fired nine employees Ibid., July 2, 1941.

136 "emergency" spending Ibid., July 1, 1941.

"The hand that held" Ibid., October 13, 1941.

Mattice bolted Ibid., November 3, 1941.

"The gang" Ibid.

"the remains" Ibid.

137 requisitioned *New York Times*, August 28, 1942.

"Sentamentalist" See Will Friedwald, liner notes to *Frank Sinatra and the Tommy Dorsey Orchestra: Love Songs*, RCA Victor, 090206–68701–2.

FOURTH OF JULY, 1956

140 Negro population and employment figures See Joseph A. Clarke, *Migration and Housing Among the Negro Population of Asbury Park, NJ* (Trenton, NJ: The Urban Colored Population Commission, 1945).

African-American scientist See interview with William J. Jones by the New Jersey Historical Commission, http://www.infoage.org/jones.html.

"During the war years" Clarke, *Migration and Housing.*

colored patrol themselves Interview with Thomas S. Smith by June West, under the auspices of the Monmouth County Library Headquarters, 1999, http://www.visitmonmouth.com/oralhistory/bios/SmithThomas.htm.

141 Smock family *Asbury Park Evening Press*, September 2, 1911.
Some observers thought Ibid., June 8, 1944.
"There was no sleight" Ibid.
"a conservative economic government" Ibid., February 10, 1956.
under investigation Ibid., November 1, 1947.
Indictments *New York Times*, May 2, 1947.

142 "All of our actions" *Asbury Park Evening Press*, September 3, 1947.
"similar to that" Ibid.
Nine million Kenneth T. Jackson *Crabgrass Frontier: The Suburbanization of the United States* (New York: Oxford University Press, 1985), 238.
Housing starts Ibid., 233.
slums *Asbury Park Evening Press*, March 7, 1956.
Catalina ranch Ibid., July 1, 1955.
Oldsmobile Ibid., July 5, 1955.
New Jersey Turnpike Ibid., July 1, 1955.
Garden State Ibid.

143 Detroit Ibid.
"City dwellers by the thousands" July 2, 1955.
The next day Ibid., July 3, 1955.
Asbury police Ibid., July 5, 1955.
Photos of the beach Ibid.
widening of feeder roads Ibid., June 10, 1955.
Convention Hall Ibid., July 2, 1955.
Monroe Ibid., July 1, 1955.
1956 survey Ibid., May 3, 1957.
"major beachfront improvement" Ibid.
merry-go-round lease Ibid., January 10, 1956.
resign Ibid.

144 "no specific complaint" Ibid., February 10, 1956.
"Coney Island type venue" Ibid., May 3, 1957.
for description of Coney Island amusements See Judith A. Adams and Edwin J. Perkins, *The American Amusement Park Industry: A History of Technology and Thrills* (Boston: Twayne, 1991), 44.

145 "catchpenny game" *Asbury Park Evening Press*, July 5, 1956.
for history of pinball See Edward Trapunski, *Special When Lit: A Visual and Anecdotal History of Pinball* (New York: Doubleday Dolphin, 1979).

146 "Pinball feeds on" Ibid.
big new department stores Ibid.
$8,000 a year *Asbury Park Evening Press*, April 4, 1946

147 the state of New Jersey ruled For a history of gaming laws in New Jersey, see the New Jersey Law Revision Commission memorandum from its staff, re "Games of Chance," November 6, 2000.
Judge confirmed *Asbury Park Evening Press*, June 8, 1955.
Lembke Ibid.
"disguised w.... a phony 'skill'" Ibid., July 1, 1956

"the immediate dollar" Ibid., June 28, 1956.

"If Asbury Park's prosperity" Ibid.

148 local clergyman Ibid., July 9, 1956.

Toms River man Ibid., July 8, 1956.

Another concessionaire Ibid.

Beach Merchants' Association Ibid., July 3, 1956.

Billy Graham Ibid., September 2 and 3, 1955.

Long Branch Ibid., July 5, 1956.

"Everyone will sell hot dogs" Ibid., July 9, 1956.

history of Palace Amusements personal communication with Bob Crane, savetillie.com.

149 for "teenagers" *Asbury Park Evening Press*, June 7, 1955.

For Amusement Only Ibid., July 9, 1956.

"dark rides" personal communication with Bob Crane, savetillie.com.

"denigrate" *Asbury Park Evening Press*, May 3, 1957.

150 "Wildwood" Ibid., July 7, 1955.

for Haley history See James Miller, *Flowers in the Dust Bin: The Rise of Rock and Roll 1947–1977* (New York: Simon and Schuster, 1999).

151 the Redicker brothers *Asbury Park Sun*, March 12, 1946.

kicked off with Ibid.

"We can show the youngsters" John Swenson, *Bill Haley: The Daddy of Rock and Roll* (New York: Stein & Day, 1983), 88.

152 $1.50 *Asbury Park Sun*, July 1, 1955.

$250 lease Ibid., July 11, 1956.

"This newspaper" *Asbury Park Evening Press.*, March 24, 1956.

153 even deeper poverty For a profile of the West Side, see *Asbury Park Evening Press* three-part series, March 7, 8, and 9, 1956.

Asbury Park Village Clarke, *Migration and Housing*.

"official skeleton" *Asbury Park Evening Press* three-part series.

slumlords Ibid.

154 Cuba's *Asbury Park Evening Press*, July 2, 1956.

"Jolly Farmer" Ibid., July 7, 1956.

"I fell in love" Miller, *Flowers in the Dust Bin*, 113.

155 white cheerleader sweaters Ibid.

156 "unlawful" Ibid., March 12, 1946.

civil rights law Ibid., March 10, 1946.

"three hundred white folks" Author's interview with David Parreott Jr.

Freddie Price *Asbury Park Evening Press*, July 12, 1956.

twenty-seven hundred Ibid., July 2, 1956.

"reserved policemen" Ibid., July 3, 1956.

"Boardwalk crowds" Ibid.

157 "When they started singing" Ibid., July 11, 1956.

custodian Ibid., July 2, 1956

Redicker said Ibid.

ordered the doors closed Ibid.

seventy-five thousand Ibid.

158 support Ibid.

"Convention Hall Riot"   Ibid.

"roving cars"   Ibid.

159 "only the prompt"   Ibid., July 3, 1956.

Twenty-five were injured   Ibid., July 2, 1956.

"hot music and cold beer"   Ibid., July 3, 1956.

"From the information I got"   Ibid., July 2, 1956.

Of the eight kids arrested   Ibid., July 3, 1956.

"definitely not"   Ibid., July 2, 1956.

"mass fighting"   Ibid.

160 "Whereas psychologists"   Ibid., July 3, 1956.

"rock and roll and the rest"   Ibid., July 11, 1956.

winning ticket   Ibid., May 15, 1957.

"the best showing"   Ibid.

161 the batting cage   Ibid., May 29, 1957.

Bamberger's   Ibid., March 6, 1956.

write off   Kenneth T. Jackson, "All the World's a Mall: Reflections on the Social and Economic Consequences of the American Shopping Center," *American Historical Review* 101 (October 1996): 1111–21.

"dead"   *Asbury Park Evening Press*, July 5, 1956.

hadn't been self-sustaining   Ibid., May 7, 1957.

"Here," its founder   See Disney Paper Resource Center, http://disney-paper.tripod.com.

162 "visualize a vital, growing"   *Asbury Park Evening Press*, May 6, 1957.

"social stagnation"   Ibid., October 8, 1960.

FOURTH OF JULY, 1970

164 "a series of extraordinary"   Dr. Robert M. Fogelson and Dr. Robert B. Hill, "Who Riots? A Study of Participation in the 1967 Riots," in *Supplemental Studies for the National Advisory Commission on Civil Disobedience* (New York: Praeger, 1968).

two white cops roughed up   Tom Hayden, *Rebellion in Newark: Official Violence and Ghetto Response* (New York: Random House, 1967).

"The spirit and the feeling"   Amiri Baraka, *The Autobiography of Leroi Jones* (Chicago: Lawrence Hill Books, 1984), 367.

165 "a city in open rebellion"   *Asbury Park Evening Press*, July 15, 1967.

"The line between the jungle"   Hayden, *Rebellion in Newark*, 38.

"planned, open insurrection"   *Asbury Park Evening Press*, July 17, 1967.

35 percent "West Side Story."

"Yea, I paid attention"   Author's interview with Gregory Holland, June 6, 1997.

special meeting   For all quotes, see minutes of "Special Meeting," July 17, 1967, author's collection courtesy David Parreott Jr.

166 Howard University   Monmouth County Historical interview with Thomas Smith.

"Tell Tommy"   Author's interview with Donald Hammary and David Parreott Jr. August 12, 1997.

"It has been next to impossible"   *Asbury Park Sunday Press*, July 16, 1967.

167 "standpat"   Fletcher Knebbel, "A Cop Named Joe," *Look*, July 27, 1971, 15–19.

168 Mesnikoff   Author's interview with Norman Mesnikoff, June 10, 1997.

"riffraff theory"   Fogelson and Hill, "Who Riots?" 222.

169 At about that time   *Asbury Park Evening Press*, July 18, 1967.

Detroit   *New York Times*, July 23, 1997.

"civil unrest"   Fogelson and Hill, "Who Riots?" 244.

"the greatest wave of urban violence"   Howard Zinn, *Postwar America: 1947–1971* (Indianapolis: Bobbs-Merrill, 1973), 132.

110 U.S. cities   I. F. Stone, *Polemics and Prophecies: 1967–1970* (New York: Random House, 1970), 96.

170 silent protest   *Asbury Park Evening Press*, April 10, 1968.

Mattice elected   Ibid., May 27, 1969.

A TRADITIONAL 4TH   *Asbury Park Evening News*, July 2, 1970.

a hundred deaths   Ibid.

a million drafted   See Selective Service System History and Records, http://www.sss.gov/lotter2.htm.

New Jersey's population   Thomas P. Norman, ed., *New Jersey Trends* (New Brunswick: Institute of Environment Statistics, Rutgers University, State University of New Jersey, 1974).

171 30 percent   Knebbel, "Cop Named Joe."

Mrs. Jay's   *Asbury Park Evening Press*, July 7, 1970.

172 Monterey Hotel   *New York Times*, November 24, 1963.

a thousand cars   *Asbury Park Evening Press*, July 18, 1967.

"We may not know much"   Ibid., July 7, 1970.

Mitch Ryder   Ibid., July 2, 1967.

173 I EAT THE GREEN MERMAID   Jim Wheelock, "Growin' Up—Pt. 1, Early Asbury Park," memoir, author's collection.

Head Shop   *Asbury Park Evening Press*, July 16, 1967.

174 "At first glance"   Wheelock, "Growin' Up."

Built into one whole wall   John Davidson, "John Luraschi," http://www.chorusandverse.com/content/200208/20020811_JohnLuraschi.htm.

Margaret Potter   Robert Santelli, "Remembering the Upstage," *Backstreets*, Fall 1987.

Van Zandt   Author's interview with Steve Van Zandt, July 23, 1997.

"it was a place for the local musicians"   Santelli, "Remembering."

a local reporter   Joan Pikula, "Vibrating Steel Mill," *Asbury Park Evening Press*, April 20, 1970.

175 "glory hog"   Davidson, "John Luraschi."

"his desire and"   Santelli, "Remembering," 19.

"do these blues songs"   Author's interview with David Sancious, October 1, 1997.

178 Tony Blair   *Asbury Park Evening Press*, June 5, 1968.

181 fifty policemen   Knebbel, "Cop Named Joe."

"I need some back-up" Hammary interview.

out at a club Author's interview with Thomas Smith, June 10, 1997.

182 "large groups of teenagers" Asbury Park Evening Press, July 6, 1970.

"I seen more people" "West Side Story."

seventy-five teenagers Asbury Park Evening Press, July 6, 1970.

"just like a party" Ibid.

183 "I've been here twenty years" Asbury Park Evening Press, July 6, 1970.

the local market Parreott interview.

The uprising targeted Asbury Park Evening Press, July 6, 1970.

three quarters of the buildings Ibid., July 7, 1970.

three A.M. Ibid., July 6, 1970.

"cool it" Ibid.

184 harassing Ibid., July 7, 1970.

Fisch's Ibid., July 8, 1970.

Cahill Ibid., July 7, 1970.

"We feared" Ibid.

"this has been brewing a long time" Ibid.

185 ransacking Ibid.

"There seemed to be no organization" Ibid.

Mayor Mattice Ibid., July 11, 1970

MCAP meeting Ibid., July 7, 1970.

186 "This doesn't take any more time" Ibid.

noon Tuesday Ibid., July 8, 1970.

"Hey, they're going east!" Ibid.

"several hundred blacks" New York Times, July 8, 1970.

Black Liberation flag Asbury Park Evening Press, July 8, 1970.

around three thirty Max Gunther, "TV Coverage of Racial Riot," TV Guide, September 26, 1970, 8–11.

187 "like a corpse" Asbury Park Evening Press, July 8, 1970.

television reporter Gunther, "TV Coverage."

"In any organization" Smith interview.

Forty-six people injured Asbury Park Evening Press, July 8, 1970.

twenty-five troopers Ibid., July 9, 1970.

188 neighboring Neptune Ibid., July 8, 1970.

Hamm "West Side Story."

the mayor met again Asbury Park Evening Press, July 10, 1970.

black peace patrol New York Times, July 9, 1970.

Governor Cahill Asbury Park Evening Press, July 10, 1970.

troopers withdrawn Ibid., July 12, 1970.

Hamm emerged from the meeting Ibid.

By eleven that night Ibid.

180 persons injured Knebbel, "Cop Named Joe."

189 "a particular irony" New York Times, July 9, 1970.

"urban pathology" Asbury Park Evening Press, August 11, 1975.

"The riots was just the end of it" Author's interview with Carl Williams.

Parreott Author's interview.

FOURTH OF JULY, 1978

191 Tallent   Author's interview.
192 Springsteen on water tower   Conversation with author.
193 "The best parts of those days"   Ken Viola, Vini Lopez interview "Growin' Up, Pt. 3," *Thunder Roads* magazine, 1979.
194 "was going to do original songs"   Robert Santelli, "Vini Roslyn," *Backstreets*, Winter 1987.
    "We used to play"   Marc Eliot with Mike Apel, *Down Thunder Road: The Making of Bruce Springsteen* (New York: Simon and Schuster, 1992), 38.
    Steel Mill was touring   Allen C. Schery, "California Dreaming," *Backstreets*, Fall 1987.
    "We were popular in a small area"   Eliot, *Down Thunder Road*, 41.
    the band's "following"   *Asbury Park Press*, July 17, 1970.
    "jam-packed"   Author's interview with Sancious.
    driven across country   Randy Cepuch, "Robbin Thompson," *Backstreets*, Fall 1986.
195 "rocks a little differently"   Eliot, *Down Thunder Road*, 41.
    Springsteen didn't hang on Springwood   Conversation with author.
    Glory Road   Author's interview with Tallent.
196 "When we first played together"   Dave Marsh, *Born to Run: The Bruce Springsteen Story* (Garden City, NY: Dolphin Books, 1979), 95.
    Springsteen recalls   Conversation with author.
    Ku Klux Klan had reappeared   *Asbury Park Press*, April 25, 1971.
    Crosses burned   Ibid.
    eight feet in the air   *Asbury Park Press*, April 28, 1971.
197 gotten into a shouting match   Knebbel "Cop Named Joe."
    The police accused Hammary   *Asbury Park Press*, April 24, 1971.
    stabbed to death   *Asbury Park Press*, April 25, 1971.
    Parreott's eulogy   Ibid.
    kerosene-soaked cross   Ibid., April 28, 1971.
    Sundance Blues Band   Ibid., April 30, 1971.
    performing with Springsteen   Ibid., July 2, 1971.
198 Bill Graham   Ibid., April 30, 1971.
    "We had to fight our way"   Ibid., July 1, 1971.
    "Basically"   Author's interview with Tallent.
    Delores Holmes   Author's interview with Holmes.
199 "the darkest, dingiest, dampest"   Marsh, *Born to Run*, 16.
    $13.75   Ibid., 10.
    "Don't you bring those people"   Author's interview with Holmes.
200 Tom Potter's old apartment   Springsteen conversation with author.
    "Amidst the old hairdryers"   Bruce Springsteen, *Songs* (New York: Avon Books, 1998), 6.
    "primarily an acoustic record"   Ibid., 23.

"great funky riffs"   Peter Knobler with Greg Mitchell, "Who Is Bruce Springsteen and Why Are We Saying All These Wonderful Things About Him?" *Crawdaddy*, March 1973; reprinted in *Very Seventies: A Cultural History of the 1970's* (New York: Simon & Schuster, 1995).

201   another cross   *Asbury Park Press*, January 12, 1973.
      last payment on its debt   Ibid., October 26, 1975.
      The Casino had burnt   *New York Times*, May 18, 1979.
      Convention Hall   Ibid., May 14, 1972.
      "swimming pool"   Ibid., April 26, 1971.
      Wesley Lake   Ibid., October 12, 1975.
      defeated Mattice   Ibid., August 11, 1975.
      eighty-seven-count   Ibid., July 16, 1973.
      "conspiring to retain"   Ibid., November 15, 1975.
      baby parade   Ibid., August 27, 1973.
      A fifth of the city's income   Ibid., June 29, 1975.
      ten percent wage reduction   Ibid., December 19, 1974.
      "We have no money"   Ibid., June 29, 1975.
202   "cast of characters"   Springsteen, *Songs*, 25.
      "watched the town"   Ibid.
203   "We all wanted to get out"   Sancious interview with author.
      "a metaphor"   Springsteen, *Songs*, 25.
      "my getaway"   Ibid., 26.
204   "It was . . . like they shelved it"   Viola interview of Vini Lopez.
      Dr. Lorenzo Harris   *New York Times*, August 11, 1975.
      almost sixty percent   Ibid.
      maybe $200 a week   Springsteen conversation with author.
      The Magic Touch   *Asbury Park Press*, September 30, 1973.
      Convention Hall   Ibid., August 1974.
      "turning point"   Springsteen, *Songs*, 44.
      "longest and deepest recession"   Thomas M. Superl, "The U.S. Economy in 1977 and 1978," Federal Reserve Bank of Minneapolis, *Quarterly Review* 2, no. 1 (Winter 1978).
      ninety percent in service industry   Robert Hamrin, *America's New Economy: The Basic Guide* (New York: Franklin Watts, 1988), 14.
206   That bill died   Stephen Piccolo, "Gaming in Atlantic City: A History of Legal Gambling in New Jersey." http://www.chequers.com/magazine/piccolo/part3.htm.
      state-run casinos   *Asbury Park Press*, November 1, 1974.
      Byrne   Ibid.
      unemployment rate   *Asbury Park Press*, November 2, 1974.
      Tourism Development Council   Ibid., November 3, 1974.
      sixty percent in favor   Ibid., November 4, 1974.
      No Dice coalition   Ibid., November 6, 1974
      "a carnival atmosphere" and other religious-leader quotes   Ibid., November 1, 1974.
207   bishop of United Methodist Church   Ibid., November 4, 1974.
      twenty of twenty-four newspapers   Ibid., November 3, 1974.
      "handing the casinos"   Ibid., November 1, 1974.

"The very same interests"   Ovid Demaris, *The Boardwalk Jungle* (New York: Bantam, 1986), 51.

three-to-one margin   *Asbury Park Press*, November 6, 1974.

"to come to the aid"   Ibid.

extend the boardwalk   *New York Times*, August 11, 1975.

Forty percent   "West Side Story."

208 "elderly black man"   *New York Times*, October 12, 1975.

a small item   *Asbury Park Press*, October 26, 1975.

209 full of dread   Springsteen, *Songs*, 46.

210 "You're not necessarily"   Ibid., 47.

"When the Upstage closed"   Robert Santelli, "Twenty Years Burning Down the Road," in *Racing in the Street: The Bruce Springsteen Reader*, ed. June Skinner Sawyers (New York: Penguin Books, 2004).

small item   *Asbury Park Press*, October 26, 1975.

Berkeley-Carteret   *Asbury Park Press*, May 30, 1976

211 New Jersey's unemployment   Ibid., November 3, 1976.

"the elderly and disabled"   Demaris, *Boardwalk*, 57.

Mayor Kramer opposed   *New York Times*, May 7, 1978.

war chest   *Asbury Park Press*, November 3, 1976.

"painless"   See State of New Jersey, *Gambling Study Commission*, 1973.

"a unique tool"   "Impact of Gambling: Economic Effect More Measurable Than Social Effect," United States General Accounting Office, Report to the Honorable Frank R. Wolf, House of Representatives. Hereafter, "Gambling Study."

NAACP   *Asbury Park Press*, November 1, 1976.

"undercutting" the Mob   Gambling Study.

"puritanical"   Ibid.

"money-tight"   *Asbury Park Press*, November 3, 1976.

212 Chalfonte-Haddon   See Demaris, *Boardwalk*, 54.

fifty thousand jobs   Dave Schwarz, "Jurisdiction Summary: Atlantic City, New Jersey," http://gaming.unlv.edu/research/subject/AtlanticCity.html.

By 1985   See Demaris, *Boardwalk*, x.

"The laws that established"   Schwarz, "Jurisdiction," quoting Dennis P. Rud, "The Social Impact of Atlantic City Casino Gambling."

Twentieth Century Fund   Demaris, *Boardwalk*, x.

Meyer Lansky   Gary Potter, "Meyer Lanksy: His Inner Circle," Part 1, http://glasgowcrew.tripod.com/Lansky.html.

213 Joey Gambino   Demaris, *Boardwalk*, 91.

twelfth most distressed   *New York Times*, May 7, 1978 (see same for quotes in this paragraph).

"small-scale model"   Ibid.

214 "It is not so much a question"   Ibid.

Lang's Guest House   *Asbury Park Press*, July 5, 1978.

high-density use   *New York Times*, July 12, 1992.

"a dumping ground"   *Asbury Park Press*, July 5, 1978.

"dead space"   *New York Times*, May 7, 1978.

215 Three people died   *Asbury Park Press*, July 5, 1978.

"You can't have community pride"   "West Side Story."
"in the middle of a community"   Springsteen, *songs*, 68.
"sense of accountability"   Ibid., 65.
"any hint of escapism"   Ibid., 68.
217 Santa Monica pier, etc.   Dave Marsh, "Bruce Springsteen Raises Cain,"
in *Bruce Springsteen: The Rolling Stone Files* (New York: Hyperion, 1996), 81.

EPILOGUE: FOURTH OF JULY, 2001

219 a parade in Ocean Grove   *Asbury Park Press*, July 4, 2001.
221 new, comprehensive waterfront-redevelopment   Ibid., November 8, 1984.
Added   Ibid., April 29, 2001.
a quarter lived below poverty line   "Missouri State Census Data Center:
Basic Demographic Trend Report," Asbury Park city, http://www.oseda.-
missouri.edu/mscdc/census/us/trend/places/S34NJ/P340070.
median annual income   Ibid., West Side data from "West Side Story."
housing units   Ibid.
"Reagan is reality"   "West Side Story."
adopt (unanimously)   *Asbury Park Press*, November 8, 1984.
222 "exchanging its character"   Ibid.
"elderly, deinstitutionalized"   Ibid.
loans to boardinghouse   *New York Times*, July 12, 1992.
seven hundred beds   Ibid.
"socially disadvantaged"   *Asbury Park Press*, November 8, 1984.
$325,000   *New York Times*, September 17, 1986.
immigrant grandfather   *Asbury Park Press*, February 29, 2000.
largest landlord   "West Side Story."
local banks refused   *Asbury Park Press*, December 4, 1991.
$16 million   Ibid., February 4, 1991.
223 reported $8 million   Henry Vaccaro call to *Restore by the Shore* radio
show, hosted by Maureen Nevin, transcript at http://www.restoreradio.-
com.
Kramer guitar   "About the Company," Vaccaro Guitar Co., http://
www.grandcentralmusic.com/mall/vaccaro/about.html.
Johnny Cash   *New York Times*, September 17, 1986.
seventy percent capacity   Ibid., November 22, 1987.
"the private sector"   *Asbury Park Press*, April 16, 1986.
$164 million   *New York Times*, November 22, 1987.
unemployment   Ibid.
twenty-four hundred residential units   *Asbury Park Press*, April 16, 1986.
"a new Asbury Park"   *New York Times*, September 25, 1988.
a third of the project   *Asbury Park Press*, April 16, 1986.
Carabetta family   Ibid., February 14, 1991.
224 sixteen town houses   *New York Times*, September 17, 1986.
burned down   Ibid., November 22, 1987.

subcontractors   *Asbury Park Press*, October 1, 1987.
"It just means"   Ibid.
Jefferson Motel   Ibid., November 22, 1987.
224 luxury residential units   *New York Times*, September 25, 1988.
tripling   *Asbury Park Press*, June 30, 1997.
tax abatement   Ibid., November 3, 1988.
hadn't turned a profit in three years   Ibid., December 1, 1991.
225 stopped making payments   Ibid., February 14, 1991.
$12 million   Ibid., December 1, 1991.
Thomas Smith   Ibid., September 26, 2002.
"the five or six year depression"   *New York Times*, September 4, 1994.
"The right things just didn't"   *Asbury Park Press*, April 13, 1991.
"raped"   Ibid., September 27, 1993.
Toms River bank   *Asbury Park Press*, December 1, 1991.
Chapter 11   *Boston Globe*, June 10, 1992.
Back in 1986   *New York Times*, September 17, 1986.
226 *Born in the U.S.A.*   Dave Marsh, *Glory Days: Bruce Springsteen in the 1980s*
(New York: Pantheon Books, 1987).
Michael Jackson's family   *Asbury Park Press*, October 10, 2000.
227 three hundred thousand cubic yards of sand   "Asbury Park to Manasquan Beach Restoration Project," U.S. Army Corps of Engineers, http://
www.usna.edu/NAOE/courses/en420/bravo/.
3.1 million   Ibid.
230 Asbury Park Rock & Roll Museum   *Asbury Park Press*, July 15, 1998.
in January of 1989   Claire Whiteside, "Last Ride in Asbury Park: New
Jersey Bids Farewell to Its Greatest Carousel," *New Jersey Monthly*, June 1989.
231 Wonderland Ibid.
"Save Tillie"   See savetillie.com.
dropped by almost thirty percent   *Asbury Park Press*, June 30, 1997.
shell game   Ibid., July 21, 1998.
232 $9.25 million   Ibid.
Asbury Park politics   Ibid., January 29, 2001.
$30,000   Ibid.
arrested for buying cocaine   Ibid., February 1, 1994.
233 "men started taking women"   Author's interview, June 1997.
MOVE OVER FIRE ISLAND   *New York Times*, August 6, 2000.
234 St. Stephen's plan   *Asbury Park Press*, April 29, 2001.
the council vetoed   Ibid.
"hidden agendas"   Ibid.
1981 study   Ibid.
"private money"   Ibid.
"The city can't do anything"   Ibid.
seventy-two lots to Konvitz   *Asbury Park Press*, July 7, 2000.
sold only seven   Ibid.
235 Fourth of July, 1912   Ibid., July 20, 2000.
$100 million   Ibid.
$20 million   Ibid.
"non-descript people"   Ibid.

$35,000 loan   Ibid., July 17, 2000.

"respect my opinion"   Ibid., July 20, 2000.

"business acumen"   Ibid., July 17, 2000.

236 "There is one person"   Ibid., July 25, 2000.

237 "My City of Ruins"   Ibid., December 22, 2000.

"rock'n'roll entertainment Mecca"   *Shopping Center World* magazine, January 1, 2003.

"gentrification"   Ibid.

$4 million deficit   *Asbury Park Press*, August 17, 2001.

238 five percent affordable   Ibid., December 21, 2001.

"the new Asbury Park"   Ibid., October 24, 2004.

thirty percent in poverty   U.S. Bureau of the Census, Census 2000.

"not necessarily"   *Asbury Park Press*, November 20, 2001.

city manager indicted   Ibid., October 11, 2002.

"dying for this"   *New York Times*, April 2, 2004.

Tillie's face   Ibid., June 12, 2004.

2004 parade   *Asbury Park Press*, July 5, 2004.

SELECTED BIBLIOGRAPHY

Adams, Judith A., and Edwin J. Perkins. *The American Amusement Park Industry: A History of Technology and Thrills.* Boston: Twayne, 1991.

"The Asbury Park Bank-Fraud Case: *Twining v. New Jersey.*" www.soc.umnie-du/~samaha/cases/twining%20facts.html.

Asbury Park Historical Society. "New Jersey Register of Historic Places Nomination" for Palace Amusements, April 26, 2000. (See www.homestead.com/savetillie/apl7.html.)

Baker, Edward A. *King of Ragtime: Scott Joplin and His Era.* New York: Oxford University Press, 1994.

Baraka, Amiri. *The Autobiography of Leroi Jones.* Chicago: Lawrence Hill Books, 1984.

Basie, William, as told to Albert Murray. *Good Morning Blues: The Autobiography of Count Basie.* New York: Random House, 1985.

Benjamin, Richard. "Arthur Pryor: Ragtime Pioneer." Paragon Ragtime Orchestra (1998–99). www.paragonragtime.com/pryor.html.

Blesh, Rudi, and Harriet Janie. *They All Played Ragtime.* New York: Oak Publications, 1971.

Board of Commerce and Navigation, New Jersey. *Report on the erosion and protection of New Jersey beaches.* Victor Gellineau, director and chief engineer, MacCrellish & Quigley, Trenton, NJ. 1922, 1924, and 1930.

Burrows, Edwin G., and Mike Wallace. *Gotham: A History of New York City to 1898.* New York: Oxford University Press, 1999.

Cameron, Richard M. *Methodism and Society in Historical Perspective.* New York: Abingdon Press, 1961.

Chalmers, David M. *Hooded Americanism: The History of the Ku Klux Klan.* Durham, NC: Duke University Press, 1987.

Clarke, Joseph A. *Migration and Housing Among the Negro Population of Asbury Park, NJ.* Trenton, NJ: The Urban Colored Population Commission, State of New Jersey, 1945.

Crane, Bob. savetillie.com.

Crane, Stephen. *The Complete Short Stories and Sketches of Stephen Crane.* Ed. Thomas A. Gullason. New York: Doubleday, 1963.

_____. *Maggie: A Girl of the Streets.* Ed. Thomas A. Gullason. New York: W. W. Norton Critical Edition, 1979.

Defoe, Daniel. *Robinson Crusoe.* New York: Dell, 1982.

Demaris, Ovid. *The Boardwalk Jungle.* New York: Bantam, 1986.

Di Beneditto, Allesandra. *Italian Immigration to the United States.* Institutus Survey Paper 1/2000, A FAST-US-2(PP2D) U.S.

Eliot, Marc, with Mike Apel. *Down Thunder Road: The Making of Bruce Springsteen.* New York: Simon and Schuster, 1992.

Fass, Paula S. *The Damned and the Beautiful: American Youth in the 1920's.* New York: Oxford University Press, 1977.

Fogelson, Dr. Robert M., and Dr. Robert B. Hill. "Who Riots? A Study of Participation in the 1967 Riots." In *Supplemental Studies for the National Advisory Commission on Civil Disobedience.* New York: Praeger, 1968.

Friedwald, Will. Liner notes to *Frank Sinatra and the Tommy Dorsey Orchestra: Love Songs.* RCA Victor, 090206-68701-2.

Frizane, Daniel F., and Frederick P. Williams. "Historical Notes" to *Arthur Pryor, Trombone Soloist of the Sousa Band.* Crystal Records, CD451

Gioia, Ted. *The History of Jazz.* New York: Oxford University Press, 1997.

Hamrin, Robert. *America's New Economy: The Basic Guide.* New York: Franklin Watts, 1988.

Hasse, John Edward. *The Life and Genius of Duke Ellington.* New York: Simon and Schuster, 1993.

Hayden, Tom. *Rebellion in Newark: Official Violence and Ghetto Response.* New York: Random House, 1967.

Hodges, Graham Russell. *Slavery and Freedom in the Rural North: African Americans in Monmouth County, New Jersey, 1665-1865.* Madison, WI: Madison House, 1997.

Jackson, Kenneth T. "All the World's a Mall: Reflections on the Social and Economic Consequences of the American Shopping Center." *American Historical Review* 101 (October 1996): 1111-21.

_____. *Crabgrass Frontier: The Suburbanization of the United States.* New York: Oxford University Press, 1985.

_____. *The Ku Klux Klan in the City: 1915-1930.* New York: Oxford University Press, 1967.

Josephson, Matthew. *The Robber Barons: The Great American Capitalists, 1861-1901.* New York: Harcourt, Brace and Company, 1934.

Knebbel, Fletcher. "A Cop Named Joe," *Look,* July 27, 1971, 15-19.

Knobler, Peter, with Greg Mitchell. *Very Seventies: A Cultural History of the 1970's.* New York: Simon & Schuster, 1995.

Kobbé, Gustav. *The New Jersey Coast and Pines: An Illustrated Guide-Book (With Road Maps).* Portsmouth, NH: Walking News Inc., 1982. First published 1889.

Ku Klux Klan. *Inspirational Addresses.* Second Imperial Klonvokation, September 23–26, 1924. Author's collection.

_____. "TriState Klonklave." July 4, 1924, souvenir program. Author's collection.

Luccock, Halford E., and Paul Hutchinson. *The Story of Methodism.* New York, Cincinnati: The Methodist Book Concern, 1926.

Marsh, Dave. *Born to Run: The Bruce Springsteen Story.* Garden City, NY: Dolphin Books, 1979.

_____. *Glory Days: Bruce Springsteen in the 1980s.* New York: Pantheon Books, 1987.

McKay, Leonora Walker. *Mama and Papa: Volume II, The Blacks of Monmouth County.* Self-published, 1984.

McMahon, T. J. *The Golden Age of the Monmouth Shore: 1864–1914.* Fairhaven, NJ: T. J. McMahon Publishing, 1964.

Mihalic, Nick. *History of Local 400.* http://www.ibew400.org/history.html.

Miller, James. *Flowers in the Dustbin: The Rise of Rock and Roll, 1947–1977.* New York: Simon and Schuster, 1999.

Naughright, W. Stanley. *Final Report of the Special Committee,* appointed by resolution of the General Assembly, adopted March 19, 1934, to inquire into alleged Corrupt Conduct, Crimes and Misdemeanors of Civil Offices of the State, December 17, 1934, Chairman W. Stanley Naughright.

New Jersey, State of. *Gambling Study Commission.* 1973.

New Jersey Law Revision Commission. Memorandum from staff, re "Games of Chance." November 6, 2000.

Norman, Thomas P. *New Jersey Trends.* New Brunswick: Institute of Environment Statistics, Rutgers University, State University of New Jersey, 1974.

Piccolo, Stephen. "Gaming in Atlantic City: A History of Legal Gambling in New Jersey." http://www.chequers.com/magazine/piccolo/part3.htm.

Pike, Helen-Chantal. *Images of America: Asbury Park.* Portsmouth, NH: Arcadia Publishing, 1997.

Pine, Dr. Alan S., Jean C. Hershenov, and Dr. Aaron H. Lefkowitz. *Peddler to Suburbanite: The History of the Jews of Monmouth County, New Jersey.* Deal Park, NJ: Monmouth Jewish Community Council, 1981.

Rolling Stone, the editors of. *Bruce Springsteen: The Rolling Stone Files.* New York: Hyperion, 1996.

Santelli, Robert. "Remembering the Upstage." *Backstreets,* Fall 1987.

_____. "Twenty Years Burning Down the Road." In *Racing in the Street: The Bruce Springsteen Reader.* Ed. June Skinner Sawyers. New York: Penguin Books, 2004.

Schuller, Gunther. *Early Jazz: Its Roots and Musical Development.* New York: Oxford University Press, 1968.

Schwarz, Dave. "Jurisdiction Summary: Atlantic City, New Jersey." http://gaming.unlv.edu/research/subject/AtlanticCity.html.

Simpson, Matthew. *A Hundred Years of Methodism.* New York: Phillips and Hunt, 1876.

Sousa, John Philip. *Marching Along.* Westerville, OH: Integrity Press, 1994. Originally published 1928.

Springsteen, Bruce. *Songs.* New York: Avon Books, 1998.

Stallman, R. W. *Stephen Crane: A Biography.* New York: George Braziller, 1968.

Stanger, Frank Bateman, ed. *The Methodist Trail in New Jersey: One Hundred and Twenty-Five Years of Methodism in the New Jersey Annual Conference, 1863–1961.* Camden: NJ: Annual Conference of the Methodist Church, 1961.

Stone, I. F. *Polemics and Prophecies: 1967–1970.* New York: Random House, 1970.

Sweet, William Warren. *Methodism in American History.* New York: Abingdon Press, 1933, 1954.

Swenson, John. *Bill Haley: The Daddy of Rock and Roll.* New York: Stein & Day, 1983.

Thomas, Gordon, and Max Morgan Witts. *Shipwreck: The Strange Fate of the Morro Castle.* New York: Dell, 1973.

Thomas, James S. *Methodism's Racial Dilemma: The Story of Central Jurisdiction.* New York: Abingdon Press, 1992.

Trapunski, Edward. *Special When Lit: A Visual and Anecdotal History of Pinball.* New York: Doubleday Dolphin, 1979.

Uminowicz, Glenn. "Sport in a Middle-Class Utopia: Asbury Park, New Jersey, 1871–1895." *Journal of Sport History* 11, no. 1 (Spring 1984).

United States General Accounting Office. "Impact of Gambling: Economic Effect More Measurable Than Social Effect." Report to the Honorable Frank R. Wolf, House of Representatives.

Utilities Power and Light Corporation. Annual reports, 1927–34.

Wade, Wyn Craig. *The Fiery Cross: The Ku Klux Klan in America.* New York: Simon and Schuster, 1987.

Walton, Ortiz. *Music: Black, White and Blue.* New York: William Morrow, 1972.

Wertheim, Stanley, and Paul Sorrentino. *The Crane Log: A Documentary Life of Stephen Crane, 1871–1900.* New York: G. K. Hall and Co., 1994.

Wheelock, Jim. "Growin' Up—Pt. 1, Early Asbury Park." Author's collection.

Whiteside, Claire. "Last Ride in Asbury Park: New Jersey Bids Farewell to Its Greatest Carousel." *New Jersey Monthly,* June 1989.

Wilson, Harold F. *The Jersey Shore: A Social and Economic History of the Counties of Atlantic, Cape May, Monmouth, and Ocean.* New York: Lewis Historical Publishing Co., Inc., 1953.

——————. *The Story of the Jersey Shore.* Princeton, NJ: D. Van Nostrand Co., Inc., 1964.

Zinn, Howard. *A People's History of the United States.* New York: HarperPerennial Library, 1980.

——————. *Postwar America: 1947–1971.* Indianapolis: Bobbs-Merrill, 1973.

INDEX

A NOTE ON THE AUTHOR

Daniel Wolff is the author of *You Send Me: The Life and Times of Sam Cooke*, which won the Ralph J. Gleason Award for best music book of 1995. He was nominated for a Grammy for his liner notes to *Complete Recordings of Sam Cooke with the Soul Stirrers*. His journalism has appeared in *Vogue*, the *Nation*, and *Doubletake*, and his poetry in the *Paris Review*, the *Partisan Review*, and the *Threepenny Review*.

A NOTE ON THE TYPE

The text of this book is set in Linotype Goudy Old Style. It was designed by Frederic Goudy (1865–1947), an American designer whose types were very popular during his lifetime, and particularly fashionable in the 1940s. He was also a craftsman who cut the metal patterns for his type designs, engraved matrices, and cast type.

The design for Goudy Old Style is based on Goudy Roman, with which it shares a "hand-wrought" appearance and asymmetrical serifs, but unlike Goudy Roman its capitals are modeled on Renaissance lettering.